AF773491

Cybercrime and the Law

This book provides a comprehensive and synthetic analysis of the legal acts of the Council of Europe and the European Union affecting regulation of cybercrime in EU countries. Technical aspects relating to cybercrime are also discussed. The work explains core ideas, including background, nomenclature, a definition of computer crime and a history of its criminalisation. It examines the Council of Europe's Convention on Cybercrime, the first international law act governing the subject, and the additional Protocol to the Convention on Cybercrime, dealing with the criminalisation of computer-generated racist and xenophobic acts. The volume discusses European Union regulations, including applicable European Union laws on cybercrime such as the Council Framework Decision 2005/222/JHA and Directive 2013/40/EU on attacks against information systems, and Directive 2011/93/EU on Combating the Sexual Abuse and Sexual Exploitation of Children and Child Pornography. Finally, the work explores issues of cyberterrorism including the dissemination of terrorist content online. The book will be a valuable resource for academics, researchers and policy-makers working in the areas of criminal law, IT law, EU law and cyber security.

Filip Radoniewicz is legal advisor, adjunct at the War Studies Academy in Warsaw. He has worked as an assistant judge and an expert at the Ministry of Justice and at the Academic Center for Cybersecurity Policy at War Studies Academy. Graduate of post-graduate studies: "European Union Law" at the Jagiellonian University, "Human Rights and Freedoms" co-organised by the Institute of Legal Sciences of the Polish Academy of Sciences and the Helsinki Foundation for Human Rights and "Computer Network Administration" at the Lublin University of Technology; author or co-author of approximately eighty publications, mainly in the field of broadly understood criminal law, new technology law and human rights.

Cybercrime and the Law

An Analysis of Legal Governance in Europe

Filip Radoniewicz

Routledge
Taylor & Francis Group
LONDON AND NEW YORK

First published 2025
by Routledge
4 Park Square, Milton Park, Abingdon, Oxon OX14 4RN

and by Routledge
605 Third Avenue, New York, NY 10158

Routledge is an imprint of the Taylor & Francis Group, an informa business

© 2025 Filip Radoniewicz

The right of Filip Radoniewicz to be identified as author of this work has been asserted in accordance with sections 77 and 78 of the Copyright, Designs and Patents Act 1988.

All rights reserved. No part of this book may be reprinted or reproduced or utilised in any form or by any electronic, mechanical, or other means, now known or hereafter invented, including photocopying and recording, or in any information storage or retrieval system, without permission in writing from the publishers.

Trademark notice: Product or corporate names may be trademarks or registered trademarks, and are used only for identification and explanation without intent to infringe.

British Library Cataloguing-in-Publication Data
A catalogue record for this book is available from the British Library

ISBN: 978-1-032-74201-4 (hbk)
ISBN: 978-1-032-76042-1 (pbk)
ISBN: 978-1-003-47677-1 (ebk)

DOI: 10.4324/9781003476771

Typeset in Galliard
by Apex CoVantage, LLC

For my daughter Dorothy, my wife Monica . . . and my friend Flipper, wherever he is . . .

Contents

Preface

Since the beginning of the last century, we have been dealing with technological progress on an unprecedented scale. Information technology is a sector which is experiencing rapid development in all spheres of life, including in particular information and communication technology. This is owing to the progressing convergence of information technology and telecommunications, this being the outcome of the development of computer networks and the internet, which necessitates the fast and effective processing and transmission of information, whose role has greatly increased. Information has not only become a commodity, gaining immense economic significance, but it is also a vital instrument in the sphere of politics and power. Therefore, the view that we are living in an "information revolution", "information" or even "information technology" society is becoming increasingly popular.

Of course, in addition to undeniable advantages, it is also a source of threat. Janusz Barta and Ryszard Markiewicz compare the internet to the Wild West, as an area "where law does not exist, or it is difficult to enforce it".[1] There is no doubt that the development of legal regulations ensuring secure information transfer constitutes a considerable challenge for lawmakers. It is a challenge which is not easy for legislators to meet.

This study focuses primarily on European legal acts of an international (Council of Europe law) or supra-national nature (EU law which is regarded as a body of laws separate both from national laws and international laws)[2] targeting computer crime (cybercrime in the strict sense) or offences against the confidentiality, integrity and availability of computer data (computers or networks are the target of crime, e.g., hacking) and – to a lesser extent – legal acts relating to "computer-related crime" (computers or networks are a tool used for committing a crime, e.g., the dissemination of child pornography,

1 Barta, Markiewicz (1998), p. 9.

2 See, judgements of the CJEU of 5 February 1963, *NV Algemene Transport en Expeditie Onderneming van Gend & Loos v Netherlands Inland Revenue Administration* (26/62), and of 15 July 1964 – *Flaminio Costa v E.N.E.L.* (6/64)

fraud), hate crimes and (in addition) cyberterrorism.[3] The monograph deals with the issue of substantive criminal law, so procedural issues are only signalised.

The book comprises six chapters. The first two chapters are introductory to the discussed issues, and the next four are dogmatic in nature. The first chapter contains the basic information intended to explain the technical side of cybercrime, i.e., methods used by criminals, called colloquially, hackers (e.g., spoofing, DDoS attacks, phishing, pharming, spyware, etc.).

While the aim of the first chapter is a general introduction to the topic of hacking by discussing its technical aspects, chapter 2 constitutes a proper introduction to this study. It presents attempts to define computer crimes and their classification, the history of the criminalisation of this phenomenon along with binding regulations difficulties and explains the basic concepts: information, computer data, computer program, cyberspace, information society and knowledge-based economy. In addition to explaining certain core notions and terms, as mentioned earlier, this chapter features a concise discussion of the creation and development of IT systems and the internet. Moreover, the author decided to include subchapters in which technical issues are discussed. However, they were limited to the issues of intrusion detection systems and securing electronic evidence, whereas the forms of attack against data security were described in chapter 1.

Chapter 3 refers to the Council of Europe – Convention on Cybercrime opened for signature on 23 November 2001 in Budapest (it is the first international law act which governs the issues discussed in this study). The great importance of the Convention has led to a separate chapter being devoted to it.

Chapter 4 discusses other legal acts of the Council of Europe regarding the issue of broadly understood cybercrime, in particular the Protocol to the Convention on Cybercrime, concerning the criminalisation of acts of a racist and xenophobic nature committed through computer systems, open to signature on 28 January 2003 and Convention on the Protection of Children against Sexual Exploitation and Sexual Abuse open to signature on 25 October 2007 in Lanzarote.

Chapter 5 discusses European Union regulations, including applicable European Union laws on cybercrime: the Council Framework Decision 2005/222/JHA of 24 February 2005 on attacks against information systems, Directive 2013/40/EU of the European Parliament and of the Council of 12 August 2013 on attacks against information systems and Directive 2011/93/EU of the European Parliament and of the Council of 13 December 2011 on Combating the Sexual Abuse and Sexual Exploitation of Children and Child Pornography.

3 The issue of nomenclature and classification will be discussed in chapter 1, constituting an introduction to the issues of computer crime.

The last chapter goes beyond the framework of this monograph, as it concerns the issues of cyberterrorism and combating terrorist content on the internet in EU law [(Directive 2017/541 of the 15th of March 2017 on combating terrorism and Regulation (EU) 2021/784 of the European Parliament and of the Council of 29 April 2021 on addressing the dissemination of terrorist content online (TERREG)].

Filip Radoniewicz

1 Technical aspects of cybercrime

Classifications of computer attacks

Attacks on computer systems and IT networks can be divided in different ways, using various criteria. Depending on the source of the attack, attacks are distinguished as follows:

1) local (internal) – the perpetrator already has access to the attacked network or has physically connected to it;
2) remote – the attack is carried out from a system located outside network (usually from the internet).

Taking the number of computers involved as a criterion, attacks can be:

1) direct – when the attacker uses one computer for this purpose;
2) distributed – when the perpetrator uses many computers without their users' knowledge after taking control over them. These are the so-called zombie computers or agents. In this situation, it is difficult to detect the perpetrator, because thousands of computers from all over the world may participate in the attack. For this purpose, the perpetrator may use several computers (masters), each of which controls intermediary computers (so-called zombies), using installed ones' (without users' knowledge – e.g., as a result of hacking) attack programs (demons), waiting in sleep for a given moment. When everything is ready, the perpetrator issues commands to the masters, which run the controlled ones' demons themselves. Such networks of zombie computers are called botnets. They may number several hundred thousand hosts. They are currently serving no longer just for conducting distributed denial of service attacks (DDoS – see subchapter "Denial of service attacks"), but for other purposes, in particular sending spam, stealing from bank account holders and trading in illegally obtained information from infected zombie computers. Within 10 days the botnet assembled from 183 thousand computers is able to accumulate

DOI: 10.4324/9781003476771-1

310,000 data records (bank account numbers, payment cards and logins and passwords).[1]

Based on the degree of the perpetrator's interaction with the attacked system, attacks are distinguished:

1) passive – the attacker gains access to the transmitted data by being able to read them but does not modify them (e.g., eavesdropping and monitoring data transmitted between network users);
2) active – the attacker participates in the processing of transmitted data, being able not only to read them, but also to falsify or modify them, so as to obtain the intended target of the attack, e.g., "man in the middle".

Assuming the perpetrator's intention as a criterion, we can distinguish attacks as:

1) intentional;
2) unintentional – contrary to appearances, many attacks are of this nature, being accidental or resulting from ordinary human carelessness.

For example, most viruses are spread over the internet by unaware users. The network may also become disabled by a user experimenting with the software.

It is also possible to gain access unintentionally. With this situation we would be dealing with – for example – an ordinary user who as a result of a program error, would gain administrator privileges (e.g., by accidentally entering unexpected data inputs).

Currently, the attacker can use ready-made programs for attacks. They replace him in issuing subsequent commands during the entire process. It wasn't that long ago that you had to use one program for scanning ports, another for network penetration and another for carrying out the attack itself. Moreover, these applications were not easy to use – they were demanding at least basic knowledge of computer science. Currently, everything can be done by one easy-to-use program (e.g., Cain and Abel),[2] thanks to which a complex and dangerous attack can be performed by a layperson.

You can also come across a taxonomy according to which acts that are harmful in the security of IT systems are referred to as attacks, and these include attacks and system intrusions. An attack is considered an action that does not result in gaining access to the network or computer. For example, DoS attacks (discussed later) lead only to disabling the computer or network. But it is an intrusion when the hacker gains access to the network or computer. For this reason, it was proposed to name the perpetrators of the attacks attackers, while

1 Adamski (2013), pp. 68–69.
2 Easttom, Taylor (2010), pp. 440–443.

perpetrators of intrusions are intruders. This nomenclature was basically not accepted. Rather, there is a convention according to which the term "attacks" is used to describe all attacks on security networks, while attacks aimed at gaining access (i.e., hacking) are one of their types. Moreover, some attacks (e.g., buffer overflow) may seek both to disrupt the program and to gain access.[3]

Stages of computer attacks

The process of carrying out an attack is often broken down into stages. It should be noted that in practice such a division is difficult. In addition, not all phases are always present (it depends, among others, on the type of attack and its success; all of which can in principle only occur if successful). Before the attack, the perpetrator performs certain preliminary steps necessary to take appropriate action. First of all, it selects a goal and collects information about its topic. Several preparatory phases can be distinguished (similarly as final). It should not be forgotten that sometimes they overlap, and not all of them are always present. Moreover, sometimes the same activities are classified as both preparatory and preliminary activities (constituting part of the actual attack). It's probably safest to recognise that the attack consists of three main phases, within which the following steps can be distinguished:

1) preparatory activities, which may include reconnaissance, port scanning and target designation;
2) "proper" attack;
3) final activities (modification of the system enabling the perpetrator to return, covering up traces, using the effects of the attack – the so-called propagation).

Preparatory activities

Before launching the actual attack, a hacker conducts a kind of "intelligence" or "reconnaissance" mission. This consists in determining the target, its security measures and weaknesses. This stage is also known as the "passive phase" or "passive search", as it does not involve interacting with the target system.[4] The perpetrator may obtain a lot of information about the target from the internet. For example, if the network of a company chosen by the hacker is to be the target of the attack, useful data can be obtained from the company's website (such as the software or hardware used, if it boasts of having purchased

3 Shinder, Tittel (2002).

4 It should be noted that these activities are not always the first stage of the preparation phase. It sometimes happens that a hacker does not choose a specific system (vulnerable) to attack and in the first place he is searching it, carrying out actions usually performed at a later stage of the preparation phase (e.g., port scanning).

it). Additionally, the websites of software and hardware suppliers often contain reference letters from satisfied customers. It can be useful to obtain the names of employees on the web in order to log in using their accounts (even former ones – they are often active for some time after their departure from the given company).[5] Even rubbish thrown away by company employees (including documents cut up in a shredder) can be a source of information.

Another type of activity preceding the actual attack is port scanning (a place assigned to each service or application from and to which "its" data reaches). This is the active phase of the attack – it involves interacting with the system under attack (computer, server) but is not yet invasive. Port scanning involves checking which ports in a given system are open. This is done using software simply called scanners. They facilitate determining which devices in the network are vulnerable to attack, which TCP/IP services are running, and then examining them for security vulnerabilities. The scanner takes steps to establish a TCP connection by sending data packets to all ports in the system and waits for responses – if the port is listening, in other words, if it is open, it responds. This is the simplest and most reliable method of scanning, but this action exposes the perpetrator to detection. In addition, the victim's computer records IP addresses from the moment the connection is established. There are more sophisticated ways to avoid this. For example, half-open scanning (SYN scanning), FIN, X-mas and Null. The first of these involves initiating a connection – the so-called three-way handshake process[6] – which is initiated but does not continue. The port scanner generates a SYN packet. If the port is open, it will respond by sending a SYN-ACK packet. The scanning computer responds with an RST (Reset) packet, breaking the connection before the "handshake" is complete. As methods have emerged to detect and protocol this type of action, new scanning techniques have been developed, including the afore-said FIN, X-mas and Null. They are all based on the same principle, namely sending erroneous packets: in the case of the FIN method – packets with FIN (finish) flag, X-mas – FIN, URG (priority) and PSH (push flag – a packet forcing packet to be sent); in the case of Null – a packet without tags, to all ports of the target system and awaiting a response or its lack. Closed ports respond to the packet with an appropriate RST packet, while open ports will ignore it. This method is currently ineffective on Microsoft systems, which have implemented a patch that does not allow the RST packet to be sent. There are methods to avoid scanning detection, such as using an idle computer (finding a computer on the network that does not produce or receive

5 Krysiak (2005), pp. 474–475; Easttom, Taylor (2010), pp. 422–425.

6 The three-way handshake consists of three (hence the name) steps: first, the client sends a synchronisation request packet (SYN packet, i.e., with a SYN flag), secon, the server sends an acknowledgement packet (ACK) and a SYN segment – it itself requests synchronisation, third, the client sends an ACK packet in response confirming the server's request – the connection is established when both computers acknowledge their requests.

any network traffic and somehow impersonating it) and making multiple connections from a larger number of IP addresses and "hiding" the actual connection responsible for port scanning between them. It is worth adding that scanners are programs available on the internet (AngryIP, NSAuditor), often as applications used by administrators to check network security (e.g., Microsoft Baseline Security Analyser). Using them does not cause any damage.[7]

Additional activity included in preparatory activities is so-called enumeration. Unlike scanning, enumeration is an invasive method that requires an active connection to a computer and consists in sending a query about the resources provided by a given system. The answer is given without checking whether the questioner is authorised to it. Enumeration is performed by appropriate programs, namely FreeNetEnumerator, NSAuditor or ShareEnum.[8]

Port scanning (not to mention reconnaissance) is a non-punishable form of preparation for a crime. It is not criminalised in any legislation except the British one (Computer Misuse Act 1990 (CMA)[9]).[10]

Types of computer attacks

Computer eavesdropping

The surveillance of ICT networks is commonly referred to as computer eavesdropping. There are two types of computer eavesdropping – passive, where the perpetrator only becomes familiar with the intercepted information, and active, which involves modifying the transmitted data, e.g., by redirecting it to other network locations.

One example of passive eavesdropping is so-called sniffing – intercepting packets (put simply: "portions" into which data is divided to facilitate its transmission over a network). Before describing the essential aspects of this technique, it is important to explain that the network device which provides access to the network, i.e., a network interface card, filters the packets to make sure only the data intended for the computer on which the card is installed can reach it. The purpose of this mechanism is not so much to ensure security but to protect the computer against being overwhelmed. Many network interface cards can be switched to the so-called promiscuous mode to intercept all

7 For more on the subject, see: Easttom, Taylor (2010), pp. 425–432; Erickson (2008); Amoroso (2013), pp. 42–45; Shinder, Tittel (2002); Jajodia, Shakarian, Subrahmanian, Swarup, Wang (2015), pp. 67–56.

8 For more on the subject, see Easttom, Taylor (2010), pp. 433–436.

9 An Act to make provision for securing computer material against unauthorised access or modification; and for connected purposes (c. 18); the text of the Act is available on the official service www.legislation.gov.uk; CMA applies throughout the whole territory of the United Kingdom.

10 Radoniewicz (2021d), pp. 411–414; Tehrani (2017), pp. 183–184.

traffic within a local area network (LAN) using a protocol analyser,[11] a software tool used by network administrators to monitor the network (hence its alternative name – a network monitor). This may include the network monitor implemented in all newer Microsoft operating systems or the popular Wireshark (formerly ethereal). In addition to software that is, at least by design, intended for administrators, there are many sniffers developed specifically as "hacker tools", such as Sniffer Pro and Esniff.c. Also of note is the highly specialised software developed by the FBI, including Carnivore, dSniff and Cain and Abel. The general purpose of this software is to filter the intercepted packets for data of interest. A sniffer must be installed on a computer that is connected to a local network within which the targeted computer operates. Currently, the large majority of networks comprise multiple segments that are "separated" from each other by hubs or switches. In the former case, data can be intercepted only within a segment, whereas in the latter even this possibility is excluded, because switches filter data to allow only that which is specifically addressed to a computer (regardless of the network interface card's operating mode). This makes it impossible to operate entirely from the outside (from another network segment), especially from the internet, unless the switch or router is intercepted, or one of the more advanced methods is used (for instance, MAC flooding – overwhelming the switch with MAC addresses). Other available methods involve active forms of attack, such as session hijacking and man-in-the-middle attacks. These are discussed further on in this publication.

With the development of wireless LANs, however, we have recently seen a "revival" of the classic sniffing technique. In these networks, radio waves act as the transmission medium. They are primarily used by portable devices (including laptops, palmtops, mobile phones), as well as desktops and peripherals, both in office and home use. Any device with a WLAN[12] interface can connect to these networks. Since the transmission medium (radio waves) can be shared not only by the connected devices, but also by devices from other wireless networks, everyone can eavesdrop on data transmission within a network that has no or very weak protection. This especially may happen in home networks, which often lack password protection, or when they do have a password in place, it is too simple or is the default option (set by the device manufacturer and left unchanged by an unaware user). As in the case of sniffing in wired networks, the perpetrator needs a (wireless) network interface card that is set to

11 Network protocols – sets of rules defining communication processes. They need to use the same network protocol in order for the exchange of data between computers to be possible.

12 WLAN (wireless local area network) – they usually "supplement" local area networks – they are used where the use of cables is impossible or unprofitable. For uploading, the data uses radio waves (microwaves) at a frequency of 2.4 GHz or 5 GHz (depending on the standard). The term Wi-Fi is often used as a synonym for WLAN Wireless Fidelity which means a set of standards created for building wireless networks.

monitor mode (it can be considered a counterpart of the promiscuous mode in network interface cards).

An example of active eavesdropping is a man-in-the-middle attack. In the most simple term, it involves the attacker "inserting themselves" into data transmission between two computers and "relaying" information between them. The attacker redirects communications sent by the victim's computer (Computer A) to the intended receiver's computer (Computer B), to their own computer before they reach Computer B, and only then relays them to Computer B. As a result, all messages between Computer A and Computer B pass through the attacker's computer, allowing the attacker to read them. What is more, the attacker can modify the relayed communications. Even encrypted connections are not protected against such attacks. Having redirected communications from Computer A to their own computer, the perpetrator gains access to the encrypted connection by using a false certificate or public key (allegedly belonging to Computer B, which is, for instance, the server of a bank providing services to the user of Computer A). Subsequently, they establish a connection with Computer B, "pretending" to be Computer A, to relay data between Computer A and B (both ways). Consequently, all traffic between Computer A and Computer B (including login and the password to an online bank account) passes through the attacker's computer.[13]

Another example of active eavesdropping is session hijacking. Session hijacking takes place when an authorised connection between two computers is compromised and their session is "taken over". The session continues but the trusted host (or server) has been replaced by an attacker. This is achieved by "injecting" transport-protocol segments into streams exchanged through an authorised (properly established) connection between the victim and the trusted system. The attacker fabricates a correct segment and sends it as a valid one, originating from the previous sources. To this end, they must be able to view the content of a data stream (e.g., through sniffing).[14] The next group of computer and network surveillance methods based on specialised equipment involves electromagnetic wave analysis. An electromagnetic field is produced around each conductive object. For instance, cables connecting a computer with a printer are comparable to small radio transmitters.[15]

Computer data is converted into binary language and sent through electrical impulses. Consequently, an electromagnetic field is produced during transmission, and this field can be turned back into a legible form to read the encoded information.

Electromagnetic waves emitted by computer equipment can propagate in three ways:

13 Radoniewicz (2021g), p. 217. Cf. Krysiak (2005), pp. 495, 497–498; Russell (ed.) (2002); Ghernaouti (2013), pp. 235–238, Teach (2020), pp. 214–216.

14 Radoniewicz (2021g), pp. 217–218. For more on the subject, see Russell (ed.) (2002).

15 Adamski (2000), p. 59.

1) in free space (this includes, for instance, radio frequency waves);
2) in the form of surface waves on metal wires and objects;
3) on wireways (electrical wires).

Data interception technology, based on the analysis of an electromagnetic field produced by broadly defined computer equipment, is referred to in American literature as TEMPEST (Transient Electromagnetic Emanation Surveillance Technology). The same acronym also refers to a standard defining security conditions for the registration and analysis of electromagnetic radiation emitted by computer equipment (Transient Electromagnetic Pulse Emanation Standard). It was developed for military technology purposes and can be further applied to define the very phenomenon of electromagnetic radiation form cathode-ray tubes and the possibility of using it to intercept information displayed on the screen of a remote monitor (the so-called van Eck effect).[16] Of course, this method is historical – cathode ray tube monitors are currently unheard of.

More sophisticated devices used nowadays to intercept and analyse electromagnetic waves are fully computerised. They have digital-to-analogue converters that automatically correlate data from a received signal with the binary form of intercepted data. Converters can reproduce signals immediately (online) or later, e.g., in a lab (offline).

This surveillance method is of particular interest to criminals, as it allows them to operate from a safe distance without having to worry about leaving a trace.

Until recently, such techniques were very expensive, and as such could be used almost exclusively by intelligence and police services. Now, however, they are utilised by organised crime groups engaging in "professional" information "theft", such as gaining access to business secrets to sell them to competitors, as well as by private detectives. There are two main factors that have exacerbated this problem. One is the emergence of "demand" for such "services", and the other is the increased affordability of equipment.

Of course, it is even easier to capture computer data within wireless networks, in which electromagnetic waves are the medium.

The methods of cracking passwords

The most common way of securing access to a system is to require the user to confirm their identity using a login and password (other verification methods include the use of smart cards or biometrics). There are several methods of defeating this protection. If passwords are sent via a network, the perpetrator may try to intercept them, just like other data, using the so-called packet

16 Adamski (2000), p. 59; Grabosky, Smith (1998), pp. 38–39. Currently, this technology no longer has any practical application, since CRT monitors have long become obsolete.

sniffer; a keylogger or Trojan placed in the victim's computer may also be used for this purpose.[17] Apart from that, he may also simply phish for them (social engineering, discussed further in this publication).

The most effective way to get into the system is simply to deceive it by "presenting" yourself as an authorised person.

There are three basic methods of verifying a user's identity. The most popular of them is asking for a password (the "something you know" method – this "something" is the password). Sometimes we can come across a requirement for a person whose identity is being verified to possess an object for identification (e.g., a chip card – it is the "something you have" method). Identification methods which are seldomly employed are those that are based on a user's biometric data (e.g., fingerprints, iris – the "what you are" method).

The most common method of user authentication is, of course, the first one indicated earlier, the method that uses a login and password.

The least complicated method is the brute force method, which simply involves trying to guess the password by entering successive combinations. It is especially effective in situations when the hacker deals with a system belonging to a private user and knows the user's data, which the user could have used when creating the password (for instance their birthday, cat's name, etc.). If the perpetrator breaks into a computer to which he has physical access, he may look around the surroundings. It is possible that the user has written down the password somewhere. Contrary to what may be expected, this is often the case, especially in internal networks belonging to corporations or offices, where there is – for security reasons – a requirement to frequently change a rather complicated, and therefore difficult to remember, password. There are special programs that have a dictionary (hence the name "dictionary attack"), which allows the perpetrator to type in successive combinations of characters. The more complex the security system is, the more complex the password cracking program must be. The best of them allows the breaking of passwords with the help of several computers, for example by dividing the password into parts and using a separate computer to work on each of them. The process of breaking passwords protecting access to encrypted archive files is analogous. Moreover, the hacker may use other methods. For instance, if he has at least one decrypted file, he can decrypt other files encrypted with the same algorithm (the so-called text decryption method). Passwords are often stored in the system. It is simply enough to know where and how to look for them. This is due to the fact that the average user usually uses many passwords – to log in to their mailbox, to log on to websites, etc. Therefore, they usually "outsource" remembering them to the system, which then enters a password automatically for the user when needed.[18] The examples of popular password

17 See further comments in this chapter.

18 Shinder, Tittel (2002). For more on the subject, see Erickson (2008).

cracking tools – in addition to the already mentioned Cain and Abel – are John the Ripper and Hashcat.

While discussing the methods of cracking passwords, it is impossible not to refer to the method of cracking said passwords using so-called rainbow tables. It is, in a way, a combination of two techniques already discussed (brute force and the dictionary method). This method is used in cracking passwords encrypted with a one-way hash function.[19] It saves the computing power required to crack passwords with the dictionary method and thus saves time.[20]

Security breaches are just one of many techniques (and not even the most common) used by hackers to penetrate computer systems. Other methods boil down to bypassing them and consist of:

1) misleading people (social engineering);
2) misleading the system – these methods of bypassing security include spoofing (masquerading);
3) exploiting vulnerabilities (bugs) in operating systems, applications or protocols (sets of rules defining communication processes responsible for the identification of computers in a network), which is often carried out by programs called exploits (enabling exploitation of a specific vulnerability in a specific application).

Spoofing

Spoofing, on the other hand, consists in falsifying addresses, i.e., misleading the system. IP addresses which are most often falsified are IP addresses in packet headers (that is "portions" into which data is divided in order to be sent through a network), but it is also possible to falsify WWW (World Wide Web) and e-mail addresses, as well as entries in ARP tables and DNS servers. Therefore, we can talk about spoofing as:[21]

1) IP spoofing (masquerading), which aims to deceive the attacked system as to where messages are sent in order to sneak them past a firewall or router. It involves modifying packet headers to indicate a trusted address. Currently, it is not possible to eliminate IP spoofing. However, it can be limited by a properly configured firewall;
2) ARP spoofing, ARP poisoning. ARP (Address Resolution Protocol) is responsible for translating IP addresses to MAC physical addresses. In the dynamic ARP table, computers store IP addresses and corresponding MAC

19 "hashing function" (hash function) – a function that assigns a certain value (key, hash, hash-code) to any set of data, which is a "hash" of this data (generated on its basis according to a specific algorithm).

20 For more on the subject, see, e.g., https://en.wikipedia.org/wiki/Rainbow_table, access 19 June 2024.

21 Radoniewicz (2016), pp. 92–94.

addresses of hosts on their network. When the sending computer does not have in its table the MAC address corresponding to the host's IP address it wants to send data to, ARP protocol sends a message to all computers on the network (subnet) requesting the computer with a given IP address to provide its MAC address. When a response is received, the protocol makes an appropriate "entry" in the ARP table. ARP spoofing consists in the attacker's sending incorrect replies indicating a false MAC address (e.g., that of the perpetrator), which leads to the creation of false entries in the table. This results in data being sent to the wrong computer (indicated by the perpetrator);[22]

3) DNS spoofing, DNS poisoning. The Domain Name System is responsible – as indicated earlier – for translating domain names to appropriate IP addresses. The user, wishing to gain access to a specific website, enters its address in the mnemonic form. The operating system then sends a query to the DNS server to obtain the IP address of that website. If hackers manage to replace a valid address in a DNS server with another one, they will make the user, by typing the name of the website in which he is interested, go to a completely different site. This can be, for example, a page created by a hacker imitating the "original" page of a bank's website;
4) e-mail spoofing, such as actions aimed at concealing the real sender of an e-mail or impersonating the person or institution (e.g., a bank) trusted by the addressee. This technique is used in attempts to obtain confidential data by deception (like gaining access data to electronic banking accounts) and to send so-called spam.[23]

Social engineering

One of the most common methods used by hackers is the so-called social engineering[24] method. It involves obtaining confidential information by interacting with people. Unlike the methods mentioned earlier, it does not rely on technical means but on human weakness – gaining access to a system, either by earning the authorised person's trust or by cheating them out of passwords, by taking advantage of someone's carelessness and lack of attention, or by using deception. The most famous hacker – Kevin Mitnick – did most of his hacking

22 Network Basics Companion Guide, Cisco Networking Academy, pp. 504–505.

23 The term "spam" means mass messages sent that are unwanted by the recipients they reach. The origin of this term is explained in various ways, e.g., as an abbreviation of stupid pointless annoying messages. In fact, this term comes from one of Monty Python's sketches, in which restaurant guests who ordered various dishes listed on the menu received one and the same dish – luncheon meat). Generally, there are two types of spam: commercial advertising spam (unsolicited commercial information) and non-commercial spam, sent, e.g., as part of a smear campaign, aimed at extorting money, receiving financial support or spreading viruses.

24 Adamski (2000), p. 50.

using this method.[25] Usually, although it is not a rule, social engineering is used when a hacker is not able to gain access to a system by "technical" methods, i.e., with the use of a computer (by finding a security loophole, introducing a Trojan, etc.). It is sometimes used as a way of obtaining the information needed by a hacker in the course of preliminary activities.

This may involve, for example, contacting an administrator and claiming to be a new employee who is having problems with access to his account, or contacting a company employee and – after posing as an IT specialist or maintenance person – phishing for passwords. Information that can be obtained in the manner mentioned in the subchapter "Preparatory activities" (e.g., information posted on the company's website) will be helpful in carrying out these types of activities. Recently, obtaining data from various types of rubbish, especially printouts (also cut in a shredder), has become a popular method. The literature also distinguishes reverse social engineering, which consists in causing the victim, for example an employee of the company whose network is to be the target of the attack, to contact the hacker. This can be done by sending an e-mail with information on how to solve a common technical problem or new IT solutions, for instance. The advantage of this solution is that the victim may be less suspicious of the perpetrator offering to help and will not report it to an administrator as an incident.[26]

Social engineering constitutes a part of a large quantity of attacks. It often happens that, in order to carry out an attack by technical means, it is necessary to force certain actions on the part of a potential victim. It may be persuading them to click a link on a webpage, which results in the installation of spyware on the user's computer, or opening an attachment in an e-mail, and as a consequence "infecting the computer" (as it was, for example, in the case of the I Love You virus). In such situations, however, social engineering is not the most important element of the attack (viruses, Trojans or spyware may spread in other ways, without forcing the potential victim to take certain actions), whose uniqueness is determined by other elements, mainly of a technical nature, hence they are discussed elsewhere. In the next subchapter, phishing will be discussed as an example of a threat based on exploiting the user's gullibility.

Phishing

The aim of phishing (usually it is indicated that the term comes from "password harvesting fishing") is to obtain confidential data by impersonating

25 As emphasised by K. Mitnick, "The weakest link in the security chain is the human element. I obtained confidential information in the same way government employees did, and I did it all without even touching a computer. . . . I was so successful with this line of attack that I rarely had to go towards a technical attack" – as cited in Easttom, Taylor (2010), p. 63.

26 Casey, Daywalt (2011), p. 375; Krysiak (2005), pp. 475–476; Shinder, Tittel (2002).

entities and institutions, usually known and trusted (such as banks, online shops, auction services or mail services). Sometimes the perpetrator falsifies source addresses in order to authenticate e-mails sent (using IP spoofing). It is not necessary, because often addresses of specially created accounts associated with a given institution (e.g., a bank) are sufficient. Phishing is based on sending mass e-mails directing users to a false website that looks very much like the original one, which in fact intercepts information entered by the user. As an illustration, attackers send emails with a link to a website created by them that imitates the website of a bank (not necessarily the user's bank – emails are usually sent in bulk, and the perpetrator assumes that the bank's clients will be among the addressees) with a request to log in due to the introduction of new security measures and the related necessity to change settings. When an unknowing user tries to log in, the data he/she enters (password, login and other data requested by the attacker, for example a one-time password used to confirm banking operations) reaches the website author, who gains access to the user's bank account this way. The most common variants of phishing include spear phishing, when the perpetrator's emails are targeted at a specific group of entities (such as the employees of a specific company), with a clearly defined goal in mind (in the example earlier – gaining access to that company's network), and they resemble "company" emails sent by that entity; whaling, where the attack is targeted at members of corporate governing bodies (hence the name of this form of phishing – whaling, which is to be associated with hunting for big fish), or social phishing, where the environment of the perpetrator's actions are social networking sites (especially Facebook, although due to the popularity of this site, we can see a separate category created for this portal – Facebook phishing).[27]

Pharming

Pharming is considered a more complicated and sophisticated form of phishing. Its aim is to direct the user to a website indicated by a hacker and, with its help, to force the users to provide specific data or induce them to undertake certain actions. The simplest example of a crime that can be perpetrated using this technique is when a hacker obtains data providing him access to the victim's online bank account. A crafted page imitating a bank website is used to do this. The login details and password entered by an unaware user are intercepted and used by the perpetrator to gain access to the victim's real account. Often at the same time the so-called one-time password is tricked out, which is used by the user to approve online operations. Pharming comes in several variants – a less complicated one, where the perpetrator installs a Trojan on the victim's computer, which modifies entries in the hosts or lmhosts files. In these files, the operating system stores information about the translation of

27 Casey, Daywalt (2011), pp. 376–377; Easttom, Taylor (2010), pp. 61–62, 174–176.

mnemonic names to IP addresses – the system accesses this information before generating a query to the DNS[28] server to obtain an IP address. Another "type" of pharming involves "poisoning" the DNS server. A simpler variant of this method is for the hacker to use a fake DNS server that listens for requests sent by hosts for the translation of mnemonic names to IP addresses. In response, it sends out fake IP addresses. The client links the domain name with the IP address sent by the fake server.

As the use of the internet by means of wireless networks via home routers (predominantly routers provided by the user's telecommunication service provider, allowing simultaneous use of the internet, television and telephone calls via the same line) or access points has become increasingly common, a new type of pharming has emerged – so-called drive-by pharming. It consists in gaining access by a hacker (by means of malicious code, i.e., a "simple computer program", which an unaware user downloaded from the internet while visiting a website prepared by the perpetrator or another website, on which he had previously placed such code, e.g., by launching an XSS attack) to a router or wireless network access point, and then in changing its settings (sometimes it simply replaces the device's firmware with an appropriately modified version) in such a way that the user, after entering a mnemonic name of a website he wants to visit in a browser, is redirected to a fake website (e.g., a fake bank website). This change boils down to redirecting DNS traffic from the home router to the DNS server controlled by the attacker. In order to gain access to the router, the perpetrator must crack the password. In many cases, this may be unnecessary. The user did not know there was a need for a password or very simply the user unknowingly left the password pre-installed in the router or the password invented is not complicated. This attack may have many other negative consequences. For example, it may hinder the smooth functioning of antivirus protection by making it difficult to download new virus signatures and software updates, as well as new security patches (by invalidating relevant DNS records).

Exploiting vulnerabilities

The next group of hacking techniques that may allow unauthorised access includes methods based on exploiting vulnerabilities. The internet is a set of applications that perform specific functions (routing packets, sharing information or resources). To fulfil their role, they must cooperate with the user.[29] This process may involve, for example, pressing a key or "clicking" a cursor in a designated field, or entering a string of characters. The user may, intentionally or unintentionally, enter into an application data which the application

28 DNS (Domain Name System) – a protocol, service and server used for the translation of mnemonic names of network devices (both servers and individual computers) into IP addresses, understandable for devices which form the network (e.g., www.sejm.gov.pl to 194.41.12.17).

29 Russell (2002). See more Khurana, Yadav, Kumari (2018), pp. 302–307.

does not expect, i.e., data which the programmers did not anticipate, and therefore did not specify what happens when such unexpected (incorrect) values appear. This may result in system suspension or in opening the path to it.[30] A classic example of such a situation is buffer overflow (or buffer overrun). Buffers are areas of main memory in which programs store data before copying them to disk. Buffer overflow occurs when the number of bytes or characters exceeds the maximum number of bytes or characters to be entered, i.e., the number of bytes allowed by the programmer. So, if 25 bytes are foreseen and 27 are entered, in this situation the memory areas directly adjacent to the buffer, which may be another buffer, will be overwritten with other variables or data responsible for the control flow of the program being executed. As a result, the program may be disrupted or even brought to a standstill. A hacker can then gain access to the system by overwriting data in such a way that the program starts to execute their commands.[31]

Another group of attacks in this group, which should be mentioned here, is those based on the introduction of appropriately crafted input data, the execution of which by an attacked application allows, for instance, the bypass of authentication mechanisms, unauthorised acquisition or the modification of data or the execution of system commands. Structured Query Language (SQL) injection will serve as an illustration. Most websites are built with the use of databases that store data according to specific rules. This can be any type of information, depending on the nature of a given site (such as the website of an online shop, bank or library). SQL, in turn, is the most popular, database-independent language for transmitting commands to the database and presenting the results in a format understandable to the user. In order for an application to function (acting as an intermediary between the user and the website, for instance between an online shop's customer and that shop), it must have access to a database (containing both the shop's assortment and customer data) with the necessary authorisation to perform specific actions in this database, such as browsing the shop's assortment. It is therefore authorised to use its resources. If an attacker modifies commands passed by the application (usually via a form or query window)[32] to the database server, the modified queries will be executed with permissions assigned to the application. In this case, the attackers do not go through any authentication process. No firewall separating the application and the database server will stop them either. This is due to the fact that if the application may use the database, so can the attacker.[33]

30 Krysiak (2005), pp. 492–493. See more: Erickson (2008).
31 Radoniewicz (2016), pp. 97–99. Holt, Bossler, Seigfried-Spellar (2017), pp. 69–72; Russel (ed.) (2002).
32 Another *SQL Injection* method of attack is, e.g., the use of adequately modified cookies.
33 Radoniewicz (2016), pp. 100–101. For more on the subject, Russell (ed.) (2002); Khurana, Yadav, Kumari (2018), pp. 307–311.

The subject of Cross-Site Scripting (XSS) attacks – similar to SQL Injection attacks that exploit web application vulnerabilities – is the user's browser, in which a hostile code is activated. Input data is usually in the form of malicious scripts[34] but may take any form. XSS is particularly dangerous in services that require authentication, as hackers can perform basically any action based on the rights of the authenticated client or intercept a session. Situations where the victim is the system administrator are particularly dangerous. An XSS attack can also be used to redirect the user to another website, connect to the installation of a malicious program (e.g., a Trojan horse), as well as alter or falsify website content. To execute hostile instructions, XSS exploits the user's trust in a web application. Depending on where the malicious code is placed, XSS attacks are divided into XSS Reflected/Non-persist and XSS Persist/Stored. As regards the former, the malicious code is part of a URL forwarded to the victim leading to a website of which the perpetrator knows it is placed on a server vulnerable to XSS attacks.[35] The link may be sent by email, through instant messaging or it may be posted on a forum or form a page crafted specifically for this purpose. It must be accompanied by an "incentive" which will cause the victim to click on it, e.g., "You have just won a million zloty. All you have to do to claim your winnings is click on the link below". If the victim clicks on the crafted link, a connection to a http server vulnerable to XSS will be established and the hostile code will be "reflected" – sent back to the user's browser along with the downloaded website, where – like other "normal" scripts from this website – it will be executed. Although the code is harmless as part of the link, after its activation in the browser it can carry out the operations it was created for. Stored attacks can be used on sites which allow data to be stored, such as forums, blogs, social networking sites and so on. They must of course be placed on a server that is vulnerable to XSS attacks. The hacker inserts the malicious code, for example as part of a post on an internet forum, from where it is sent to a database. The perpetrator's next step is usually to direct the victim to this page using various social engineering techniques. Alternatively, the code waits until the user accidentally goes to the infected site. Once the victim enters the site, it is loaded into the browser on the user's computer, which executes all the scripts from the site, including the code posted by the hacker. There are ready-to-use software packages on the internet for browser hijacking using XSS, such as XSS Proxy or BeEF (Browser Exploitation Framework).

As with SQL Injection attacks, the main defence against such attacks is thorough validation and filtering of the server's input and output data.

34 Script is an uncomplicated program (see more in subchapter "Computer programs" of the chapter 2). JavaScript, on the other hand, is a standard programming language that can be used to create scripts embedded in web pages to provide new capabilities such as menus, sounds and other interactive features.

35 Vulnerable to XSS – one whose software does not filter the input data coming from the user, and therefore allows an attacker to embed malicious code into the WWW site placed on it, and then to execute it in the user's browser.

It should also be mentioned that applications often contain some kind of "errors", which are in fact bad (default) configurations in a way that increases their vulnerability to attacks. Therefore, in order to prevent them it is enough to change the configuration appropriately (disabling some processes or limiting the sharing of resources). Moreover – as already mentioned – users are often not aware of the need to set access passwords (e.g., in wireless routers).

Malware (malicious software)

The perpetrators often use special programs – e.g. Trojans, viruses, worms and other "hacker tools" – that belong to the group known as malware (malicious software).

Trojan horses, commonly known as Trojans, are seemingly harmless programs with additional instructions. They perform actions of which the user is not aware. Trojans are used by hackers to bypass system security. Once the Trojan is installed, the hacker has access to data. In addition, the Trojan itself can perform certain actions, such as deleting data or modifying it, or sending files to the attacker. Trojans are often disguised as harmless programs (used to be primarily screen savers) or as executable scripts on websites, which then install themselves on the user's computer while entering the infected website. One example of a Trojan is the Pokemon Trojan (classified as W32.Pokemon. Worm). After running the pokemon.exe file, an animated Pikachu (a character from a Japanese anime series titled *Pokemon*) appears on the screen, and at the same time the file is sent by email to everyone in the address book and proceeds to delete all the files from the Windows catalogue. A very popular Trojan was Netbus, written in 1998 by the Swedish programmer Carl-Fredrik Neither. Once placed on the victim's computer, it allows the perpetrator – in addition to the performance of "classic actions" (amongst others, file management or intercepting the characters typed on the keyboard) – to perform many operations, such as ejecting and inserting optical drive trays (CD-ROM/ DVD-ROM), changing mouse keys (left button becomes right and vice versa), displaying graphic files on the screen, switching off the system, launching any program or closing the operating system.[36]

Here, we should also mention "back door" programs. This term can be understood in two ways: firstly, as a program that is installed on the user's system (either on a regular computer or on a server) – obviously without the user's knowledge or consent – and enables the person who placed it to access the system bypassing any security features. It may be left by the hacker after their attack in order to allow them to return to the system without the necessity to break any security again, or placed by them in any other way. In principle, this variant can be assumed to be a type of Trojan (the most famous Trojan of this type was "Back Orifice", which could be camouflaged as a component of any

36 Cf. Holt, Bossler, Seigfried-Spellar (2017), pp. 135–139, Russell (ed.) (2002).

other program). Secondly – and this is the original meaning of the term – it can be understood as a backdoor deliberately left by the programmer.[37]

Viruses are computer programs installed without the user's knowledge and consent. Among other harmful effects, they can disrupt a system's operations (e.g., by displaying various messages) or destroying data. They can clone themselves (replicate their own codes) and attack other computers either by installing themselves on physical carriers to be subsequently spread by users, or through a network, by sending themselves as email attachments. In some instances, they remain dormant for a period of time to attack on a specific date (time bomb) or following a certain action by the user, like restarting the infected program (logic bomb). The term "virus" referring to such a self-replicating computer program, was coined by the American computer scientist Frederick B. Cohen (the author of the first antivirus systems). One of the earliest such programs was the Michelangelo virus, which became active and attempted to erase data on 6 March – the Renaissance artist's birthday. Viruses can mutate. However, they do not do so entirely on their own[38] – these mutations are often upgraded versions developed by hackers based on an old code. This way, they reduce their detectability by antivirus software. Several hundreds of new viruses emerge every month.[39]

The following types of viruses can be distinguished according to a range of criteria:[40]

1) in terms of virus location, the usual distinction is made into:
   a) boot sector viruses – which install themselves in the master boot record (MBR) of the hard drive, from which they are loaded to memory before the operating system is started;
   b) file-infecting viruses – which infect files (in the past, only executable files were targeted). This is the most common type of virus. The virus code is put at the start (in the oldest viruses), at the end or in a random section (in the newer versions) of the file. When the file is loaded into the memory, the first code to be executed is that of the virus. Once the code is executed, the carrier file starts to work correctly, and consequently virus activation may go unnoticed.
   c) multipartite viruses – often referred to as hybrid viruses – these viruses combine the characteristics of MBR-resident viruses and file-infecting

37 Shinder, Tittel (2002).

38 Although some viruses can replicate themselves to produce copies that have different codes, making them appear as some kind of mutation, the process is not intentional but rather occurs randomly, and does not involve any changes in the functions of individual instructions – see further discussion in this section.

39 Brenner (2012), pp. 36–37; Willems (2019), pp. 1–8; Holt, Bossler, Seigfried-Spellar (2017), pp. 131–135.

40 Russell (ed.) (2002): Shinder, Tittel (2002); http://www.symantec.com/connect/articles/security-11-part-1-viruses-and-worms.

viruses. This makes them more difficult to remove – if the MBR-resident section is omitted during removal, the virus will regenerate based on the code stored in the MBR to infect the system again;

d) macroviruses – such a virus will run like a normal macro would (macros are small instructions within documents), i.e., within another application (office software, usually a word processor, as well as a spreadsheet). They do not attack executable files, but those that contain macro definitions;

2) in terms of their location in memory, viruses can be divided into:

a) resident viruses – which install themselves in the infected host's memory and activate once specific conditions are met (e.g., when a program is run). Most viruses belong to this group;

b) non-resident viruses (also direct-action viruses – viruses that attack files directly) – these viruses can be activated only after running an infected program. In the majority of cases, it will be activated only once (unless the infected program is run again). Once activated, it is actively searching for ways to spread (through local drives or via a network) – that is, to infect other files;

3) in terms of their distinctive features, the following virus types can be named:

a) stealth viruses – these can hide from antivirus software by, for example, removing themselves from the infected file and changing location, or executing a copy of the previously infected file without the virus code to "suggest it" to the antivirus scanner during a hard-drive scan;

b) polymorphic viruses – these can replicate, but the copies they produce are not identical (e.g., due to their code being encrypted each time using a different key), making them more difficult to be identified by antivirus programs, which cannot store all virus variations in their databases;

c) metamorphic viruses – like polymorphic viruses, these change their codes, albeit not by encryption, but through removing or adding instructions, or by changing the coding pattern for these instructions (without changing their functions);

d) armoured viruses – viruses employing a range of techniques to make it more difficult for antivirus software to detect them (e.g., by misleading it as to their drive location);

e) cavity viruses – they overwrite files without changing their length (they do not add themselves to existing sections of a file, but instead fill in its empty spaces), making detection more difficult;

f) camouflage viruses – viruses that appear as harmless software. With the evolution of antivirus software and the emergence of advanced methods of virus detection, they are now easily detectable and as such rare;

g) companion viruses – these create a separate executable file with its own code that replaces the file with the original program (which is stored under a different name or removed permanently from the system). This is a very primitive type of virus, usually created by novice developers in high-level languages;

h) time and logic bombs, as mentioned previously.

Data threats can also be posed by programs called worms. Nowadays, the difference between worms and viruses is less clear than it used to be – these programs can switch locations via a network to infect multiple computers. In the past, this ability distinguished them from viruses which did not have that ability (they could replicate only on a single computer). Moreover, worms – unlike viruses – are autonomous in that they are not connected with other programs. They often replicate and are sent through electronic mail (mailers and mass mailers) by unaware users. The main purpose of worms is to create chaos in a network without necessarily destroying data. The first worm to have appeared online was the internet Worm (or Morris Worm), created in 1988 by Robert Tappan Morris Jr. (at the time a computer science student at Cornell University, now a professor at Massachusetts Institute of Technology – MIT). Developed to demonstrate that operating-system protections were faulty, the worm was anonymously put online. It was not meant to cause any harm and had a mechanism in place to control its replication. The mechanism did not work, however, allowing the worm to replicate at a stunning pace, disabling 6,000 computers connected to the internet (about 10% of all computers at the time) within a couple of hours. Morris tried to counter these adverse effects by putting a solution online. At the same time, UCB (University of California, Berkeley) and MIT scientists found a way to contain the worm. Once the crisis was averted, Morris admitted to having caused it and became the first person convicted under the Computer Fraud and Abuse Act of 1986 (he was sentenced to three years of probation, 400 hours of community service and a fine of about 10,000 dollars).[41]

Other examples of malware include:

1) rootkit[42] – a program used to gain full system access and to conceal the attack (for instance, by hiding files, processes and logged-in users) and the attacker's presence. Rootkits are usually spread as Trojans, backdoors and other types of malicious codes pretending to be normal programs or system libraries. Some versions gain control over the kernel, making their removal much more difficult (they affect the administrator's detection measures), and can even enter the BIOS memory of the motherboard or graphics

41 For more on the subject, refer to Brenner (2012), pp. 38–39; Loundy (2003), p. 57 et seq., Holt, Bossler, Seigfried-Spellar (2017), pp. 139–141; Middleton (2017), pp. 33–35.

42 The term "rootkit" derives from Unix tools designed to provide the user with administrator privileges without being noticed by the system administrator.

card, in which case system reinstallation and hard-drive formatting cannot solve the problem. There are the following types of rootkits:

a) kernel-mode rootkit – can edit the operating system's kernel, which makes it difficult to detect and remove;
b) application rootkit – replaces binary files with rootkit files;
c) memory-based rootkit – is active in the computer's operating memory, i.e., a system restart causes its removal;
d) persistent rootkit – changes system registry entries to destabilise the operating system;
e) user-mode rootkit – can only work within the privileges of the user on whose computer it was installed;
f) root-mode rootkit – uses system administrative privileges, which means it can be modified;

2) keylogger – a program that records the keys struck on a keyboard to gather valuable information, such as passwords. Some keyloggers can also intercept web browser data to have the web browser automatically fill in various forms, log in, etc.;
3) web crawler (also referred to as web spider, web robot, web bot) – a program that collects information about internet structures, websites and content; the data it collects can vary. They can, for instance, scan websites to find email addresses and collect them into databases, which are then used to send spam mail;
4) web bug – a program embedded in a webpage to collect visitor data (e.g., website entry time, IP address, type of browser);
5) exploit – a program designed to exploit software vulnerabilities;
6) dialer – a program that connects by dial-up with a telephone number without the user's knowledge and consent. In the past, when most people used modems and telephone lines to connect to the internet, these represented a serious issue – once installed, they reconfigured the modem connection to connect with premium-rate numbers. This led to excessive call charges, and it was not until they received unusually high telephone bills that the user then realised they had fallen victim to dialler fraud;
7) bot – the abbreviation of "robot"; a program designed to execute specific automated tasks over the internet. The aforementioned web crawler is an example of a bot. Currently, however, this term is mostly used to refer to programs that co-opt computers into botnets;
8) browser hijacker – a program that modifies web browser user settings – for instance, a default start-up page;
9) wabbits and rabbits – programs that are sometimes wrongfully classified as viruses, although their purpose is not to destroy data, but to destabilise the system through a denial of service attack, in which processes proliferate to block process tables (hence the attack is referred to as "fork-bomb attack" where "fork" is the system function that creates new processes). This effect is achieved through the abrupt replication of the program;

10) tracking cookies – cookies are small text files created on a user's hard drive by some of the visited websites. Based on these files, the user is recognised by the website when revisiting it. This not only makes the website load faster, but also allows its personalisation to align with the user's requirements. Cookie analysis makes it possible to track which websites were visited and when. Therefore, while cookies are not harmful in and of themselves, they do compromise privacy (hence website owners are obliged to inform users about the use of these files). More advanced types of cookies are tracking cookies (also known as third party cookies), which are exchanged between websites to match advertisements to user's tastes and habits. As a result, users who are interested in health and beauty (visiting websites related to these subjects) will see advertisements, for instance, of cosmetics and weight-loss diets, and not of cars and computers.[43]
11) ransomware – a type of malware that permanently blocks access to the victim's data (usually using encryption techniques) unless a ransom is paid. Offenders demand a ransom in bitcoins or other virtual payment methods that ensure the anonymity of the transaction. They promise that they will send the victim a key with which the data is decrypted after payment. But there is no guarantee that this will happen. An early 2018 data report by CyberEdge found that of 1,200 survey respondents, 38.7% paid the ransom. However, only half of them (19.1% of respondents) managed to recover their data later, while the rest (19.6%) failed to recover their data despite paying a fee.[44,45]

Spyware and adware (advertising software) are also included in this category. The programs in the first group collect data on the user's computer (e.g., personal data, payment card numbers, passwords, addresses of visited websites). They may be placed on the victim's system as a result of the offender gaining unauthorised access to it (that is by breaking in), either by means of a Trojan or by means of a "back door" program (see further discussion). Other installation methods include sending such a program by e-mail as an attachment to an e-mail (when opened, the program installs itself on the system), or as a result of the XSS attacks. It happens that some spyware programs are distributed together with application programs (this was the case with AOL messenger or KaZaa – a popular p2p network client). The collected data is transmitted to the person (or company) that placed it, in various ways. First of all, it can be sent directly via the internet. However, if the attacker has access to the

43 See also Huber (2019), pp. 78–80.
44 https://cyber-edge.com/wp-contentlupload2018/03/CyberEdge-2018-CDR.pdf; accesses on 1 June 2024.
45 Willems (2019), pp. 89–91. Cf. Holt, Bossler, Seigfried-Spellar (2017), pp. 145–146, Ahn, Doupe, Zhao, Liao (2019), pp. 104–128, Kosiński (2015), pp. 93–108.

infiltrated system, he can download it "personally" by "entering" into it from time to time in order to receive it. Similarly, if the program has been installed as a result of breaking in, the hacker may provide himself with the possibility to return to the attacked system (such as by leaving a backdoor to it) and then to retrieve the data. It should not be forgotten that, apart from invigilating the system, placing a spyware program may enable an attacker to obtain system administrator privileges (if the attacker manages to intercept the system password), which entails taking full control over the system.[46]

Adware is software that is distributed free of charge but "in exchange" for the user tolerating the display of advertisements, with these being the source of income for the manufacturer (they are adware-type licensed programs), as well as software that is installed without the user's consent and is displayed obtrusively (and obviously without the user's consent). In addition, such programs usually monitor websites visited by the user and thus adapt the content of adverts to specific interests. This way they not only take up bandwidth but above all violate the user's privacy. Furthermore, they also monitor the user's computer and send the data collected this way to the manufacturer.

Bluejacking and bluehacking

Bluejacking is construed as sending unsolicited messages using Bluetooth technology, which is currently used by many devices (from mobile phones to laptops), usually using so-called vcards, which are files used to exchange personal data ("business cards"). Bluejacking is usually harmless. It serves, for example, for meeting new people. However, it can be dangerous when it uses system files. Bluehacking, on the other hand, carries specific threats. It may assume the form of bluesnarfing, i.e., winning SMS messages by exploiting software bugs, or "manual" unlocking of the system by a third party (allowing it to establish an authorised connection via Bluetooth), or gaining data through the "back door", by setting up (manually) the authorisation of connections with the attacker's device. The effect of this is to accept all connections and files coming from the attacker. Another bluehacking technique is blueBug – creating a large number of connections with a device, leading to its suspension or enabling the perpetrator to bypass security.[47]

Denial of service attacks

Acts aimed at disrupting the network, often leading to network crashes, or at blocking specific hosts (e.g., servers, computers) include denial of service attacks.[48] Essentially, they consist in generating heavy web traffic or a specific

46 Cf. Easttom, Taylor (2010), pp. 176–178.
47 https://en.wikipedia.org/wiki/Bluejacking, access 1 June 2024.
48 These attacks can also provide a gateway to other illegal acts, such as session hijacking.

type of traffic that causes servers to crash, or overloads routers or network devices. Furthermore, such attacks can be targeted against specific computers, disabling their communication with the server.[49] There is also a "boosted" version of these attacks – the so-called distributed denial of service (DDoS) attack, which uses botnets – networks of intermediate computers – without the knowledge of their users. The perpetrators install special software on them (so-called demons, which are difficult to detect because of their "dormancy" – they only become activate to mount an attack) and run it at a specific time to mount the attack. Since it is possible to use a vast number of computers spread around the world, the true source of the attack remains unknown. The internet now offers access to both DoS software and "ready-made" botnets. What is more, it is possible to rent botnets.

Depending on the underlying mechanism, there are two general forms of denial of service attacks: those that crash services (drain resources) and those that flood services (drain the bandwidth). The former are similar to system intrusion attempts. They are based on exploiting vulnerabilities in the TCP/IP stack specification of a piece of software (sometimes a specific version thereof).[50] Examples include ping of death and teardrop. The former is a method designed to block systems by sending them so-called ping packets[51] whose size is larger than the maximum size (i.e., 65.536 bytes). It causes the computer (server) to crash or reset.[52] This method is now generally a concern of the past. New operating systems are resilient against such attacks, and those that are vulnerable are largely out of use, and besides, a number of patches were released[53] to protect against them. Teardrop attacks use packet fragmentation (i.e., the fragmentation of the "portions" into which data is divided to be sent over a network). Each network technology has a defined maximum amount of data packets they can carry. Since these values can vary between networks, a packet sent from one network to another might simply prove to be too large. Therefore, it must be broken down into smaller fragments. The packets are reassembled in the target PC based on data contained in fragment headings. One way by which a 4000-byte packet can be divided is as follows:

49 Shinder, Tittel (2002).

50 Erickson (2008).

51 Ping is a tool designed to check whether a connection with an IP address can be established by sending it an ICMP echo request (ICMP – internet Control Message Protocol, used for network diagnostics and routing), commonly referred to as a "ping packet", or simply ping. The received reply (ICMP Echo Reply) provides information on the number of packets sent to the target address and the number of packets that reached it, as well as the time it took to go both ways. The name derives from active-sonar probing – a method used by ships to assess the location of an obstacle or an unidentified vessel by listening to echoes produced by acoustic waves sent to the vessel. Over time, this abbreviation began to be developed as, for instance, Packet internet Groper.

52 Chauhan, Saini (2018), pp. 261–266.

53 Patch – a set of changes usually designed to fix certain issues or errors, or to update software. Currently, the preferred term is "update".

fragment 1 – bytes from 1 to 1500; fragment 2 – bytes from 1501 to 3000, etc. Teardrop (and its newer versions) divides the packet such that its fragments overlap, e.g., fragment 1 – bytes from 1 to 1500; fragment 2 – bytes from 1500 to 3000, and so forth. In effect, the target computer has trouble putting the packet together, which causes it to crash.[54]

Flooding (bandwidth draining) attacks can be divided into two groups: those that exploit TCP/IP vulnerabilities and those that generate heavy web traffic (so-called brute force attacks).

SYN Flood is an example of a flooding attack from the former category. It relies on the so-called three-way handshake in TCP, which causes two computers to establish direct connection with each other (computer and server). The process takes place as follows:

1) the client sends a packet with a request to synchronise (SYN);
2) the server sends an acknowledgement (ACK) and a SYN packet;
3) in response, the client sends an ACK packet to acknowledge the server's request – a connection is established once both computers have acknowledged their requests.

In order to block the server for other clients, the hacker can employ the described process by flooding the server with SYN packets (SYN Flood attack).[55] To this end, they send a large number of SYN packets with false, non-existing IP addresses to the server. The server replies by sending ACK and SYN packets, and waiting for an ACK packet from the client. Since the expected ACK packet does not arrive, the server queues its pending ACK and SYN packets. Because the queue has a limited capacity, the incoming SYN packets (from "real" clients) are ignored. If continued, the attack eventually causes the server to be blocked – the expected ACK packets do not arrive, but the actual SYN packets will not reach it, either. In effect, server connection will not be established.

Instead of using packets with a non-existent IP address, it is possible to utilise a false address suggesting that the data has been sent by the attacked server (so-called LAND attack). As a result, the attacked system finds itself in a loop, trying to reply to itself.

One other option is to use the IP address of the host or server to be blocked as a false source address, and then to send the falsified SYN packets to the broadcast address of the targeted network (see previous discussion). This will cause the host or server to be flooded with ACK and SYN packets, and at the same time the computers sending them will be blocked. This is called distributed reflected denial of service (DRDoS). Currently, these attacks can be prevented by firewalls.

54 Russell (ed.) (2002), Shinder, Tittel (2002).
55 Cf. Erickson (2008), Shinder, Tittel (2002).

The latter group (attacks involving the generation of heavy web traffic) can be exemplified by a DDoS attack using DNS servers, to which the perpetrator sends minor queries with a false IP address (which is the address of the victim). What this approach takes advantage of is the fact that the reply to these queries is usually many times larger (and the attacker can ensure this by adequately preparing queries). If the number of queries is large, an equally bigger number of replies will be sent to the victim's address, causing an overload. The administrator may, however, configure the DNS server to send a refusal, which is much shorter, to all suspected queries.[56]

One example of a simple application-level attack that produces the same effects as a DoS attack is the so-called email bomb. It consists in sending messages to a selected user that are numerous enough to block that user's email box, or to overwhelm the email server. Special software is available on the internet which allows messaging while concealing sender identity. Such attacks can be successfully managed by installing a packet filter. There is one type of an email bomb, however, for which the solution will not work – namely, list linking. This form of attack takes place by subscribing the targeted user to as many (potentially thousands) mailing lists as possible. The incoming messages from these lists fill up the mailbox or block the server, and since their origin is unspecified, the filter will not be able to contain them.[57]

56 Krysiak (2005), p. 500; Shinder, Tittel (2002).
57 Krysiak (2005), p. 501.

2 Basic information

Information and computer data

The notions of "information" and "data" are often considered to be equivalent and treated as synonyms, despite the differences between them. As information is an interdisciplinary notion, numerous diverse definitions have been coined in various fields of science (law, philosophy, information theory, cybernetics, information technology). The word "information" comes from the Latin *informatio* – which means presentation or image, and *informare* – to shape or to demonstrate. This is a common "intuitive" understanding of the notion.

For the purpose of this study, the meaning of the term assigned in cybernetics and information technology should be taken into consideration.

First, it is worth stressing that the term "information" in both of the mentioned fields has the characteristics of a primitive notion (it is an essential notion everyone should know and understand intuitively, and it is used to define other terms, hence it is normally not defined, for example, the notions of "point" in Euclidean geometry or "number" in the number theory). If a definition of a primitive notion is created, it is a meaning-specific definition, described by providing information on the relationships in which the referent of the defined notion exists), hence the difficulties in the development of the definition of information. According to Norbert Wiener, referred to as "the father of cybernetics", "Information is information, not matter or energy".[1] A considerable number of attempts to define the notion can be considered as rudimentary definitions. They most often stress that "information may include any factor which reduces the extent of ignorance of a given phenomenon, allowing a human being, a living organism or a machine to better understand their surroundings, and take intentional action".[2] In colloquial language (in the humanistic understanding of the notion), it is a description of a certain state of affairs, formulated using a certain natural language and addressed to a human recipient. In cybernetics and the theory of information, the term

1 Wiener (1985), p. 161.
2 Wojnicki (1985), p. 5.

DOI: 10.4324/9781003476771-2

"information" is used in a more comprehensive meaning than the one commonly applied. It is not only a description, but also a command, an imperative, an instruction or a guideline for specific actions. Information may be expressed in any form, with the use of any code (e.g., genetic code, electric impulse including neural impulse). Hence the senders (recipients) of information can be both human beings or other living organisms, or their organs, and a machine or an organisation.[3]

As mentioned, it is vital to determine the relationship between the notions of information and data. Two approaches can be identified in this regard. The first one involves substance-related understanding, in other words, a somewhat "classical" understanding, according to which information and data (a medium transmitting information, e.g., a sequence of signs) are treated as a unity.

The notions of information and data are clearly differentiated by Wolfgang Kilian who notes that

> information is data (spatial and temporal events, states, procedures, numbers, descriptions) which pertain to a certain model (a system of a fragment of the world with real and unreal components, and relations), at the same time recording the model (describing, forming and changing it) from the perspective of a given person (data user) and due to a specified objective. Therefore, data and information are not synonymous, as data becomes information by a specific reference to a given fragment of reality (model) from the perspective of a user, and due to a certain objective.[4]

Data is a carrier of information, it can take various forms (letters, numbers, images, sounds, electric impulses). Information is what can be interpreted, decoded from data. The same data sets can be interpreted in various ways, so they might become the source of different pieces of information. Information obtained in this way may be completely unreadable to humans (n. processor commands in a computer system).[5]

Legislators and international lawmakers who prepare regulations governing computer crime adopted the latter of the positions discussed earlier.

According to the definitions included in the Annex to the OECD[6] Recommendation of the Council concerning Guidelines for the Security of

3 Wojnicki (1985), pp. 5–6. Cf. Wróblewski (1968), 12, pp. 896–898.

4 Kilian (2003), p. 15.

5 Cf. Adamski (2000), p. 39.

6 Organization for Economic Co-operation and Development (Fr. Organization Coopération et de Développement Economiques) – an international organisation with an economic profile bringing together 38 highly advanced and democratic countries. It was created by 20 countries under the Convention on the Organization of Economic Co-operation and Development, together with Additional Protocols Nos. 1 and 2 to that Convention, constituting an integral part, done at Paris on 14 December 1960. It is a direct successor of the Organization for

Information Systems of 26 November 1992[7] (hereinafter Recommendation C (92) 188):

1) data means "a representation of facts, concepts or instructions in a formalised manner suitable for communication, interpretation or processing by human beings or by automatic means";
2) information is understood as "the meaning assigned to data by means of conventions applied to that data".

In similar way defined computer data in Article 1 (b) of the Convention on Cybercrime,[8] under which this term means "any representation of facts, information or concepts in a form suitable for processing in a computer system, including a program suitable to cause a computer system to perform a function". This definition unlike the one included in Recommendation C (92) 188 – provides that term computer data also includes programs responsible for performing functions by a computer system.

In general, information is not physical, all the more so it is not an object. It is a certain non-physical, "abstract object". It can be transmitted, processed and stored only after it assumes the form of data. Data can take on various forms. These include letters, sounds, digits and so forth. Data is the carrier (medium) of information. Information includes the contents which can be interpreted or decoded from the data. The differentiation between the two notions is vital from a legal point of view. It is possible to obtain IT data without the possibility to use the information included in such data, for instance due to the lack of knowledge of the algorithm according to which the information has been encoded. The destruction of data is not always equivalent to the damage to information, while the take-over of data does not necessarily mean information theft.[9] Gaining access to data does not always mean access

European Economic Cooperation (Fr. Organization Européene de Coopération de Economique), whose task was to develop a plan for rebuilding Europe from the destruction of war based ono The Marshall Plan. It should be emphasised that despite its origins and composition (the vast majority of its members are European countries) and an organic connection with the Council of Europe (common parliamentary body), OECD is a universal organisation. OECD objectives (in accordance with Article 1 of the Convention on the Organization for Economic Co-operation and Development) are to support targeted policies to achieve the highest possible, sustainable economic growth and employment and a rising level life in the Member States, contributing to expansion based on sound principles of economic development in both Member States and non-Member States and contributing to the expansion of world trade (see Izdebski (1996), pp. 91–92, 97–98; Latoszek (2001), pp. 350–351).

7 Recommendation of the Council concerning Guidelines for the Security of Information Systems of 26 November 1992 [C(92)188/FINAL]. More on Recommendation C (92) 188 and OECD initiatives Radoniewicz (2022b), pp. 54–56.

8 Convention on Cybercrime (ETS No. 185, hereinafter "the Convention"), opened for signature in Budapest on 23 November 2001.

9 Cf. Adamski (2000), pp. 39–40.

to information (e.g., during IT data transmissions where, roughly speaking, it is "delocalised" because, for the purpose of transfer, data is divided into packets which are sent via various routes, and in different order, and then put together at the target location). Computer data has a tangible nature, but it is not an object – it is a magnetic record of information made on a data storage device, electrical impulses or electromagnetic waves when transmitted over a network. Data storage devices, such as hard drives, semiconductor memory, CDs and DVDs, are, of course, objects.

The confidentiality, integrity and availability of computer data

In the time before the information revolution, the legal protection of information concerned the secrecy of correspondence, official secrets, state secrets and trade secrets. The digital revolution, and the resulting expansion of information technologies into new spheres of human activities which, along with the emergence of IT systems significantly streamlining data processing by facilitating data concentration, copying, transmission and dissemination, have resulted in the fact that information technologies are currently used in any sphere where data processing is needed, both in the private and public sectors.

Information itself has become an essential production factor and, at the same time, a commodity ("commodification" synonymous to the notion of "commercialisation") and a valuable asset.

In addition to information confidentiality which, as already noted, was the first one to be covered by protection, information accessibility and integrity are the other two attributes to be protected.[10]

Availability means the possibility to use the information by authorised persons whenever necessary. According to the guidelines laid down in Recommendation C (92) 188, the availability of data, information and information systems means that they are accessible and usable on a timely basis in the required manner. In turn, as per Article 4 (d) of the Regulation (EC) No. 460/2004 of the European Parliament and of the Council of 10 March 2004 establishing the European Network and Information Security Agency[11] (no longer in force), the notion has a broader scope. Availability additionally refers to the availability of services, as it means that data is accessible and services are operational. System or network overload with the surge of transmitted data (denial of service attacks – DoS attacks see chapter 1) can serve as an example of attacks targeting availability.

According to the definition laid down in Recommendation C (92) 188, integrity is understood as the characteristic of data and information being

10 See more, e.g. Akhgar, Staniforth, Bosco (2014), p. 14.

11 OJ EU 2004 L 77/1. This act is obviously invalid. This issue is currently regulated Regulation (EU) 2019/881 of the European Parliament and of the Council of 17 April 2019 on ENISA (the European Union Agency for Cybersecurity) and on information and communications technology cybersecurity certification and repealing Regulation (EU) No 526/2013 (Cybersecurity Act) (Text with EEA relevance) (OJ UE 2019 L 15115).

accurate and complete, and the preservation of accuracy and completeness. It refers to the integrity of both data and computer systems. As for information processed in an IT network, integrity means that the sent and received data is identical. The most frequent attacks against data integrity include the destruction or modification of data or infection of the system with a virus with a view to deleting data.

Confidentiality means access to data only by authorised persons, excluding third parties. It involves the protection of data against the reading and copying of data by unauthorised individuals. The guidelines set out in Recommendation C (92) 188 define confidentiality as the feature of data and information being disclosed only to authorised persons, entities and processes at authorised times and in an authorised manner. The forms of attack against confidentiality include, for instance, access to data by intercepting it during transmission (computer eavesdropping).

In addition to the ("core") attributes listed earlier; one can currently speak about other properties of information. In line with the ISO[12] 27001 standard (EN IDO/IEC 27001 – an international standard specifying requirements for information security management systems), information security is interpreted as the maintenance of confidentiality, integrity and availability of information. However, other components, such as authenticity, accountability and reliability, can be taken into consideration, too. Authenticity guarantees that the identity of a given entity or resource is as declared. Accountability means the assurance that the actions of such an entity can be assigned in a straightforward way to this specific entity. Reliability is a property meaning cohesive, intentional conduct and outcomes.

12 International Organization for Standardization (in French: Organisation internationale de normalisation) – an international non-governmental organisation bringing together national standardisation bodies. Due to its non-governmental nature, the standards developed by ISO are not legally binding on individual states but are respected by them due to the prestige of the organisation. The International Organization for Standardization sets standards in all areas of life (currently there are over 25000 – see www.iso.org/about, access 1 June 2019). Examples: ISO 3 – a standard unifying a series of values; ISO 2108 – International Standard Book Number (ISBN); ISO 9407 – standard defining shoe sizes; or PN-EN ISO/IEC 27000:2020–07 – information technology, security techniques, information security management systems and PN-EN ISO/IEC 27001:2023–08 – information security, cybersecurity and privacy protection. In turn, IEC (International Electrotechnical Commission) is a global organisation that develops and publishes international standards in the field of broadly understood electrical and electronic techniques. Other organisations involved in the standardisation network are ICANN (the Internet Corporation for Assigned Names and Numbers) which is responsible for assigning internet domain names and determining their structure and for general supervision over the operation of the DNS server system (server system, communication protocol and a service supporting a distributed address database network; enables the conversion of mnemonic addresses into logical addresses – IP addresses – understandable to network devices) around the world, and ITU-T (International Telecommunications Union – Telecommunications Standardization Sector ITU) which is responsible for the creation of standards in the field of telecommunications.

Computer programs

In international law and acts governing the legal protection of computer programs,[13] the definition of a computer program has never been provided. It is not stipulated in Directive 2009/24/EC of the European Parliament and of the Council of 23 April 2009 on the legal protection of computer programs.[14] There is no such definition in Polish, French and German legislation either (similar to the majority of contemporary European legal regulations). This is owing to the fact that, as rightly noted, technological progress is so fast that such a definition would soon become outdated.[15]

A computer program is generally believed to be a set of instructions (commands), expressed in a computer-readable form (with words, mathematical symbols, graphic signs), aimed at bringing about computer action intended by the program authors, with a view to achieving a specific result.[16]

Computer programs have two principal formats – a source code in a programming language[17] and an object code, which is the outcome of computer

13 The Paris Act Relating to the Berne Convention for the Protection of Literary and Artistic Works of 9 September 1886, concluded on 24 June 1971, the WIPO (World Intellectual Property Organization) Copyright Treaty adopted in Geneva on 23 December 1996. The term "computer program" was defined in Model Provisions on the Protection of Computer Software, adopted in 1978. As stipulated in Section 1 (I), it is "a set of instructions capable, when incorporated in a machine-readable medium, of causing a machine having information-processing capabilities to indicate, perform or achieve a particular function, task or result".

14 OJ EU 2009 L 111/16.

15 It is worth mentioning here that some legislation uses the legal definition of a computer program. It is included, for example, in the American Copyright Act of 1976, where a computer program is defined as "a set of statements or instructions to be used directly or indirectly in a computer in order to bring about a certain result" § 101, Title 17, Chapter I the United States Code – USC), and in the Civil Code of the Russian Federation of 2006 (Part Four of the Civil Code of the Russian Federation, adopted by the State Duma on 24 November 2006 approved by the Federation Council on 8 December 2006 (№ 230-ФЗ от 18.12.2006)), where, in Article 1261 the definition laid down in the Act of 22 September 1992 on the Protection of Computer Programs and Databases was repeated. It differs from the definitions included in the laws of other countries, because its notional scope also covers data intended for the operation of a computer and audiovisual representations generated by it: "A computer program is a set of data and commands presented in an objective form, intended for the operation of a computer and other computer devices in order to obtain a certain result, including preparatory materials obtained during the development of a computer program, and the audiovisual displays generated by it".

16 Radoniewicz (2009a), p. 24.

17 Due to the fact that the development of a program in a computer-readable form (binary language) is a process which requires substantial skills and considerable workload, programming languages are used for this purpose. They are artificial languages with their own expressions and syntax rules. An assembler language is at a higher level than the binary code, but it is still a low-level programming language which allows the use of acronyms and names (so-called mnemonics) translated into the binary language by a program (so-called assembler). Programmers normally use high-level programming languages, e.g., Basic, C++, which resemble "human" language. The written program is automatically translated into a binary language. In other

program compilation from a source code to the form which is "understandable" for a computer.[18] It is worth noting that the division is fairly conventional, although a lot of consideration is still given to it in legal studies. In practice, numerous variations exist between these two formats. As regards such languages as Python or Perl, a program source code is translated to the form of a binary code on execution.

A program may be executed directly – if expressed in a language readable for a given device – or indirectly – if interpreted by another program (interpreter) which analyses its source code and then executes it.

The terms "software" and "application" are often used as synonyms of a computer program. It is not entirely accurate, though. The first notion might refer to both a single program or all programs installed on a given computer and, most of all, to a certain set of programs forming a functional whole, designed with a view to performing specific tasks (e.g., operating systems controlling the operations of a computer; managing its hardware and software assets; application software, e.g., office suites, language suites – programming tools, network software allowing communication, or antivirus software), which include numerous additional components, such as so-called libraries.[19] Firmware is a specific form of software which is embedded in a device (integrated with hardware), meaning system software run from ROM, in the case of PCs, and providing a set of basic procedures for the system's interaction with hardware (e.g., Bios). Firmware can also be found in other electronic devices (routers, satellite navigation systems, telephones and so forth). In turn, an application is understood as either application software intended for the performance of a specific type of task (e.g., text processing, text editors or making calculations such as spreadsheets) or a program which requires the presence of a master graphical user interface or an operating system of a specific type, such as Windows applications. Applications should not be confused with utility software (a program allowing or facilitating the management of computer assets). A program may be included in a single file (so-called executable file).[20] This, however, is currently very rare.

---

words, the source code (created by a programmer) is compiled to an object code (understandable for a computer). See more, e.g. Murray (2016), pp. 16–22.

18 To this end, computer data is recorded in a binary language (also called a machine language or machine code) in a binary system, namely in the form of a sequence of 0's and 1's.

19 A library is a set of standard tested programs and procedures (subroutines), often in a compiled form, stored in a computer system, which can be implemented in new computer programs. The implementation takes place in the course of compiling and consolidating a given program. Libraries allow the improved quality of software (through the application of well-tested components, and avoiding the performance of the same algorithms, and acceleration of the program development process).

20 A file is an organised set of data (such as a program, document) having specified attributes (e.g., size, date and time of creation, or access rights) identified by a unique name (within defined boundaries, e.g., a given directory). It is a basic unit which allows the differentiation between individual data sets. Files combine various commands, numbers, words or images in a coherent whole which users can read, edit, or sent to an output device (e.g., a printer). Upon

Hence, it should be borne in mind that a computer program is intangible and, as such, it maintains its identity despite different forms of expression or medium (paper, computer data saved on a hard drive or CD/DVD or as electrical impulses transmitted via an IT network) – as only its material form changes.

The structure of a computer program usually can be divided into two parts (corresponding to two basic types of data):

1) data which forms a code (instructions intended for the processor, and controlling its operations);
2) data used by the program.

Within a computer program, there are parts intended for the performance of specific tasks, called subprograms, or procedures.

"Script" is the term that will also be used later in this book and hence merits explanation. It is a text file intended for execution without the need for compilation, which instructs a program on how a specific task should be performed (e.g., logging in to electronic mail). Scripts are applied to adjust the parameters to the individual needs of users, or to increase site interactivity.

To conclude the discussion of issues related to computer programs, it is worth mentioning interfaces. They are parts of a program which allow mutual links and interaction between software components (between individual programs), between software and elements of hardware, or between electronic devices (as an electronic system joining two devices, facilitating the connection of hardware or software functional modules through the precise definition of standards, e.g., the definition of input/output signals, such as M.2, USB). Moreover, it is necessary to mention interfaces allowing users to communicate with software and hardware using the senses (mainly vision). They assume the form of command-line interfaces, or the look and feel of a graphical user interface (e.g., GUI or MS Windows). It consists of, for example, such elements as icons or display screens.[21]

The history of computer networks and the internet

The rapid development of computer networks, with the emergence of the internet as one of its principal aspects, has taken place within the last 30 years.

---

saving, the data included in a file may be distributed into a large number of non-adjacent clusters (basic data storage unit, entailing one or several disk sectors). Their arrangement is recorded in a file allocation table, while users see them as a whole. A division can be made between executable files, which are files containing programs that are ready for execution (with .com or .exe extensions in Windows systems, or with an "x" attribute in Unix/Linux systems), a directory (folder) – a file system which contains references to other files (including other directories), symbolic links – references to other files (most operations in these type of files will in fact be performed on files to which they refer to), FIFO queues (First in, First Out), sockets, data streams, etc.

21 Cf. Barta, Markiewicz (2010), pp. 184–185.

At first, it was impossible to imagine that technological progress would be so dramatic. The first computer was built as early as the 1940s in the United States. It occupied a space of 139 m^2, used 17,000 vacuum tubes and performed 1,000 calculations per second (today an average personal computer performs several hundred million operations per second). The first "commercial computer" was the UNIVAC (Universal Automatic Computer) built in 1951.[22] Only government institutions and universities could afford to purchase computers manufactured in the 1950s and 1960s. The breakthrough came in the 1970s when the first Altair 880, accessible to the average US citizen, was launched on the market.[23] It was followed by Atari, the Commodore 64 and the IBM PC – personal computers for home and office use (the Commodore 64 selling a total of 3.5 million units by 1986).[24] The first networks were also created in the 1970s. They consisted of a mainframe and connected terminals which used files, programs and the computing power of the mainframe. They were useless without it. Together with the emergence of relatively inexpensive personal computers, an opportunity occurred to equip every employee with such a device, not only a terminal. At the same time, users lost the possibility to use the resources stored on the mainframe, and they had to exchange the data via physical storage media (so-called *per pedes* post). To address the issue, the Ethernet standard was developed in the late 1970s, allowing the connection of personal computers in a local area network (LAN).[25] It is currently the most popular technology used in computer networks.[26]

At the same time, so-called bulletin board systems (BBSs) started developing as networks consisting of computers connected via modems and phone lines. The simplest type of a BBS is an ordinary personal computer on which

22 More details in Gates (1995), pp. 1–64.

23 Gates (1995), p. 17.

24 Lavorgna (2020), p. 11.

25 Network infrastructure can vary greatly in terms of: size of the area, number of users and number and types of services available. Based on the criterion range, it most often stands out:

1) local area network (LAN): a network infrastructure that provides access to users and end devices in a small geographical area (e.g., office, school), administered usually by a single organisation or individual;
2) wide area network (WAN): network infrastructure that provides access to other networks over a wide geographical area (such as between cities), administrated usually by multiple service providers;
3) metropolitan area network (MAN): a network infrastructure that covers an area larger than a LAN but smaller than a WAN (e.g., a city). MANs are typically operated by a single entity, such as a large organisation;
4) wireless LAN (WLAN): similar to a LAN but wirelessly interconnects users and endpoints in a small geographical area;
5) storage area network (SAN): a network infrastructure designed to support file servers and provide data storage, retrieval and replication. It involves high-end servers, multiple disk arrays (called blocks) and Fibre Channel interconnection technology (Network Basics Companion Guide, Cisco Networking Academy, pp. 28–30).

26 Shinder, Tittel (2002).

appropriate software has been installed. Its user is provided access to resources, enabling the use of, for example, electronic mail, newsgroups, games and file exchange. To use a given BBS, it was enough to know the phone number and simply "make a call". Most BBSs provided the possibility to communicate with other BBSs, which allowed the exchange of mail and files on a global scale. Very soon BBSs began to be used for illegal purposes – access to malware, the dissemination of pirated software (mainly games) and pornography. For instance, according to A. Walczak-Żochowska, the first service devoted in full to child pornography was launched in 1982.[27] In its heyday, there were over 40,000 BBS's in the United States alone. Their significance has dropped to zero, as access to the internet became significantly cheaper with incomparably greater possibilities.[28] ARPANET, the "predecessor" of the internet, was developing at the same time.

The Advanced Research Project Agency (ARPA) was established in 1957 within the structures of the US Department of Defence (and further renamed as the Defence Advanced Research Project Agency in 1972). The original objective of the ARPA was to build an artificial satellite. However, the agency soon embarked on works aimed at developing modern technologies. The development of a computer network which would communicate between universities and government institutions became one of its main tasks. The ARPANET, developed in 1969, was the outcome of the work.[29] The central idea of the authors was to build a distributed network – without any central location, so that even if a part of its structure was destroyed or damaged, the rest of the network would remain in working order. Therefore, data transmitted via such a network was to be divided into packets, and sent independently, even via various routes, and after reaching their destination the data would be reassembled based on their headings (so-called *packet switching*). If the previous path is no longer available (e.g., due to the destruction of part of the network), the packets are routed to another path. Intermediary devices (first of all hubs,[30]

27 Walczak-Żochowska (2008), p. 110.

28 Cf. Grabosky, Smith (1998), pp. 5–6; Shinder, Tittel (2002).

29 Murray (2016), pp. 16–22; Shinder, Tittel (2002).

30 Hubs – multiport devices connecting network segments. Passive hubs only join wires. More advanced hubs execute additional tasks (e.g., active hubs strengthen the signal, and so-called smart hubs can monitor transmission). Since they send electrical signals from one port (socket) to all the other ports, the data being transmitted reaches all computers connected to these hubs. Replaced by switches, these devices are now rarely in use.

switches,[31] routers,[32] repeaters,[33] gateways,[34] access points)[35] only see the source and destination IP addresses[36] (packet contents are not available to them).[37]

The precursor of today's File Transfer Protocol (FTP)[38] was launched in the 1970s, together with newsgroups and multiplayer games. At the time, ARPANET limited its range to universities and government institutions. In the early 1980s, 5,000 hosts[39] were connected to the ARPANET, while the

31 Switches – equipment that uses packet switching to connect devices in most modern local area networks (LANs). They can also be used to create virtual local networks – networks of devices logically separated within a larger physical network. Regardless of their physical location (they can be located in different segments of the network), the devices that comprise VLAN can communicate with each other as if existing in a single shared local network.

32 Router – a multiport network device (it "is a Computer" – see Network Basics Companion Guide, Cisco Networking Academy, pp. 240–241) used to connect several (at least two) different networks or for logic network segmentation (division into sub-networks). Routers also allow the physical segmentation of networks. Their primary role is associated with routing (acting as intermediaries in the transmission of data between hosts from different networks). While they can operate as dedicated devices, it is equally possible for their functions to be carried out by computers with suitable software. Furthermore, routers can filter packets and act as firewalls.

33 Repeaters (Signal Booster) – the main function of the repeater is to regenerate an incoming signal from the sender before retransmitting it to the receiver.

34 Gateways – devices that connect networks that are using different protocols or architectures. They do so by translating or converting data formats or protocols between different networks. Their function is often performed by routers. More about network devices – see, e.g. Comer (2015); Krysiak (2005, pp. 110–122).

35 Access points – devices that allow wireless-capable devices to connect to a wired network. Here, the data can be transmitted and received using radio waves or infrared signals.

36 The IP address is assigned by the network administrator. However, it has nothing to do with the MAC (Media Access Control) physical address, which is linked to the network interface card. The address comprises two elements – network prefix (network ID) and suffix (host ID). See more, e.g., Comer (2015): Krysiak (2005, p. 205). "Physical addresses" of hosts, linked to the network interface card, are MAC addresses. As opposed to IP addresses, they generally cannot be changed (although some NIC producers provide such an option). When a packet is sent to another computer in a local network, the source computer must know the MAC address of the target computer. Accordingly, using the address resolution protocol (ARP), it establishes the MAC address of the target computer with the logical IP address specified in the sent packet and sends the address. The broadcast address is a special address used to send data to all hosts within a specific network (see more, e.g. Comer (2015); Krysiak (2005), pp. 104–105).

37 Network Basics Companion Guide, Cisco Networking Academy, pp. 17–18.

38 File Transfer Protocol (FTP) – a protocol developed to enable data transfer between a client and a server. Data transfer can happen in either direction – the client can download (pull) data from the server, or the client upload (push) data to the server (Network Basics Companion Guide, Cisco Networking Academy, p. 161).

39 Host – a computer or other device that communicates with other hosts on the network. Hosts include clients (i.e., computers, tablets, smartphones) and servers that send or receive data and provide services and applications. The host category does not typically include intermediary network devices such as switches and routers, which are often classified as nodes instead. A node is therefore a broader concept that covers any device connected to the network, while in order to recognise a given device as a host, it must be assigned an IP address. In other

number increased to 28,000 by the end of the decade. A significant milestone on the way to building an open-architecture network environment, and to blurring the boundaries between various networks (the process was called internetting)[40] was to acknowledge the TCP/IP protocol,[41] developed in the 1970s, as the leading standard in network operations. In 1983, ARPANET was divided into two parts – Milnet (Military network) and NSFNet (Civil network) from which today's internet emerged. In 1987, DNS (Domain Name System) was introduced as a protocol, service and server network used for the replacement of mnemonic names of network devices (both servers and individual computers) into IP addresses, understandable for devices which form a network (e.g., www.sejm.gov.pl to 45.60.74.29).

The World Wide Web (WWW) service started operating in 1992. Thanks to the application of hyperlinks, it has made the internet a much more accessible place, allowing its use by persons who do not have specialist skills. The occurrence of web browsers additionally facilitated "surfing". The first one was Mosaic, developed in 1993. The internet had over 1 million hosts at the time.

eBay, an internet auction service, and Amazon book store launched its operations in 1995. The following year saw the beginning of Google, currently the most popular search engine in the world. The Wireless Application Protocol technology (WAP), allowing internet access from mobile phones, has been in development since 1998. The first online bank, First Internet Bank of Indiana (www.firstib.com, operating to the present day), was established in 1999. At the end of the 1990s, the first networks and peer-to-peer programs (p2p, e.g., Gnutella, Napster, Kazaa, BitTorrent) were launched, allowing internet users to exchange files on an unprecedented scale. Skype, a web messenger (IM – Instant Messenger) based on p2p architecture has been present on the internet since 2003. Then came social networking sites – services facilitating the exchange of opinions, views and works. Facebook was launched in 2004, YouTube was established in 2005 and Twitter in 2006. In 2005, the number of internet users worldwide exceeded 1 billion; in 2007, it amounted to approximately 1.319 billion (accounting for 20% of the world's population at the time), reaching 1.6 billion in 2010, and it currently sits at

---

words, all hosts are nodes, but network nodes are not hosts unless they require an IP address to function. Commonly, the concept of a host is narrowed down to a client, treating servers as a separate category.

40 The term "internet" was used for the first time in 1974 by V. Cerf and B. Kahn in their research report titled "A Protocol for Packet Network Interconnection", concerning the TCP protocol.

41 Computer identification in a network is done by network protocols. Network protocols are sets of rules defining communication processes. They need to use the same network protocol in order for the exchange of data between computers to be made possible. Two or more protocols in various layers of the network create a stack. Currently, the most popular stack is the aforementioned TCP/IP (Transmission Control Protocol/Internet Protocol). For more on the subject, e.g. Network Basics Companion Guide, Cisco Networking Academy, pp. 105–106, 175.

5.4 billion, which is around 64% of the global population of 7.5 billion.[42] It should be noted here that the number of connected devices is even greater, as a lot of users connect to the internet via multiple devices (tablets, smartphones, computers).[43,44]

The arrival of hackers

It can be said that the beginning of hacking dates back to the moment when the first telephone networks were built, as it was the time when phreakers (phone freaks) started operating. They broke in to telecommunications networks to make free phone calls. Another group of offenders who became active at the time were crackers, specialising in the breaking of security features in telecommunication systems. The term is currently used to refer to "crackers" of passwords and security features. Both of the aforementioned groups can be considered as predecessors of today's hackers[45] (in fact, a lot of them started their activities as phreakers or crackers). At first, the term "hacker" had a different meaning than today – it simply meant a talented programmer. Later, after the subcultures of hackers and phreakers merged together, it acquired another meaning (similar to the one we know today) – someone acting underground, hacking into computers and networks, sometimes for noble reasons, and sometimes just for fun and fame. This image of hackers in culture was consolidated in films (in particular *War Games* directed by J. Badham in 1983 or *Hackers* in 1995 by I. Softley).[46] Currently, the term "hacker" is understood as a person who "wreaks havoc" on the internet, i.e., both breaking in to computer networks and computers, and disrupting their operation.[47] In colloquial speech, the word is often used to refer to all offenders acting on the internet, including online fraudsters. Therefore, the term "hacking" can be understood in several ways: as hacking in its strictest sense, namely conduct consisting in

42 The data comes from the ITU (International Telecommunication Union)_ website www.itu.int/itu-d/reports/statistics/2023/10/10/ff23-internet-use/; access 19 June 2024.

43 To compare, in early 1980s, 5,000 hosts were connected to the ARPANET, while the number increased to 28,000 by the end of the decade.

44 See more, e.g. Rustad (2009), pp. 1–4.

45 The term "hacker" was derived from the term "hack", used in the 1960s by students at the Massachusetts Institute of Technology to indicate clever jokes they were making (one of the examples provided was a manipulation of a control panel in a lift, as a result of which the lift would go to a totally different floor than the one indicated in the selected button). See Brenner (2012), p. 16.

46 Cf. Shinder, Tittel (2002). Ghernaouti (2013), pp. 189–192, Grabosky (2016), pp. 4–8; Gillespie (2016), pp. 42–43; Hill, Marion (2016), pp. 19–20.

47 At the same time, we are dealing with a certain type of a paradox – there is no need for hackers to have such advanced skills as their predecessors from previous years. It is enough to download appropriate software which will do everything for us. A term was even coined to define such persons – script kiddies (a script is a program written in a scripting language which performs certain tasks inside another program – in short, it is not an independent program, e.g., JavaScript on websites, or macros in MS Office documents).

obtaining access to an information system or computer data, and as hacking in a broader sense, namely any attack against the security of information systems and data (including disruptions to the operation of IT systems, or modifications to, or destruction of, computer data), and in the broadest, colloquial sense of the term – as a collective reference to practically all crimes committed online (of course, except, for example, dissemination of pornography or copyright violations). The subject of this study is hacking in the broad sense of the term.[48]

Definition of a computer crime

To date, no legislator has decided to introduce the legal definition of a computer crime into the legal system. This results from the fact that, due to the pace of technological progress, it would often need to be amended. Of course, there are many definitions of the term in criminal law theory. Probably the first, very comprehensive and general definition was proposed by Ulrich Sieber during the OECD Expert Committee meeting in Paris in 1983, according to which "computer crime (or 'computer related crime') is any illegal, unethical or unauthorised behaviour involving automatic data processing and/or transmission of data"[49] can be considered one of the first. An even more general definition of computer crime was developed several years later for Interpol.[50] According to the definition, computer crimes are "criminal activities in the scope of computer technologies". But its authors supplemented it by adding a catalog of such conducts (*inter alia* the breach of resource-access rights, fraud with the use of computers, the reproduction of software, the storage of illegal resource). Defining computer crimes in this way has become the norm – attempts have been made to provide examples of crimes rather than create general definitions.[51]

48 See more Brenner (2012), pp. 16–23; Graham, Smith (2020), pp. 31–35; Huber (2019), pp. 33–35; Hill, Marion (2016), pp. 61–64; Holt, Bossler, Seigfried-Spellar (2017), pp. 75–104.

49 Sieber (1998), pp. 20–21.

50 Interpol (International Criminal Police Organization (ICPO)). An organisation established in 1923 at the International Congress of Criminal Police in Vienna. In the years 1938–1945 it came under the control of the Third Reich authorities and its headquarters were moved to Berlin. In 1946, during a conference in Brussels, it was reactivated and its headquarters moved to Paris. In 1989, the headquarters were moved to Lyon. Interpol currently has 196 Member States. Its purpose is to support cooperation between police authorities around the world within the limits set by their regulations and in the spirit of the UN Universal Declaration of Human Rights and the creation and development of all institutions for effective prevention and combating of crime (cf. Article 2 of the Interpol Statute, the text of which is available on the official website www.interpol.int, access 1 June 2024). There is a network of operational contact points within Interpol's structure 24 hours a day, seven days a week (Interpol 24/7 Global Communication System, current name – I24/7).

51 Radoniewicz (2021a), pp. 37–38. See also Hill, Marion (2016), pp. 3–6; Payne (2020), pp. 7–11.

Along with technological advancement, the terms describing the phenomenon of computer crime are also evolving, including:

- computer crimes (the earliest name);
- computer related crimes;
- crimes by computer;
- digital crimes;
- internet crimes;
- e-crimes;
- netcrimes;
- virtual crimes;
- cybercrimes;
- IT-crimes.[52]

Without doubt, the term which has gained the greatest popularity is "cybercrime", used both in literature on the subject and in some international documents (in particular, the Convention on Cybercrime).

During the Tenth United Nations Congress on the Prevention of Crime and Treatment of Offenders[53] it was found that cybercrime refers to any crime that can be committed by means of a computer system or network, in a computer system or network, or against a computer system or network. At the same time, the following classification of cybercrime was proposed:

1) cybercrime in a narrow sense (computer crime), meaning any illegal behaviour directed by means of electronic operation that targets the security of computer systems and the data processed by them, i.e.,
   - unauthorised access;
   - damage to the computer, computer data or applications;
   - computer sabotage;
   - unauthorised interception;
   - computer espionage;
2) cybercrime in a broader sense ("computer-related crime"): any illegal behaviour committed by means of, or in relation to, a computer system or network, including such crimes as illegal possession and offering or distributing information by means of a computer system or network.[54]

52 Adamski (2000), pp. 32–33; Clough (2015), p. 9; Hill, Marion (2016), pp. 3–4.
53 The Tenth United Nations Congress on the Prevention of Crime and Treatment of Offenders. Vienna, 10 to 17 April 2000.
54 Cf. Gercke (2011), p. 26; Shinder, Tittel (2002).

Classification of computer crimes

First, it is important to point out the simplest possible dichotomous classification of computer crimes, with a distinction between "old" and "new" crimes. The first group includes common ("plain", conventional) offences that have gained a new or modified form as a result of technological developments (e.g., the dissemination of child pornography, fraud). "New" crimes are those that have emerged with the development of information technology and its convergence with telecommunications (e.g., unauthorised access to information system, unauthorised modification of computer data or network disruption).[55]

Computer crimes can be broken down into the following groups:

1) crimes which do not require the connection of computers to a network;
2) crimes which can only be committed on the internet (internet, virtual crime);
3) crime generally related to modern technology, including those related not only to computers and computer networks, but also crime in the field of nanotechnology or bioengineering.[56]

Of course, the preceding classification is outdated – crimes committed without the use of a computer network (e.g., involving physical connection to a computer or server) are extremely rare.

However, the most common and the most practical classification (as it is the least refined and corresponds to reality to the greatest extent) is the one that divides cybercrime into crimes in which:

1) computers or networks are the target of crime (in a sense, "victims"; "the computer as a target"), also simply referred to as computer crimes – namely, hacking in the broad sense, in line with the convention proposed earlier, i.e., crimes with which this book is concerned (new offences);
2) computers or networks are a tool used for committing a crime ("computer as an instrument or a tool"), in other words, "computer-related crime", e.g., the dissemination of child pornography, fraud[57] ("old offences");
3) computers or networks can be used for additional tasks related to a given crime (e.g., the storage of data on illegal drug trafficking).[58]

55 Radoniewicz (2021a), p. 39. Cf. Grabosky (2006), pp. 12–14.
56 Clough (2015), p. 9.
57 This category is often broken down into two groups, i.e., ***computer assisted (related) crimes*** – crimes related to the use of a computer, such as computer fraud, and ***computer content crimes*** – cybercrime related to the contents of processed information, such as the dissemination of child pornography. See, for example, Koops, Robinson (2011), pp. 130–133; Wall (2013), pp. 49–50.
58 Brenner (2011), pp. 16–20; Clough (2015), p. 10, Grabosky (2006), p. 11.

Both in literature on the subject and in the legislations of various countries, it is possible to find a similar "tripartite" division of cybercrime into computer crimes, computer-facilitated crimes and computer-supported crimes.[59] To conclude the discussion related to the classification of cybercrime, it is worth pointing to a modification of the aforementioned divisions, presented at the Forensic Science Society Convention held in April 2001 in Huntingdon, when a classification of computer crime was made based on the criteria of the techniques applied by offenders, and the nature of their acts. It is a detailed version of the tripartite division described earlier. The classification features six categories of computer crime (cybercrime), including computer-assisted crime (where the commitment of such crime is facilitated by using computers); computer-enabled crime (where computers enable the commitment of such crime), computer-only crime (crime which cannot be committed without using computer technology), internet-assisted crime (crimes which can be committed both in a conventional (common) way and via the internet), internet-enabled crime (where it is easier to commit a given crime with the use of the internet) and internet-only crime (crime possible only via the internet), meaning those crimes where the data sets on servers or data packets sent between network nodes are used by the perpetrators in the course of their actions.[60]

The aforementioned tripartite classification was also adopted in the Convention on Cybercrime (see next chapter). Prohibited acts amounting to offences categorised in the first group were grouped together under the single title "Offences against the confidentiality, integrity, and availability of computer data and systems". Crimes from the second group can be found in three subsequent titles, as "Computer-related offences", "Content-related offences" and "Offences related to infringements of copyright and related rights".

Discussing the issue of defining and classifying cybercrime, it is worth mentioning those acts which cannot be placed in the category of computer crime.

Susan W. Brenner makes an apt distinction between computer crime and the phenomena of cyberterrorism[61] and cyber war, treating them as notions separate from cybercrime. The former term includes terrorist attacks which are carried out via computers and computer networks,[62] while the latter is defined as actions taken by states using information technology with a view to achieving military or other strategic goals.[63]

59 Clough (2015), p. 10. For information about the classification of computer crimes, see also, e.g. Brenner (2012), pp. 1–14; Ghernaouti (2013), pp. 28–35: Gillespie (2016), pp. 1–20; Grabosky (2006), pp. 11–42; Holt, Bossler, Seigfried-Spellar (2017), pp. 22–26.

60 Hołyst (2009), pp. 19–20.

61 Unlike D.L. Shinder and E. Tittel who classified cyberterrorism as cybercrimes involving the use of violence. Shinder, Tittel (2002).

62 Terrorist acts are usually crimes (e.g., murder, destruction of property). They differ from them in their purpose, which is to implement a political or social program. See chapter 6.

63 Brenner (2011), p. 16.

Cyberspace

Here, it is worth explaining the notion of cyberspace. The term "cyberspace", a combination of the two words "cybernetics" and "space", meaning cybernetic (virtual) space, emerged in the 1980s. The originator of the term is believed to be William Gibson, a Canadian writer, who used it in his novel *Neuromancer*, published in 1984, to describe the computer-generated virtual realities that the characters inhabit:

> A consensual hallucination experienced daily by billions of legitimate operators, in every nation, by children being taught mathematical concepts. A graphic representation of data abstracted from the banks of every computer in the human system. Unthinkable complexity. Lines of light ranged in the nonspace of the mind, clusters and constellations of data.[64]

The notion found its place in mass culture, and it is currently used to define virtual space, understood as space for communication via computer networks. This term is often used as a synonym of the internet.[65]

In American law the term "cyberspace" means "the interdependent network of information technology infrastructures; and includes the internet, telecommunications networks, computer systems, and embedded processors and controllers".[66] This definition limits cyberspace to network infrastructure. However, we also encounter cases in which the legislator (or legislators) tried to indicate that cyberspace consists of certain non-physical (immaterial) elements. In the light of UK National Cyber Security Strategy, cyberspace is "the interdependent network of information technology infrastructures that includes the Internet, telecommunications networks, computer systems, internet connected devices and embedded processors and controllers. It may also refer to the virtual world or domain as an experienced phenomenon, or abstract concept".[67] The so-called Tallinn Manual (version 2.0) assumed that it is an environment covering three layers: physical, logical and social.

> The physical layer comprises the physical network components (i.e., hardware and other infrastructure, such as cables, routers, servers, and computers). The logical layer consists of the connections that exist between network devices. It includes applications, data, and protocols

64 Gibson (1984), p. 69.

65 Radoniewicz (2021a), p. 33 Cf. Karpiuk (2023), p. 188; Wall (2013), pp. 10–11. See more Chałubińska-Jentkiewicz (2021), pp. 23–27; Pehlivan (2018), p. 5–10; Shackelford (2015), pp. 55–57.

66 50 § 1708(d)(2) the United States Code (USC).

67 UK National Cyber Security Strategy 2016 to 2021, p. 75, www.gov.uk/government/publications/national-cyber-security-strategy-2016-to-2021, access 19 June 2024.

that allow the exchange of data across the physical layer. The social layer encompasses individuals and groups engaged in cyber activities.[68,69]

In Polish Law, cyberspace is defined in: Article 2 (1a) of the State of Emergency Act of 21 June 2002,[70] Article 3 (1)(4) of the Natural Disasters Act of 18 April 2002[71] and in Article 2 (1b) of the Act of 29 August 2002 on Martial Law and the Competences of the Commander-in-Chief of the Army and the Rules of the Commander-in-Chief's Subordination to the Constitutional Authorities of the Republic of Poland,[72] according to which the term is understood as "the space for the processing and exchange of information, created by together with their mutual interrelations and interactions with users". Tele-information systems is defined in Article 3 (3) of the Act of 17 June 2005 on the computerisation of the operations of entities carrying out public-service task[73] as "a set of cooperating IT devices and software, providing processing and storage, as well as sending and receiving data via telecommunications networks by means of a terminal device appropriate for a given type of network".

Therefore, based on the definitions cited earlier, cyberspace can be assumed to include not only ICT systems, i.e., the devices that constitute them (hardware) along with the programs (software) that ensure the performance of functions by these systems (computer data processing), but also the interactions between devices and their users.

It should be emphasised that cyberspace has been declared the fifth domain for conducting military operations – among sea, land, air and cyberspace. As pointed out by Tadeusz Zieliński: "cyber conflicts and cyber crises involving national and non-national parties, including cyberwars, are likely to happen. In other words, cyberspace was considered among the domains which can serve as yet another battlefield for military operations".[74] It has sometimes been suggested that it should – like the high seas, international airspace or outer space – constitute a "global community" (a "res communis omnium").[75]

Overview of the history of cybercrime criminalisation

The issue of perceiving information technology as a source of threat was evolving along with its development. An American scholar researching the issue, Reed C. Hollinger, lists four essential periods of the evolution, based on American circumstances:

68 Tallinn Manual 2.0, p. 12.
69 Radoniewicz (2024), pp. 44–46.
70 Consolidated text Polish Journal of Laws of 2017, item 1928.
71 Consolidated text Polish Journal of Laws of 2017, Item 1897
72 Consolidated text Polish Journal of Laws of 2022, item 2001.
73 Consolidated text Polish Journal of Laws of 2024, item 307.
74 Zieliński (2021), p. 3.
75 Tallinn Manual 2.0.

1) 1946–1976. At first, there was no awareness of any threat whatsoever. In addition, no such threats had existed before computer networks were developed. The initial two decades are mainly the operations of the phreakers mentioned earlier. In the 1970s, BBSs were launched in the United States, arousing the interest of state authorities;
2) 1977–1988. This period saw the gradual process of criminalising computer abuse. As a result, 48 state laws (with Florida as the first state – 1978) and two federal laws were adopted by 1988. The FBI began carrying out carefully planned operations against hackers (e.g., the most famous hacker, Kevin Mitnick, was arrested).[76]
3) 1989–1993. Hollinger calls this stage "the period in which hackers were demonised". During that time, several spectacular events took place, and they actually evoked a sense of threat not only in the USA, but also in Europe. A special group for a rapid response to computer incidents was established in the USA (CERT – Computer Emergency Response Team). The direct cause for appointing the team was the emergence of a bug in the ARPANET, the first self-replicating program developed by Robert Tappan Morris Jr., which disabled 6,000 computers connected to the network (10% of all computers) (see chapter 1.). In Europe, law enforcement authorities stopped the operations of a Hanover-based group of hackers who penetrated British and American military computer networks in search of information which they could sell to the KGB.
4) 1993. In the 1990s, according to Hollinger, the "censorship" period began. Attempts were made to limit the flow of information on the internet. Relevant legal regulations were introduced in all legal systems, both in democratic and totalitarian states. It is notable that in democratic states, more restrictive legal acts were repealed after a while as unconstitutional. For instance, the US Communication Decency Act of 1996, prohibiting the dissemination of "obscene, lewd, lascivious, filthy, or indecent" material, was considered non-compliant with the Constitution of the United States in 1997. China currently has very strict regulations in force.[77]

In turn, Ulrich Sieber lists six main "waves" of computer crime legislation:[78]

1) the 1970s when it was realised that developing information technology allowed state governments to collect, store and analyse immense quantities of information about citizens, hence the first regulations enacted at the time focused on the protection of confidentiality of communication and the right to privacy;

76 See more Middleton (2017), pp. 3–9.
77 Hollinger (1997), p. XVIII et seq. Cf. Adamski (2000), pp. 2–4.
78 Sieber (1998), p. 66 et seq.; see also Grabosky (2006), pp. 7–9.

2) the 1980s when it was realised that unauthorised interference with the operation of computers might result in economic loss. Therefore, legislators banned any actions involving unauthorised access to computers and damage to computer data;
3) the next wave of legislation activities was related to the protection of intellectual property and, more specifically, to the protection of rights to computer programs. It was the outcome of pressure on the part of software producers who began to feel the impact of others copying their products without consent;
4) the moment the internet became a place of disseminating harmful (illegal) content (pornography, hate speech, libel or offensive contents), legislators began enacting regulation aimed at counteracting the phenomenon;
5) the fifth wave concerned procedural provisions, in particular those referring to the search and collection of evidence in electronic form, with the related issue of taking initiatives allowing international cooperation in relation to jurisdictional controversies arising from the cross-border nature of computer crime, and the cooperation between providers of telecommunications and network services, and law enforcement authorities;
6) the last (sixth) wave, which is still taking place, entails legislative measures in the shadow of terrorist threats aimed at ensuring widely understood security in the network, as a part of state infrastructure (the protection of critical infrastructure), often at the expense of civil liberties.

Challenges related to the emergence of computer crime

New technologies have many features that facilitate criminal activity while making crime prevention and prosecution more difficult:[79]

1) the reach of the phenomenon. The internet has provided opportunities for communication on an unprecedented scale. In 2023, approximately 67% of the world's population, or 5.4 billion people, used the internet.[80] It is an enormous number of potential perpetrators and their victims;
2) availability. The use of computers and the internet has never been easier or cheaper. On the one hand, the prices of computer hardware and computer network communications have fallen considerably and, on the other hand, the use of technological advancements has become far easier than in the past. The times when computers were enormous and expensive devices, requiring additional advanced knowledge to be operated, are long gone. The internet can currently be used on mobile phones. Computer programs

79 Radoniewicz (2021a), pp. 41–42; Clough (2015), pp. 5–8. See also Hill, Marion (2016), pp. 105–109.
80 The data comes from the ITU (International Telecommunication Union) website, www.itu.int/itu-d/reports/statistics/2023/10/10/ff23-internet-use/; access 19 June 2024.

have a user-friendly graphical interface, and the vast majority of users cannot imagine operating a computer in the so-called text mode (using command lines in MS Windows systems or consoles in Unix/Linux systems);

3) ability to remain anonymous (often not as reliable as it might seem) which both internet users and potential perpetrators of crimes committed via the internet can enjoy. It creates an illusion of full confidentiality (or even secrecy) of all the activities performed by network users, and the related chance for avoiding potential penal liability;
4) possibility to collect a substantial amount of information across a small space from where the data can be easily retrieved, and in which it can be reproduced and disseminated without limitation;
5) global reach, which means that the prohibited acts committed by perpetrators in one country can have a negative effect in another. This can give rise to extremely complex situations. For instance, this is the case when a perpetrator based in country A carries out a DdoS attack (distributed denial of service)[81] against a server located in country B, using thousands computers located in countries C, D, E, F, G, H, I and J, while residents of countries K, L, M, N, O, P and Q can suffer the consequences of such activities;

81 DoS (denial of service attacks) – the aim of this group of attacks is usually to disrupt the functioning of the network (including its complete blocking). Sometimes they are a preliminary stage leading to other harmful activities (e.g., session hijacking). In principle, it can be assumed that they consist in causing large network traffic or traffic of a specific type, which results in the server hanging or overloading the router or other network devices. Sometimes they are directed against specific hosts, e.g., computers of ordinary users (e.g., to take over a customer's session with his bank's website), or by blocking the server to prevent users from communicating with it (e.g., suspending the servers of an online store). Their "enhanced" variant is DDoS attacks (distributed denial of service), carried out using botnets – networks created from computer systems (usually computers, routers or other network devices, and now also smartphones or other devices connected to the network, such as an autonomous car, a smart refrigerator, etc.), over which the botnet creator gains control as a result of installing special devices in the programs (so-called bots or daemons). These are the so-called zombie computers or agents. These programs lie dormant and wait for the commands of the botnet operator in order to take the actions for which they were created, e.g., carrying out distributed denial of service (DDoS) attacks, massive spam sending or data theft (such as logins and passwords to banking websites). They may number several hundred thousands of hosts. Sometimes they create a pyramid structure – infected computers gain control over other hosts, becoming the so-called masters. Infected hosts are scattered all over the world, so determining the source of the attack is basically impossible. It is assumed that within 10 days the botnet consisting of 183,000 computers is able to collect 310,000 data records (bank account numbers, payment cards, logins and access passwords). Currently, carrying out even a very complicated attack involving a huge number of hosts is not very difficult – appropriate programs for creating botnets are available on the internet. Additionally, it is possible to purchase a "ready-made" botnet. Or even renting one for a specific period of time. For more on DDoS attacks and their examples, see Lloyd (2017), pp. 228–230, Ghernaouti (2013), pp. 229–233. Amoroso (2013), pp. 7–9. Holt, Bossler, Seigfried-Spellar (2017), pp. 141–144; Kosiński (2015), pp. 12–125.

6) circumstances related to investigating crimes and conducting criminal proceedings. The ephemeral nature of computer data is a source of problems related to collecting and securing evidence. Furthermore, there are problems arising from the international reach of the network and the private nature of a lot of them, which obstructs access to, for instance, traffic data which is stored on servers only for a specified period of time. The obvious consequence of the "technical" nature of computer crime is the fact that individuals dealing with the prosecution of perpetrators must have knowledge of state-of-the-art technology and appropriate hardware.

Information society and knowledge-based economy

The digital revolution has led to the development of a new notion describing modern society – information society. The term was introduced in 1963 by the Japanese anthropologist Tadao Umesao (the original version: *jōhōka shakai*), in his article on the theory of society evolution based on information technologies, and popularised by K. Koyama in 1968 in his dissertation titled *Introduction to Information Theory*. It came to Europe thanks to French sociologists A. Minc and S. Nora, who used the term in their report submitted to the French Prime Minister Raymond Barre in 1978. The notion of an information society was popularised in Europe in relation to the publication of the Bangemann Report (owing its name to Martin Bangemann, EU Commissioner for Information and Telecommunications Technologies),[82] in which a need to build a European information society, as one of the European Union's priorities, was expressed. Yet no definition of information society was provided, either in this document or in any other Community legal acts.

Numerous academic definitions of the term were developed. All of them are similar,[83] hence two, relatively universal definitions will be cited for the purpose of this study. According to T. Goban-Klas and P. Sienkiewicz, the term should be understood as a society which has found ways to apply technologically advanced means of information processing and communication with a view to creating foundations for national income, thanks to which a source of livelihood is provided to a substantial proportion of the society.[84] In line with the definition proposed by K. Krzysztofek and M. Szczepański, it is a society in which information has found a widespread application in social, cultural, economic and political life. Information society is a society equipped in well-developed means of communication and information processing which

82 Bengemann Report titled "Europe and the Global Information Society – Recommendations to the European Council", published in Brussels on 26 May 1994.

83 For more on the subject, see an article by J.S. Nowak, in which he collected and analysed 30 definitions of information society (Nowak (2008), pp. 29–33).

84 Goban-Klas, Sienkiewicz (1999), p. 53.

forms the basis for generating the majority of national income and ensures the source of livelihoods for the majority of the population.[85]

Information society is strictly related to the notion of knowledge-based economies. These two terms are sometimes used interchangeably. The concept of "knowledge-based economies" was first used in the 1980s in OECD documents. These documents also included the definition of the term, according to which it means "economies which are directly based on the production, distribution and use of knowledge and information", which was further repeated in the assumptions of the Lisbon Strategy.[86]

Detection of attacks and intrusions

The detection of intrusions or attacks is made possible thanks to audit mechanisms. It involves recording all events taking place in the network and in individual computers in the form of logs as mentioned earlier. On their basis, it can be determined whether a hacking incident or an attack has occurred (unless the perpetrator, as discussed earlier, has not disabled log records prior to the attack, or deleted relevant logs after his/her operations were completed).[87] Log records are stored in various places, depending on the type of data collected. Firewalls, routers or servers store traffic data which is information on events on the network and details of participating entities. Operating systems on individual computers record user activity – logging in and out of the system and addresses of websites visited – as well as analyse the contents of electronic mail and "monitor" various forms of user activity (including the use of games or programs).[88] In addition, the history of visited websites is stored by browsers. And we should not forget about cookie files in which website services visited by users save "their data".

Additionally, there are Intrusion Detection Systems (IDS)[89] and Intrusion Prevention Systems (IPS).[90] They operate in the background, and inform the administrator if any disturbing event occurs. Unlike IDS, which is a passive system, IPS's are active systems – they can automatically take certain specific actions (e.g., block a suspicious internet connection, try to identify the attacker or reprogram the firewall). There are two models of intrusion detection systems:

85 Krzysztofek, Szczepański (2002), p. 170.
86 The Lisbon Strategy – a socio-economic development plan for the European Union adopted by the European Council on 23–24 March 2000, whose objective was to make Europe the most dynamic and competitive economic region in the world through the development of knowledge-based economies.
87 For more on the subject, see Russell (2002).
88 Bilski, Pankowski, Stokłosa (2001), pp. 32–33.
89 See https://en.wikipedia.org/wiki/Intrusion_detection_system, access 19 June 2024.
90 They are also called Intrusion Detection and Prevention Systems (IDPS), see https://en.wikipedia.org/wiki/Intrusion_prevention_system, access 19 June 2024.

1) a model entailing the detection of anomalies, consisting in the search for single events or sequences of events departing from the regular system usage profile, determined with the use of statistical methods on the basis of audit analysis and other data (most of all these are protocol anomalies demonstrated in appropriately applied communication and traffic protocols – several connections that might be part of a complex attack);
2) a model entailing the detection of malicious activity, consisting in the comparison of a sequence of events with the recorded signature of known intrusion techniques (there are individual signatures – identifying specific forms of attacks, and generic signatures – identifying an entire attack methodology).[91]

Examples of Intrusion Detection Systems include a commercial Tipping Point[92] and Snort,[93] available under the open-source licence.

Securing evidence in electronic form

There are several important issues to bear in mind in relation to collecting evidence in electronic form. Firstly, appropriate preparation is required. It is recommended that thorough reconnaissance is performed – it is advisable to obtain from a network administrator or other competent person information concerning the location of a server, internet service providers (who might have useful information) or rules of making backup copies in a given network. Of course, an action plan should be prepared (for instance, it is necessary to identify the possible location of the computers being seized – it might turn out that they are placed in different buildings, and communicate via a network). It is necessary to consider the need to disconnect the computers being seized from the network, in order to secure the data, as it is possible that the data may be deleted remotely.

A certain proportion of the seized data constitutes so-called ephemeral data, not saved on hard drive (but, for instance, in RAM, in cache or on the onboard memory of peripherals), which is lost the moment a computer is turned off. Therefore, it is logical that such data should be secured first, and at the site of the crime. We should bear in mind that the actions aimed at collecting such data modify the contents of computer memory, which is why it is advisable to intercept data as running processes, and as a "dump" of data in RAM. There are appropriate programs to this end. They should be run from a CD/DVD or a USB drive prepared beforehand, not from the hard drive of the computer being examined (so as not to launch any processes or programs

91 For more on the subject, see Bilski, Pankowski, Stokłosa (2001), p. 38; Muszyński (2004), pp. 213–217.
92 See https://en.wikipedia.org/wiki/TippingPoint, access 19 June 2024.
93 See https://en.wikipedia.org/wiki/Snort_%28software%29, access 19 June 2024.

saved on its hard drive or memory). *Guidelines for Evidence Collection and Archiving*, developed by the IEEE, stipulate that the most volatile evidence should be collected first, starting from the most ephemeral data, i.e.:

1) registers and cache;
2) routing tables, ARP cache, kernel statistics;
3) the contents of system memory;
4) temporary file systems;
5) data on disk.

Since computer data is fragile and prone to alteration, it is advisable to immediately make a copy in the form of a bit stream image of a storage medium on which the data has been saved. All further actions should be performed on such copies, not on the "original" storage media. The process of making such a copy is called disk imaging. It is compressed and saved as an image file. In logical and physical terms, it is identical to disk contents – it differs in this respect from a backup copy which contains only active files. In order to prepare a disk image, you can connect to a computer from the outside (e.g., by connecting a disk in order to make a copy, or using a network connection), or stand-alone imaging devices (such as DIBS – Disk Image Backup System, RAID – Rapid Action Imaging Device), or simply dismantling the hard drive and connecting it to another workstation.[94]

Let us not forget that storage media is susceptible to high temperatures or electromagnetic radiation. To prevent data loss, they should not be exposed to the operation of such factors. Of course, it is required to secure them properly – to place in an antistatic bag, and use bubble wrap during transport.

There are cases when perpetrators try to destroy data. In many instances, it is possible to recover it. Neither simple deletion nor disk formatting, even together with partitioning, can remove data permanently. It is not easy to obtain the data, but it is still possible. Special programs have been developed for that purpose. Of course, there are methods which make data recovery completely impossible. They can be destroyed irretrievably, both in logical terms (with the use of "cleaning" or "resetting" programs, which overwrite data on the disk with random binary values – 0 or 1), and in physical terms – by simply destroying the disk itself (demagnetising, burning, or exposing to high temperature or acids).

Special multifunctional programs were developed for computer forensics purposes, such as for instance, EnCase[95] or PTK Forensics.[96]

94 Shinder, Tittel (2002); Holt, Bossler, Seigfried-Spellar (2017), pp. 529–535.
95 For more on the subject, see https://en.wikipedia.org/wiki/EnCase, access 19 June 2024.
96 For more on the subject, see https://en.wikipedia.org/wiki/PTK_Forensics, access 19 June 2024.

3 Cybercrime in the law of the Council of Europe (part I) – Convention on Cybercrime

Road to Convention on Cybercrime

The statement that international cooperation plays an enormous role in the fight against crimes committed on computer networks is undoubtedly a truism. The range of telecommunications networks is vast and worldwide. The conduct of a perpetrator may have simultaneous effects in many countries located at opposite ends of the globe. In addition to close cooperation between law enforcement authorities, it is also important to criminalise computer crime in as many countries as possible until the so-called hackers' paradise, i.e., countries in which their actions remain unpunished, are completely eliminated. This is in fact one of its formal conditions (due to the principle of dual criminality). I think it's safe to say that this has already happened. Currently, it is necessary to harmonise the regulations in force in individual countries (due to the *nullum crimen sine lege* principle).

For these reasons, work on creating a legal framework for interstate cooperation to ensure the security of IT data and systems has continued on an international forum since information and communication networks became interstate and thus crimes committed through them became transboundary.

It is important to emphasise that the requirement for international cooperation between states is not the only defining characteristic of the fight against computer crime. It also requires the involvement of private entities – representatives of the IT industry, mainly providers of network services.

It is believed that the first international initiative relating to the fight against computer crime was taken by the Council of Europe.[1] The initiative in question

1 Council of Europe (French: Conseil de l'Europe) – international organisation bringing together almost all European countries and several countries from outside this continent (e.g., Armenia). It was established on 5 May 1949, as a result of the signing of the Statute in London by 10 countries. The Council of Europe currently consists of 46 countries. Its seat is Strasbourg. The main objective of the Council of Europe is "to achieve a greater unity between its members for the purpose of safeguarding and realising the ideals and principles which are their common heritage and facilitating their economic and social progress" (Article 1(a) of the Statute of the Council of Europe). By pursuing such a defined goal, the organisation is primarily concerned

DOI: 10.4324/9781003476771-3

was the Conference on Criminological Aspects of Economic Crime,[2] held in Strasbourg in 1976, at which an attempt was made to define certain categories of computer-related crimes.[3]

In 1985, the Committee of Ministers of the Council of Europe instituted a panel of experts made up of 15 members (Select Committee of Experts on Computer-related Crime – PC-R-CC), chaired by Manfred Moehrenschlager, in which Ulrich Sieber participated as a scientific expert-consultant, whose task was to develop certain "guidelines" to be followed by Member States in penalising computer-related abuse. The committee finished its work in April 1989, the outcome of which was the report and draft Recommendation,[4] approved by the European Committee on Crime Problems (CDPC) in June 1989 and adopted by the Committee of Ministers of the Council of Europe on 13 September 1989 as Recommendation R (89) 9 on Computer-related Crime[5] (hereinafter Recommendation R (89) 9).

with promoting and protecting human rights, democracy and cooperation among Member States in the field of culture.

2 Twelfth Conference of Directors of Criminological Research Institutes: Criminological Aspects of Economic Crime in Strasbourg.

3 Schjølberg (2008), p. 2.

4 Recommendations of the Committee of Ministers are – besides conventions – a tool for the harmonisation of law. They differ from conventions in that their provisions are general and non-binding. They are used by the Council of Europe to indicate the objectives of its policy in a given discipline, or the directions of legislative actions to be taken by Member States. The lack of detailedness is, however, an advantage, as in consequence they are more flexible than conventions, allowing Member States greater freedom to choose how to implement their provisions. Further advantages of recommendations are that they are easier to revise and above all that they enter into force upon adoption and are addressed to all Member States. They may recommend the adoption of regulations inspired by solutions provided therein or annexed thereto. They additionally happen to supplement conventions, particularly on sensitive issues (e.g., the 1981 Convention No. 108 for the Protection of Individuals with Regard to Automatic Processing of Personal Data, referred to further in this volume, is supplemented by a number of recommendations, including the Recommendation R (99) 5 on the protection of privacy on the internet of 23 June 1999 (https://search.coe.int/cm#{%22CoEIdentifier%22:[%2209000016804f4429%22],%22sort%22:[%22CoEValidationDate%20Descending%22]}; access 1 June 2024) and Recommendation CM/Rec(2021)8 of the Committee of Ministers to member States on the protection of individuals with regard to automatic processing of personal data in the context of profiling of 3 November 2021, https://search.coe.int/cm?i=0900001680a46147, access 1 June 2024)). Without the binding power, the recommendations enjoy "moral" authority as they express the common position of Member State governments, reinforced additionally by the institution of the monitoring of their implementation by the Member States. This is confirmed by the fact that they sometimes have effect in the public international law (they are mentioned in many bilateral collaborations and good neighbourhood treaties), and they are sometimes referred to in constitutional court decisions.

5 Recommendation No. R (89) 9 on computer-related crime and final report of the European Committee on Crime Problems, Council of Europe, Publishing and Documentation Service, Strasburg 1990. The text of Recommendation R (89) 9 is available online at: https://wcd.coe.int/wcd/com.instranet.InstraServlet?command=com.instranet.CmdBlobGet&InstranetImage=610660&SecMode=1&DocId=702280&Usage=2, access 1 June 2024.

This document imposed on Member States the obligation to take into account, when preparing legislation on combating computer-related crimes, the proposals for solutions contained in the Report of the Committee of Experts, in particular the guidelines for national legislation, and the obligation to inform in 1993 the Secretary General of the Council of Europe about progress in this area.[6]

In 1993, the Secretariat of the Council of Europe ordered a study on the extent of the implementation of the Recommendation. This task was undertaken by Professor H.W.K. Kaspersen. According to his report prepared on the basis of the study, the majority of states adjusted their regulations accordingly.[7] The report prepared by Kaspersen called for the creation of an international agreement as an instrument better suited to harmonise substantive and procedural criminal law, which is a prerequisite for more effective action against computer crime than a recommendation, which is a soft law instrument.[8]

Bearing in mind the suggestions contained in the aforementioned reports, in November 1996, by way of Decision No. CDPC/103/211196, the CDPC decided to recommend to the Committee of Ministers the setting up of a special committee of experts to prepare the draft convention.

Through the decision of the Committee of Ministers of the Council of Europe No. CM/Del/Dec (97) 583, taken at the 583th Meeting of the Ministers' Deputies held on 4 February 1997, a new body, the Committee of Experts on Crime in Cyberspace – PC CY, was established pursuant to the said decision of the CDPC. The committee began work on a draft convention in April 1997, originally scheduled to be completed by 31 December 1999, but this date was postponed until 31 December 2000. In total, there were 10 plenary meetings of the committee and 15 meetings of the open-ended working group. Finally – after certain amendments following the opinion of the Parliamentary Assembly of the Council of Europe – the Convention on Cybercrime was adopted by the Committee of Ministers of the Council of Europe at its

6 For more on the subject, see the Explanatory Report to Convention on Cybercrime (comments made to the Convention on Cybercrime by their authors). It does not constitute an authoritative interpretation (which is emphasised in Section II, indicating that it may "facilitate the application of the provisions contained therein"). Its text is available on the web pages of the Council of Europe at the following address http://conventions.coe.int/Treaty/en/Reports/Html/185.htm, access 1 June 2024.

7 Implementation of Recommendation N° R (89) 9 on computer-related crime, Report prepared by Professor Dr. H.W.K. Kaspersen [doc. CDPC (97) 5 and PC-CY (97) 5] www.google.com/url?sa=t&source=web&rct=j&opi=89978449&url=www.oas.org/juridico/english/89-9%26final%2520Report.pdf&ved=2ahUKEwjtq5-IsKuHAxXtQvEDHdMoDngQFnoECBEQAQ&usg=AOvVaw0_cCGOSaJvfDiYrZt-jJbR, access 1 June 2024. Cf. Adamski (2000), pp. 6–9.

8 See more Iougleux, Mitrou, Tatianu-Eleni (2016), pp. 20–21.

109th Session on 8 November 2001. It was then opened for signature on 23 November 2001 at the International Congress on Cybercrime in Budapest.[9]

The Convention on Cybercrime[10] (hereinafter Convention on Cybercrime or the Convention) is the first international agreement on combating crimes committed through and on the internet and computer networks.

Introductory remarks

The work, which lasted for more than four years, involved not only representatives of most Member States of the Council of Europe, but also, as observers, delegates from the USA, Japan and Canada, representatives of European institutions and independent experts. The purpose of the Convention on Cybercrime is to create a legal framework for prosecuting international crimes. It provides many innovative solutions (at least at that time, given that the Convention was drawn up at the end of the previous century). It contains not only provisions concerning the types of computer-related crimes, but it also accommodates the introduction of penalisation for particular stages of committing a crime and for accessory liability, and the criminal liability of legal persons (the term "legal persons" also means organisational units without legal personality). Furthermore, it provides for a number of procedural solutions, such as data security, search and seizure of data, real-time collection of traffic data, etc.[11]

The Convention – as most acts of this type – established a certain "common minimum standard"[12] with regard to the penalisation of the offences listed therein. This means that Member States may adopt more stringent solutions regarding both the scope of criminal liability and the grounds for such liability, which the Convention on Cybercrime limits to the intent.[13] As emphasised in

9 For more on the subject, see the Explanatory Report, or e.g. Hill, Marion (2016), pp. 233–235; Holt, Bossler (2020), pp. 224–226; Janczewski, Colarik (2008a), pp. 471–472; Schjølberg (2020), pp. 94–95.

10 Convention on Cybercrime (ETS No. 185), opened for signature in Budapest on 23 November 2001, www.coe.int/en/web/conventions/full-list?module=signatures-by-treaty&treatynum=185, access 19 June 2024.

11 Radoniewicz (2021b), p. 57. Cf. Rowland, Kohl, Charlesworth (2016), pp. 325–326.

12 Explanatory Report, point 33.

13 This does not mean that national legislators cannot create types of unintentional computer crimes. Generally, there are very few of them. There are two types of them – acts involving disruption of the operation of an IT system or causing data loss due to lack of the required caution or carelessness. Many internal network failures (one could even say the vast majority) are the result of user actions. Hence the saying popular in the IT community that a secure network is one that is not connected to a public network and has no users (see Article 257 (1) Criminal Code of the Republic of Iceland Act 1940/19, Journal of Laws No. 19 of June 12, 1940). Secondly, crimes involving failure to fulfil obligations by entities responsible for network security – administrators, security inspectors (See Article 232 Criminal Code of the Czech Republic of June 8, 2009, Zakon č. 40/2009 Sb.). See more Radoniewicz (2024), pp. 125–131.

the Preamble, the Convention on Cybercrime is intended to supplement (not compete against) the existing international agreements (bilateral and multilateral, including other conventions of the Council of Europe) concluded between Member States of the Council of Europe on combating cybercrime.

It is obvious that the provisions of international law in the field of substantive criminal law cannot, in principle, be applied directly because they are not self-executing norms, i.e., such norms which are so precise that a right or obligation of an individual can be derived from them, and which are so complete that it is not necessary to enact corresponding provisions of national law in order to apply them.[14] However, they may be used indirectly as a guide for the interpretation of the national law provisions transposing them.

The undoubted advantages of the Convention on Cybercrime is its open-ended nature – it is possible for Non-Member States of the Council of Europe to accede to it[15] – and the use of optional clauses. They allow the adoption of the Convention on Cybercrime with the exclusion of certain provisions, so that the states acceding to it may, when implementing it into their internal law, reconcile its solutions with their legal tradition and culture and with the regulations already in force. Accordingly, until 1 June 2024 the Convention on Cybercrime had been signed by all Member States of the Council of Europe and ratified by almost all of them (only Ireland hasn't done it). In addition, the Convention has been signed by four non-European countries (Canada, Japan, the United States, South Africa; the United States and Japan have already ratified it), while another 27 countries (e.g., Australia, the Dominican Republic, Mauritius, Panama and Sri Lanka) have acceded to it (and ratified it). Incidentally, it should be added that many countries, such as Egypt and Pakistan – without signing the Convention on Cybercrime – have in fact

14 These comments do not however apply to the definitions provided in Article 1 of the Convention on Cybercrime, which are constructed so precisely and transparently that they could be applied directly. An exception is the definition of an information system (and in fact a computer system) due to the doubts regarding the scope of this term. This matter will be discussed in detail hereunder.

15 Non-Member States of the Council of Europe may accede to the Convention on Cybercrime if they have participated in its elaboration or have been invited to accede to it by the Committee of Ministers (which committee shall take the decision by majority of votes, after consulting with, and obtaining the unanimous consent of, the Contracting States to the Convention, which are entitled to sit on the committee (i.e., those Contracting States which are members of the Council of Europe – see Article 37 in connection with Article 36 of the Convention on Cybercrime). There is currently a trend towards opening up the Council of Europe's treaties to third countries. The vast majority of conventions are open to third countries, although some of them only allow accession by European states only. Forty-four out of a total of 224 conventions remain closed, and the most notable of these are the Convention for the Protection of Human Rights and Fundamental Freedoms, signed in Rome on 4 November 1950 as amended by its Protocols, and the European Social Charter of 18 October 1961. There is no doubt that some conventions (including the Convention on Cybercrime with Additional Protocols) would be much less effective if they limited their scope only to the Member States of the Council of Europe.

drawn on its provisions, creating their own national regulations.[16] Of course, apart from the Convention on Cybercrime there are some other regional legal acts (i.e., the 2001 Commonwealth of Independent States Agreement on Cooperation in Combating Offences related to Computer Information or the 2014 African Union Cybersecurity Convention), but they do not have the scope of the Convention on Cybercrime.[17]

The Convention on Cybercrime entered into force on 1 July 2004 after ratification by five states.[18]

The Convention on Cybercrime consists of a preamble and four chapters:

Chapter I – "Use of terms";
Chapter II – "Measures to be taken at the national level";
Chapter III – "International co-operation";
Chapter IV – "Final provisions".

Given the subject matter of this book, only Chapter I and Chapter II: Section 1 and 3, Title 1 will be discussed herein. Chapter II of the Convention on Cybercrime consists of three sections covering substantive criminal law (Articles 2–13), procedural law (Articles 14–21) and jurisdiction (Article 22). The part relating to substantive criminal law contains definitions of nine types of prohibited acts, divided into four categories, grouped under four headings:

Title 1 – "Offences against the confidentiality, integrity and availability of computer data and systems";
Title 2 – "Computer-related offences", containing offences committed with the use of a computer, i.e., computer forgery and computer fraud, being aggravated types of conventional offences;
Title 3 – "Content-related offences";
Title 4 – "Offences related to infringement of copyright and related rights", namely, computer "piracy".

Use of terms

Chapter I, consisting of one article (Article 1), explains the basic concepts of computer system, computer data, service provider and traffic data.

16 Gercke (2011), p. 200.
17 Brunst, Gecrke (2009), p. 53; Janczewski, Colarik (2008a), pp. 473–474; Lavorgna (2020), pp. 15–16; Radoniewicz (2021b), p. 58.Cf. De Arimateia da Ruz (2020), pp. 230–234.
18 Article 36 (3) of the Convention on Cybercrime provides that it shall enter into force on the first day of the month following the expiration of a period of three months after the date on which five states (including at least three Member States of the Council of Europe) have expressed their consent (i.e., have ratified, accepted or approved it – depending on their internal procedures) to be bound by the Convention. The first Member States were: Albania, Croatia, Estonia, Lithuania and Hungary.

As intended by the drafters of the Convention on Cybercrime, the State Parties are not required to transpose verbatim the concepts defined in Article 1. What is important is that, under domestic law, these four concepts are understood in a manner consistent with the Convention on Cybercrime.

Under the Convention on Cybercrime, a computer system is "any device or a group of interconnected or related devices, one or more of which, pursuant to a program, performs automatic processing of data".

The definition uses the words "interconnected or related", which means that the devices do not need to be physically connected (e.g., by wires), but that the transfer of data between them may take place via another medium (electromagnetic waves). The concept of "the automatic processing of data" can be explained with the use of the Convention of the Council of Europe for the Protection of Individuals with regard to Automatic Processing of Personal Data, open to signature in Strasbourg on 28 January 1981.[19] According to the definition contained in Article 2 I of the Convention, automatic processing of data includes the following operations if carried out in whole or in part by automated means: the storage of data, the carrying out of logical and/or arithmetical operations on those data, their alteration, erasure, retrieval or dissemination. Automated means should be construed as such operations which are carried out in whole or in part without human intervention. They are carried out by means of computer programs.

According to the Explanatory Report to the Convention on cybercrime[20] (hereinafter Explanatory Report), a computer system is a device consisting of both hardware and software. The hardware consists markedly of input, output and storage facilities. A computer program – as mentioned in chapter 2 of this book – is a set of instructions that can be executed by the computer to achieve the intended result. The term software includes only programs that provide automatic processing of data by a computer system (operating systems only, not applications).[21]

A computer system usually consists of many devices. An essential component is the processor or central processing unit. Other "non-obligatory" components are peripherals (devices that perform certain specific functions in interaction with the processing unit, such as a data storage device, monitor, printer, DVD drive, etc.). In the light of the Convention on Cybercrime, computer systems include smartphones, routers, decoders and most of all a device which is commonly understood as a personal computer (PC – but it seems that nowadays terms such as – desktop, note-book, laptop are used more often) aiming, namely a single host.[22] However, at least two independent

19 Convention for the Protection of Individuals with regard to Automatic Processing of Personal Data (ETS No. 108), open to signature in Strasbourg on 28 June 1981, www.coe.int/en/web/data-protection/convention108-and-protocol, access 19 June 2024.

20 Explanatory Report, points 23 and 24.

21 Walden (2016), p. 162.

22 Cf. Network Basics Companion Guide, Cisco Networking Academy, pp. 24–25.

interconnected (i.e., capable of exchanging data with each other) computer systems will make up a network. They are generally called hosts.[23] Data within a network can be transmitted via various media: by wire (cables) and wirelessly (for instance, via radio transmission). Networks may have varied territorial range – from a small local network consisting of several computers to a wide-ranging network covering larger areas. Computer systems included in the network may be its terminals (individual hosts: computers, smartphones, etc.) or may participate in the data transfer process, such as routers or servers. In order for a structure to be considered a network, computer data must be transmitted through it.[24]

Mathew Richrdson takes a different position, pointing out that not every device that processes computer data can be considered a computer (author uses term "computer", not "computer system"). He gives the example of a washing machine, which, like a computer, processes data and information (the author erroneously equates these concepts), but does so to a much lesser extent. According to this author, if one assumes that a washing machine is a computer, one would have to consider that a calculator is also one.[25] This is wrong reasoning. A computer system is a broader concept than a computer. Every computer is a computer system, but not every computer system can be classified as a computer – an example of such a situation is a washing machine. Whereas a calculator meets the definition of the Convention, while it does not process computer data in accordance with a computer program.

Computer data means "any representation of facts, information or concepts in a form suitable for processing in a computer system, including a program suitable to cause a computer system to perform a function". The use of the term "form suitable for processing in a computer system" means that computer data is a carrier or a medium of information (facts or concepts), which is readable by a computer system only when reduced to the form of computer data. In the light of this definition, computer data are also programs responsible for the performance of functions by a computer system.

Data is represented in binary code (also called machine code) in the binary system, i.e., in the form of strings of characters "0" and "1". Each digit is called a bit. The larger unit is a byte, which consists of eight bits. It represents one character (alphabet letter, number or symbol). The use of binary language is due to the fact that it is easiest to convert them into energy impulses (through coding). There are many encoding methods, depending on how "0" and "1" are represented. One of the most popular is the Manchester scheme,

23 Host – a computer or other device that communicates with other hosts on the network. More – see subchapter "The history of computer networks and the internet" of chapter 2.

24 Host – a computer or other device that communicates with other hosts on the network. More – see subchapter "The history of computer networks and the internet" of chapter 2, pp. 161–162. Mitrou (2016), p. 11.

25 Richardson (2019), p. 48.

in which the "1" is represented by a low voltage in the first half of the bit and a high voltage in the second half. The opposite signal means "0". This is more practical than defining logical values (i.e., "0" and "1") as specific voltage levels (e.g., +5V for "1") because capturing the signal level changes themselves is simply easier.[26]

The term "service provider" is construed as defined in the Convention on Cybercrime (Article 1 (c)):

1) any public or private entity that provides to users of its service the ability to communicate by means of a computer system; and
2) any other entity that processes or stores computer data on behalf of such communication service or users of such service.

Generally, two categories of entities are defined as service providers: content providers, namely entities that provide their own, or third party, services (content) (e.g., web portal operators); and internet service providers – i.e., domain name registry providers, mailbox providers and intermediary service providers, including network providers, access providers and service providers that transmit, store and make information available on the internet.[27] These services include:

1) mere conduit – the transmission of information provided by a recipient of the service in a communication network, or the provision of access to a communication network;
2) caching – temporary and automatic storage of data to speed up access to it – e.g., downloading to a local network server the pages most frequently accessed by its users to enable faster access;
3) hosting – storage of data from third parties (service recipients) by a service provider. It usually involves the service provider making its own servers (or virtual digital platforms) available. This will be, for instance, maintaining the service recipient's website on a server.[28]

Sometimes the same entity acts in both roles. For example, a portal operator may at the same time publish its own content (and thus be a content provider) and provide services to other entities, e.g., a hosting service, in which case it acts as an intermediary for access to services.[29] This distinction is important from a legal perspective due to the exclusion of liability in the case of provision

26 See more, e.g. Comer (2015); Shinder, Tittel (2002).
27 Sea also Rowland, Kohl, Charlesworth (2016), pp. 75–76.
28 Cf. Articles 12–15 of Directive 2000/31/EC of the European Parliament and of the Council of 8 June 2000 on Certain Legal Aspects of Information Society Services, in Particular Electronic Commerce in the Internal Market (the e-Commerce Directive) (OJ EC 2000 L 178/1) (hereinafter Directive 2000/31). See also Rowland, Kohl, Charlesworth (2016), pp. 75–76.
29 Savin (2017), pp. 120–121.

of certain services by entities from the latter group (entities intermediating in access to services).

As it stems from the definition provided in Article 1 (c), for the purposes of the Convention on Cybercrime, the term "service provider" applies to a group of entities intermediating in access to services. Given that, these are public or private entities that provide the users of its service the ability to communicate by means of a computer system or other entities that process or store computer data on behalf of such communication service providers or users of such service (as it were, mere conduit, hosting or caching).[30]

The provision of Article 1 (d) of the Convention on Cybercrime defines "traffic data" as any computer data relating to a communication by means of a computer system, generated by a computer system (such as a telephone, a computer but also a router or a server – as points along the data transfer route) that formed a part in the chain of communication, indicating the communication's origin (the place where the data transfer was initiated, as primarily an IP number, possibly a telephone number or otherwise similarly identified communication device for which the internet service provider is providing the service) and destination (analogous data identifying the communication device to which the transmission is addressed, as in the case of the communication device being the place where the data transfer was initiated), route, time, date, size, duration and/or type of underlying service (e.g., file transfer, electronic mail). Traffic data may be in dynamic form, for instance as data during transmission (data contained in packet headers), and in static form, as system logs stored in firewalls, routers or servers (containing information about all events occurring in the network and the entities involved). Traffic data undoubtedly includes e-mail addresses and IP addresses. Doubts may arise in the case of URL qualification or search criteria typed into a search engine. On the one hand, it is a set of simple instructions in a binary code allowing the user to obtain information from the web. In this context, it is in a way traffic data. On the other hand, it is a form of communication, as it indicates what the user is thinking about when typing in a URL address or a term in a search engine. Similar problems also arise with HTTP requests, which may contain information such as the user's email address, the last web page viewed or search criteria.[31]

Access to a computer system

Article 2 of the Convention on Cybercrime requires the State Parties to establish as criminal offence, when committed intentionally, the access to the whole or any part of a computer system without right.

30 The subjective scope of the term "service provider" adopted for the purposes of the Convention on Cybercrime is therefore identical to that of intermediate service providers in Directive 2000/31.

31 Clough (2015), pp. 153–154.

Gaining access to a computer system should be interpreted as obtaining the possibility of using its resources (specifically the data stored in it and the use of hardware, which also means access to the data – the software controlling it) – using colloquial language – entering it. Of course, access construed in this way does not include sending electronic mail (opening the email by the recipient). The type of network through which the perpetrator breaks in – gains unauthorised access – is of no significance for the attribution of liability. It is irrelevant whether he/she does it through a public telecommunications network or by acting within the same network, through a LAN (local area network) for instance. It is also irrelevant which medium is used for this purpose (e.g., a terrestrial telecommunication network, a wireless mobile network or Wi-Fi).

Access to the entire computer system should be understood as the possibility of using all the resources, which primarily implies obtaining full administrator rights. Access to only a part of the system may mean, for example, obtaining the rights of an ordinary user, without the right to use all the data stored in the system, or limited use, such as only browsing, without the possibility of performing other operations.

The act in question, which consists in "only" gaining unauthorised access to the whole or part of a computer system, is the so-called mere unauthorised access, computer trespass, cracking or hacking in the strict sense. Hacking, as construed in this way, affects the confidentiality[32] of processed computer data (gaining access to a computer system – as mentioned earlier – consists in accessing its resources). However, gaining unauthorised access enables the perpetrator to undertake actions which are directed against other aspects of data security – availability and integrity, such as blocking access to data (e.g., by changing passwords or the scope of user rights) or deleting data. It makes it possible to obtain passwords, personal data and other confidential information, as well as to install spyware, Trojans or to include the attacked computer – by installing appropriate software – in a network of "zombie computers", i.e., a botnet. It can therefore be a prelude to committing other serious crimes, both computer-related, such as computer fraud, computer forgery, disruptions of network functioning by launching a DDoS attack using a botnet, as well as common offences such as obtaining confidential data in order to blackmail the victim, or the use of a hijacked account in an auction website to commit "ordinary" fraud consisting of the offering to sell goods without the intention to fulfil an obligation assumed under the concluded agreement.[33]

We deal with (unauthorised) access "without right" when the perpetrator is neither an authorised user of the system (or exceeds his/her powers by gaining

32 Confidentiality of data means that they can be used only by authorised persons; the availability of data, information and computer (and information) systems means that they are accessible and usable at any time and in any way required, while integrity is a property of data and information indicating that they are accurate and complete and are maintained (see subchapter "The confidentiality, integrity and availability of computer data" of chapter 2).

33 Cf. Explanatory Report, point 44. About malicious software see next chapter.

access to a part of the system which he/she is not authorised to enter), nor a right holder (such a holder may be, for example, a person who gains access to the system by breaking its security features in order to test it). Entering into a public system, namely a system that is open to all (a Wi-Fi network in a restaurant, for example, through which its customers can connect to the internet) may not be regarded as unauthorised access. Neither is "entering" a website (whether directly or via links), because the owner of the website has consented to this by making it available on the internet. Similarly, placing tools such as cookies (see subchapter "Data interference" of this chapter) in the systems of users visiting a given website will not be a crime. Firstly, it happens automatically and is a "natural" element of the process of communication on the internet, and secondly, by surfing the web, users agree to have them placed in their systems. Furthermore, it is possible to configure the browser to disable this feature. It is also possible to simply delete such files at the end of a session, i.e., each time you "disconnect the internet connection".[34]

Parties may limit the punishability of the act in question by requiring that the perpetrator must breach security measures or must have a specific intent to obtain computer data or act with other, fraudulent intent. Furthermore, it is possible to apply the limitation of criminal liability to cases where the computer system attacked is connected to another system. If the national legislators adopt this solution, the crime consists in gaining illegal access to a computer system connected to a network (the requirement of gaining access via that network), both public and private (such as, for example, an intranet). However, a situation where the perpetrator gains physical access to a single computer system – without intermediation of another system (for example in a situation where, having gained physical access to a computer, the perpetrator browses the contents of its hard drive) remains outside the scope of this provision.

Illegal interception

Article 3 of the Convention on Cybercrime provides for a criminal offence involving the intentional interception without right, made by technical means, of non-public transmission of computer data to, from or within a computer system, including electromagnetic emissions from a computer system carrying such computer data.

The starting point for establishing this category as a prohibited act was "the unauthorised interception of data transmission" provided for in Recommendation R (89) 9. However, the wording of Article 3 of the Convention on Cybercrime makes it clear – as opposed to the corresponding stipulation of Recommendation R (89) 9 – that the punishable conduct thereunder involves both the interception of computer data being transmitted over a network and

34 Explanatory Report, points 46–49.

the analysis of electromagnetic waves emitted by equipment or cables during data transmission.[35]

Article 3 of the Convention on Cybercrime aims to protect the right of privacy of communication in every form (correspondence, oral telephone conversations, communication via the internet). The right to privacy of correspondence, it was emphasised in the Explanatory Report, is protected by Article 8[36] of the European Convention on Human Rights[37] (hereinafter ECHR) as "the right to respect for private and family life, home and his correspondence".[38]

In accordance with Article 3 of the Convention on Cybercrime, the State Parties are required to criminalise all conduct breaching the confidentiality of communications effected through a computer system, i.e., primarily online data transmissions and telephone conversations, as well as within that system (e.g., from computer to printer). The State Parties may, however, restrict criminalisation to the interception of only distance communications between computer systems (within the network).

This provision affords protection to private (non-public) communication. The term is understood to denote information shared between individual entities or specific groups of entities. As noted in the Explanatory Report, the non-public nature of such correspondence derives not from the type of data transmitted, but from the wish to keep this data confidential. The reasons for preventing third-party access to data can be purely commercial. This is the case, for instance, with the provision of chargeable services, such as cable television. Additionally, the use of a public (and, by extension, generally accessible) network, instead of a private one, for transmission purposes has no bearing for such a qualification of transmission.

35 The doubts around whether or not this surveillance method fell within the wording of Recommendation R (89) 9 stemmed from the fact that – technically speaking – such surveillance does not involve the interception of computer data, but it consists in the interception of electromagnetic waves emitted while such data is being transmitted. It is only through the analysis of these waves that the data itself is obtained.

36 In accordance with Article 8 (1) of the Convention "everyone has the right to respect for his private and family life, his home and his correspondence". Under the European Court of Human Rights case law, the term "correspondence" refers to all forms of direct communication between specific individuals, in writing and by using all forms of providing information with technical means. In particular, it relates to telephone conversations, as well as information exchange through means of electronic communication (e.g., electronic mail or other web services). See ECHR Decision of 29 June 2006 on *Weber and Saravia v Germany*, Application No. 54934/00, point 77; ECHR Judgement of 3 April 2007 on *Copland v the United Kingdom*, Application No. 62617/00, points 41 and 42; judgement of 1 July 2008 on *Liberty And Others v United Kingdom*, Application No. 58243/00, point 56. Cf. Radoniewicz (2021f), pp. 292–301, Radoniewicz (2021e), pp. 196–206.

37 Convention for the Protection of Human Rights and Fundamental Freedoms, done at Rome on 4 November 1950, amended by Protocols Nos. 3, 5 and 8 as well as supplemented by Protocol No. 2.

38 Explanatory Report, point 54. Cf. Hubbard, Schjølberg (2005), p. 12.

The scope of criminalisation stipulated in Article 3 of the Convention on Cybercrime is limited to cases in which surveillance is carried out by technical means. As emphasised by Andrzej Adamski, this solution "is designed to prevent the over-criminalisation of public life by eliminating eavesdropping and the secret watching of others without the use of technical means from the sphere of punishable conduct".[39]

The term "technical means" is fairly broad. It encompasses devices designed to intercept computer data (transmitted using various media through telecommunication networks, including wireless mobile networks), equipment used for electromagnetic radiation analysis, software (e.g., sniffers), access codes and passwords.

In the light of Article 3 of the Convention on Cybercrime, penal liability should apply to both direct eavesdropping and monitoring (where data is obtained as a result of gaining direct access thereto while it is being transmitted with a computer system) and indirect measures based on various types of covert listening devices.[40]

The Explanatory Report[41] notes that the use of the term "computer system" in Article 3 – which may also comprise radio devices designed for data transmission (such as Bluetooth) – does not result in the State Parties' obligation to expand criminalisation in order to include the interception of any radio transmission, even non-public ones. The underlying reason is that this means of communication is relatively open and easy to eavesdrop on, even by ordinary users.

In order to be held criminally liable, a perpetrator must act unlawfully (without right). In other words, surveillance will not be considered a crime if the person carrying out the surveillance is authorised to do so by the parties involved in the transmission that is being intercepted (for instance, as part of system testing processes), or has the legal right to mount surveillance – as in the case of state officers assigned with statutorily defined security and law enforcement tasks within their powers and responsibilities.[42] Common commercial practices, such as the use of cookies, may not be considered as representing interception.[43]

Article 3 of the Convention on Cybercrime imposes the obligation to criminalise conduct involving the interception of communications (i.e., their

39 Adamski (2001). p. 26.
40 Explanatory Report, point 53.
41 Explanatory Report, point 56.
42 This is mentioned in Article 8 (2) of the ECHR, which stipulates when the right to a private life may be limited by the state: "There shall be no interference by a public authority with the exercise of this right except such as is in accordance with the law and is necessary in a democratic society in the interests of national security, public safety or the economic well-being of the country, for the prevention of disorder or crime, for the protection of health or morals, or for the protection of the rights and freedoms of others".
43 Explanatory Report, point 58.

content).[44] As follows from the definition in Article 1 (d) of the Convention on Cybercrime, traffic data means "computer data relating to communication". This means that Article 3 imposes an obligation to criminalise only the interception of content data, without addressing the issue of traffic data.

It is worth mentioning that the European Court of Human Rights (hereinafter ECtHR) maintained that the use of traffic data also constituted interference with the right of respect for private life, within the meaning of Article 8 of the ECHR. In the judgement in the *Malone v the United Kingdom* case,[45] the Court found that so-called metering (recording phone calls made from a given device by registering the dialled numbers with the date and duration of each connection), which is a standard procedure of telecommunications service suppliers, per se cannot be considered as interference in the right to privacy, but the disclosure of the data obtained this way without the consent of the subscriber concerned constitutes a violation of ECHR Article 8. In the view of the Court, this results from the fact that it is an integral element in communications made by telephone. In addition, in the aforementioned judgement in the Copland case the Court stressed that the data related to e-mail and internet usage (i.e., traffic data) were subject to protection equivalent to that of telephone conversations.[46]

Nevertheless, the interception of traffic data is criminalised under some legislation. This includes, for instance, in the United States.[47]

As noted earlier, the State Parties may limit the scope of criminalisation – as in the case of illegal access under Article 2 of the Convention on Cybercrime – by requiring that the computer system under surveillance be connected with another computer system, thus criminalising data interception only within computer networks and allowing the surveillance of single computer systems by technical means to remain unpunished. Furthermore, Member States may require that the perpetrator acts with specific intent, or "dishonest intent", in order to be subject to penal liability.[48] One of the reasons this is possible is because, in a lot of legislations, crime involving illegal access is connected with the interception of communication. The purpose of

44 Cf. Explanatory Report, point 53.

45 Judgement of the European Court of Human Rights of 26 April 1979, case *Malone v the United Kingdom*, Application No. 6538/74.

46 CF. Cole (2017), p. 109; Gearty (2017), p. 277. See more about the issue of surveillance conducted by technical means in the case law of the European Court of Human Rights: Radoniewicz (2021e), passim; Radoniewicz (2021f), passim.

47 See § 2510 and § 2511, § 3121 and § 3127 (3) and (4) of the USC. See more, e.g. Rustad (2009), p. 258.

48 Such a construct can be found in the Polish Penal Code, specifically Article 267 § 3, in which the perpetrator acts to obtain information without right. Apart from this limitation, it applies to a broader scope of acts than those required by the Convention on Cybercrime, penalising those acts which serve to prepare for the crime of interception through the installation of certain equipment (this also includes the perpetrator installing data interception software). Cf. Adamski (2005), pp. 55–56.

this solution is to allow the State Parties to keep their regulations consistent and uncontradictory.[49]

As discussed in chapter 1 (see subchapter "Computer eavesdropping"), the surveillance of ICT networks is commonly referred to as computer eavesdropping. There are two types of computer eavesdropping – passive, where the perpetrator only becomes familiar with the intercepted information (sniffing), and active, which involves modifying the transmitted data, e.g., by redirecting it to other network locations (e.g., man in the middle attack).

Data interference

Article 4 of the Convention on Cybercrime stipulates that the State Parties shall criminalise intentionally committed acts involving the damaging, deleting, deteriorating, altering or suppressing (preventing access to) of computer data without right. The aim of this provision is to ensure the uninterrupted use of data processed in computer systems and of software (note that under Article 1 of the Convention on Cybercrime, the term "data" is understood to include software). It can be assumed that the direct object of protection is the integrity of data and software, and their accessibility.

Article 4 of the Convention on Cybercrime requires that the State Parties criminalise attacks that are primarily logical in nature, i.e., involve operations on computer data aimed at their destruction or deterioration (according to the Explanatory Report, the two terms overlap in that they both refer to adversely altering the information contained in data),[50] deletion (meaning the total and irreversible obliteration of data, not to be confused with erasure, which involves data removal that is not necessarily irreversible, usually allowing the erased data to be retrieved, sometimes without loss), alteration (modification of data that does not necessarily affect the information contained therein, but which may involve, for instance, compromising software performance) and suppression (e.g., by relocating data within a computer system or setting up a password to render the information contained therein inaccessible).

In the light of Article 4 of the Convention on Cybercrime, installing malware in a victim's computer system alone represents data interference without right – it is modification content (computer data) on disk.

Perpetrators of logic attacks often deploy Trojans, viruses and other malware. The attacker must act intentionally and without right. Unintentional acts of data interference are, therefore, not punishable. These may consist of the involuntary spread of viruses (for example, through data carriers or malware such as "infected" emails) by an unaware user.[51] What is more, acts falling outside the scope of criminalisation include certain operations on data and

49 Explanatory Report, point 59.
50 Explanatory Report, point 61.
51 See subchapter "Introductory remarks" of chapter 3.

software conducted by authorised entities. These primarily include activities undertaken by network administrators or internet providers to, for instance, alter software that gives users access to the web. "Permissible" acts also include certain normal and necessary interference during data transmission, e.g., where data is modified through encryption while being sent over a network, or where traffic data is modified to support user anonymity[52] (for example, by some proxy servers). The only way the State Parties may limit punishability under Article 4 of the Convention on Cybercrime is by requiring that the perpetrator's conduct results in "serious harm". The scope of this term is left to the discretion of national legislators implementing the Convention on Cybercrime.

Perpetrators, when carrying out attacks of a logical nature, often use programs such as Trojans, viruses or malware (see chapter 1).

It should be noted that data attacks can be carried out physically. These can take the form of damaging or destroying data – not only by erasing it, but also by damaging carriers on which they are recorded. And it can also involve concealing computer data by obstructing access to the carrier.

System interference

Article 5 of the Convention on Cybercrime governs the intentionally committed crime of the serious hindering without right of the functioning of a computer system by inputting, transmitting, damaging, deleting, deteriorating, altering or suppressing computer data. It is equivalent to "computer sabotage" from Recommendation R (89) 9. In this case, the object of protection is the free and uninterrupted use of a computer system.

The conduct criminalised under this provision consists in influencing a computer system through logical measures by entering computer data (e.g., viruses), transmitting it (for instance, a denial of service attack) or interfering with the data processed by the targeted system. The interference must be serious. The precise definition of this term has been left to the discretion of national legislators. Since the provision relates to acting "without right", routine acts carried out by authorised entities should not be punishable. This particularly includes system maintenance and reconfiguration (e.g., the installation of new software), or security tests, which can result in system interference as well as the inoperability or limited operability of the system.

Andrej Savin points out that Article 5 concerns the same subject as Article 4. The differences between these provisions relate to the intention of the perpetrator – in offence of Article 4, the purpose of data interference is to hinder

52 However, as noted in the Explanatory Report, the State Parties may criminalise some abuse related to anonymisation aimed at obstructing or preventing the identification of criminals (Explanatory Report, point 62). This may include spoofing or identify theft.

the functioning of the ICT system, in Article 5 – interference only without affecting the system.[53]

The authors of the Explanatory Report examine the possibility of criminalising the hindering of computer system functions by distributing unwanted messages (spam). There are two types of such messages: commercial spam for advertising purposes, i.e., so-called unsolicited commercial correspondence, and unwanted non-commercial correspondence sent, for instance, to conduct a smear campaign, to extort money through requests for financial aid or to spread viruses. Spammers gain access to email addresses primarily through email address extractors, which automatically search internet resources (websites, discussion groups) for email addresses. Other ways to obtain email addresses are, for instance, breaking into a user's email account or the email server, or purchasing an address database on the black market. Since spammers can be blacklisted, they send spam by using special accounts, randomly generated addresses, false addresses or addresses belonging to random individuals to which spammers have gained access. Email accounts can be protected against spam by filters, which analyse the content of incoming messages and block those they consider to be unwanted. According to the authors of the Explanatory Report, such conduct should be punishable if the spammer intends to seriously hinder the functions of a computer system.[54]

State Parties can take different approaches to transposing Article 5 of the Convention on Cybercrime into their legal systems by providing that some conduct (less serious) may be subject to administrative liability.[55] They are also left to decide what degree of disruption, if any, should be subject to administrative sanction and what degree should entail criminal liability (for instance, should the disruption affect the whole system or only its part, should it be temporary or permanent?).

An examination of Article 5 of the Convention on Cybercrime leads to the conclusion that, unlike Article 4, the provision does not relate to physical attacks (which could involve, for instance, the destruction of network infrastructure). This, however, does not prevent the State Parties from criminalising this type of conduct.

Article 5 of the Convention on Cybercrime does not allow the State Parties to limit the scope of criminalisation.

Acts aimed at disrupting the network, often leading to network crashes, or at blocking specific hosts (e.g., servers, computers) include denial of service attacks[56] (see chapter 1).

53 Savin (2017), p. 333.
54 Explanatory Report, point 69.
55 For example, spamming is subject to an administrative sanction under Polish law, representing a petty offence under Article 24 of the Act on the Provision of Services by Electronic Means (consolidated text: Polish Journal of Laws of 2020, item 344.).
56 These attacks can also provide a gateway to other illegal acts, such as session hijacking.

"Misuse of devices"

Article 6 of the Convention on Cybercrime imposes the obligation to expand the scope of criminal offences to include acts preceding those set out in Articles 2–5. Accordingly, the State Parties should prohibit the production, making available, distribution and ownership of so-called hacker tools, i.e., devices and programs designed or adapted primarily for the purpose of committing such acts, as well as computer passwords, access codes and other similar data by which the whole or any part of a computer system can be accessed.

Article 6 (1)(a)(i) of the Convention on Cybercrime requires that the State Parties criminalise acts, when committed intentionally and without right, involving the production, sale, procurement for use, import, distribution (understood as disseminating on a chargeable basis) or otherwise making available of a device (including by putting it online to allow its downloading by an unlimited number of users, as well as by posting links to websites with such tools), including a computer program, designed or adapted primarily for the purpose of committing any of the offences established in accordance with Articles 2–5 of the Convention. And under Article 6 (1)(a)(ii) of the Convention on Cybercrime, the State Parties are required to criminalise acts, when committed intentionally and without right, involving the production, sale, procurement for use, import, distribution or otherwise making available of a computer password, access code or similar data by which the whole or any part of a computer system is capable of being accessed, with intent that it be used for the purpose of committing any of the offences established in Articles 2 through 5.

For the purposes of Article 6 of the Convention on Cybercrime, computer programs should be understood as both programs and scripts considered to be malware, in particular so-called exploits or exploit-packs (programs that take advantage of software gaps to, for instance, enable access to a computer system), programs designed to mount denial of service attacks, viruses, worms, Trojans, rootkits, spyware and adware, dialers, port scanners, as well as programs designed to crack passwords and access codes.

In the course of the work on the draft Convention, heated discussions were held regarding the regulation of the problem of so-called dual-use programs.

Some applications have come to be used as hacker tools against their originally intended purpose. For example, network analysers, such as Microsoft's Network Monitor, which were designed for web diagnostics but can also be deployed as sniffer. A program designed to recover passwords can be used to crack them.

The authors of the Convention had several solutions to choose from regarding this issue, relying on objective or subjective criteria to qualify given programs as hacker tools. In the first case, two options were possible – the first was to completely exclude dual-use programs from the scope of the regulation by adopting the principle that only programs created solely for the purpose of committing crimes are hacker tools. However, this scope of criminalisation was ruled out as too narrow. The second option – standing in opposition to the first one – i.e., adopting the solution that all dual-use programs should be prohibited – was also rejected, this time as being too restrictive.

Relying on the subjective criterion, i.e., accepting that the perpetrator's intention would be the decisive factor for regarding a given program as a prohibited hacker tool in the light of the Convention, was rejected for obvious reasons, as it would lead to declaring illegal any software which could be used (without modification or following its appropriate "adaptation") by internet users to commit crimes, although the producer did not envisage such a possibility. The solution that was eventually adopted constitutes, according to the authors of the Convention, a compromise. It entailed adopting an objective criterion – limiting the scope of criminalisation to programs "designed or adapted primarily to commit any of the offences specified in Articles 2–5" of the Convention.[57] In fact, it is rather a "mixed" criterion (an objective one but with subjective elements) because, as a result of the adopted construction, "hacker tools" – in the light of the wording of Article 6 of the Convention – are programs which the average internet user may consider useful for committing crimes.

Andrzej Adamski stressed that, in consequence of adopting the regulation in this form, a problem arises at the evidentiary level in that the authorities of the justice system need to establish appropriate criteria to make it possible to press charges against the perpetrator and to prove his/her guilt.[58]

To emphasise that the use by network administrators and security inspectors of hacker tools sensu stricto – i.e., programs designed for the sole purpose of facilitating destructive measures (such as DDoS attack applications to test network resilience against excessive traffic) should not qualify as a crime, Article 6 (2) of the Convention on Cybercrime stipulates explicitly that Article 6 (1) should not be interpreted as imposing criminal liability where the production, sale, procurement for use, import, distribution or otherwise making available or possession referred to in Article 6 (1) is not for the purpose of committing an offence established in accordance with Articles 2–5 of the Convention, such as for the authorised testing or protection of a computer system.

Accordingly, penal liability does not apply to authorised parties (e.g., system administrators, security inspectors) that fulfil the definitional elements of the crime set out in Article 6 of the Convention on Cybercrime by engaging in conduct to test and protect a system.

The prohibition to disseminate hacker tools, as provided for in Article 6 (1)(a) of the Convention on Cybercrime, primarily relates to making them available on the internet, where they can be easily downloaded and, given that many of these programs are very easy to handle, may be used, for example, to seriously disrupt a network and computers connected thereto, even by

57 Confer Lloyd (2017), pp. 230–231.
58 Adamski (2001), p. 36. Cf. Reed, Angel (2012), p. 577.

individuals who are not particularly skilled in IT (the phenomenon of "script kiddies" – internet users who do not have sufficient skills to create or develop their own malicious programs and use programs designed by others).

Andrzej Adamski claims that it is in fact "aimed against the ostentatious publication of symbols and props of the hacker subculture on the internet", and the introduction of this solution may provoke defensive reactions from this community, leading to better concealment of resources (better camouflage or uploading resources on servers outside the jurisdiction of the State Parties to the Convention), or the emergence of a "black market" to distribute hacker tools. As a result, it may not produce the effect intended by the authors of the Convention.[59] Moreover, as Dorothy Denning points out, enforcing a ban on the production and dissemination of such software is rather costly, and it might be worth considering whether it would not be more beneficial to devote at least some of the resources used for this purpose to the prevention, detection and defence against incidents threatening network security.[60]

This regulation is nonetheless needed. Even a minor limitation of the availability of hacker tools online (achieved through both reducing their number and hindering access to them) will help to curtail attacks and to improve security. And this is extremely important nowadays given the fact that cyberspace has become a global market for the exchange of goods and services, and the internet has become the main information exchange medium.[61] In addition, the adopted solution enables law enforcement to counteract the sales of devices and the provision of services which enable bypassing various types of electronic security measures (paid TV decoders or encrypted car radios).[62] One should also remain mindful of the clear fact that the lack of any regulation regarding the production and distribution of hacker tools strengthens the sense of impunity in those committing computer abuse, while at the same time encouraging them to continue experimenting with this type of software[63] (which, as mentioned earlier, is an extremely frequent motive used by perpetrators of cybercrimes).

Under Article 6 (1)(b) of the Convention on Cybercrime, the State Parties are required to introduce penal liability for the possession of hacker tools (according to this provision, for penal liability to arise it is sufficient that the perpetrator has a single item, although the State Parties are also permitted to introduce the quantitative criterion to make punishability contingent on the possession of a number of items) with the intent that they be used for the purpose of committing any of the offences established in Articles 2–5 of the Convention.

59 Cf. Adamski (2001), pp. 37–38.
60 Denning (2000a), p. 15.
61 Adamski (2001), p. 36
62 Cf. Adamski (2001), p. 38.
63 Adamski (2001), p. 44.

It should be stressed that, for the acts prohibited both under Article 6 (1)(a) and Article 6 (1)(b) of the Convention on Cybercrime, the condition for penal liability to arise is the perpetrator's intent to enable others to use hacker tools to commit any of the offences under Articles 2–5 of the Convention. According to the authors of the Convention, this is with a view to preventing an over-criminalisation.[64]

In the light of Article 6 (1)(a) of the Convention on Cybercrime, individuals who put hacker tools online or post links to such tools, including content providers, may be held criminally liable. Conversely, penal liability may not be applied to entities belonging to the second category of service providers, i.e., service providers within the meaning of the Convention on the Cybercrime (intermediate service providers – see comments to Article 1 (c)). These entities engage in the business of providing network access (access providers and network providers) or acting as a conduit, or storing third-party data. Hence, as mentioned before, their role amounts to performing technical tasks that are passive and automated in nature. By extension, providers of such services have no knowledge of the content of transferred or stored data, nor do they have any control over it.

As rightly noted by Andrzej Adamski, the Convention on Cybercrime does not stipulate that criminal liability should be incurred for creating, possessing and distributing software designed to scan and sample networks (to check which ports in network-connected computers are listening ports, i.e., which of them are open and hence can enable an attack). This is attributable to the fact that the Convention on Cybercrime does not criminalise acts that constitute the preliminary phase of an attack against a computer system. Therefore, in the light of the Convention on Cybercrime, port scanning and network sampling should be considered non-punishable attempts and preparatory acts.

Under Article 6 (3) of the Convention on Cybercrime, state signatories may reserve the right not to apply some, or all, of the provisions of Article 6, provided that the reservation does not concern the sale, distribution or otherwise making available of passwords, access codes and similar data facilitating access to a part or whole of a computer system.

In conclusion of this part, I would like to draw the reader's attention to issues around the "nature" and form of a computer program which entail some interesting consequences. To reiterate, a computer program is generally believed to be a set of instructions (commands), expressed in a computer-readable form (with words, mathematical symbols and graphic signs), aimed at bringing about computer action intended by the program authors, with a view to achieving a specific result.

It basically comes in two forms: as a source code, written using a programming language, and as object code, which is the product of compiling

64 Explanatory Report, points 71 and 76. Cf. Gercke (2011), p. 326; Hubbard, Schjølberg (2005), p. 14.

(converting, re-writing) a computer program from the source code to a computer-readable format.[65] As mentioned earlier, numerous variations exist between these two. Moreover, in the case of such languages as Python or Perl, a program source code is translated into binary code only when executed.

The existence of these two basic forms of computer program creates some interesting problems, as noted by Krzysztof Gienas.[66]

First, the prohibitions stipulated in Article 6 of the Convention, especially under US constitutional law, may be regarded as compromising freedom of expression, with source codes constituting a manifestation of that freedom. While the European courts have yet to take a stance on this issue, I do not believe that such an interpretation would be possible. In the ECHR, the protection of the right to freedom of expression is enshrined in Article 10. This right includes three elements: the freedom to hold opinions and to receive and impart information and ideas without interference by public authority and regardless of frontiers. Of these, the freedom to impart (communiquer) information and ideas – i.e., corresponding exactly to the right to freedom of expression – occupies the most prominent position in the case law of the ECtHR, and it has shaped the actual understanding of Article 10 of the ECHR. It is essentially about the freedom to communicate to external audiences whatever the author of the utterance (message) considers worthy to be communicated. The group of addressees of an utterance is thus open and indefinite (this is where an utterance differs from correspondence – the right to which is envisaged in Article 8 of the ECHR – the latter being intended for a specific addressee). In accordance with the case law of the ECHR, the protection arising from Article 10 of the ECHR extends to all kinds of utterances expressing information (i.e., information about objective facts) or ideas (proposals as to how to interpret facts, which means the sharing of judgements, generalisations, suggestions and predictions, as well as the subjective feelings of the author of the utterance),[67] regardless of their content or communication method. It applies to political and public affairs statements, as well as to artistic statements, commercial information, popular music and advertisements broadcast via cable networks, to online content and even to certain behaviour (e.g., pinning on a red star or protesting against hunting capercaillie or motorway construction).[68,69] Other forms of social interaction (e.g., sexual life, see the decision of the European Commission of Human Rights of 12 October 1978 in case *X v United Kingdom*,[70] par. 173).[71]

65 To this end, computer data is recorded in binary language (also called machine language or machine code) in a binary system, namely in the form of a sequence of 0's and 1's.

66 Gienas (2006), pp. 36–37.

67 Garlicki (2010), pp. 593–594; Nowicki (2010), p. 583, see more Sobczak (2007a), pp. 7–8.

68 Judgement of *Steel et al. v United Kingdom*, 23 September 1998, Application No. 24838/94.

69 Nowicki (2010), p. 587. See more Sobczak (2007b), pp. 10–16.

70 Application No. 7215/75.

71 See more Garlicki (2010), pp. 595–596.

Considering the preceding, a computer program can hardly be called an utterance – whether a source code or an object code – for the simple reason that it is created for purposes other than communication of information or ideas. Its purpose namely is to produce a certain effect in the form of an operation being executed by a processor. The user often remains oblivious to the actual outcome of such a program's functioning, as it may be one of numerous applications executing operations "in the background". The argument that computer programs enjoy copyright protection similar to literary works (see Article 10 (1) of the TRIPS Agreement, Article 4 of the WIPO Copyright Treaty (WCT), and Article 1 (1) of Directive 2009/24/EC of the European Parliament and of the Council of 23 April 2009 on the legal protection of computer programs (codified version))[72,73] is irrelevant here, as they were covered by such protection not due to their similarity to literary works, but for purely practical reasons – this stemmed not only from the novelty of the good but also from the controversies surrounding the appropriate model of protection. These controversies arose as the question of whether to create a new type of intellectual property protection or use either of the existing ones, i.e., copyright or patent protection. The first solution was rejected for practical reasons – to avoid establishing a new international convention. Since the vast majority of legal commentators denied patent protection for computer programs, it was decided that they would be under copyright protection.[74]

This line of reasoning finds confirmation in the science of communication, in which the term "message" ("communication", and in the science of mass communication – especially in press studies – "utterance") is understood as "a sequence of signs (grammatical, musical or vocal) created by the sender to communicate something (to convey information, i.e., communication) to the recipient(s)".[75] An utterance consists of content and form, the latter merely conveying the former. The essence of a message is, therefore, its content, the role of the form being merely to convey the content. Hence, a computer program could at most be considered a form – one, however, that does not convey any content to the recipient(s) and as such cannot be regarded as an utterance.

The second problem highlighted by Krzysztof Gienas is less peculiar. Namely, can a computer program, in the form of a source code, be regarded a "tool"? On the one hand, presented as such, even the most dangerous virus is completely harmless, as it is incomprehensible to the computer. For example, it can be saved in a text file and sent by email without doing any harm. On the other hand, if compiled into an object code, the same virus can become

72 OJ UE 2009 L 111/16.

73 As rightly noted by Janusz Barta and Ryszard Markiewicz, this is in fact a separate (sui generis) model of protection – referring only to the principles of copyright (Barta, Markiewicz (2010), p. 132; Radoniewicz (2009b), p. 34).

74 See Barta, Markiewicz (1993), pp. 54–56, Nowicka (1995), pp. 13–22; Radoniewicz (2009b), p. 34.

75 Pisarek (2008), p. 27. CF. Morreale, Spitzberg, Barge (2007), pp. 31–39.

a dangerous tool. I, therefore, believe that the question should be answered affirmatively. At present, the source code-to-object code compilation process is fully automated and occurs without any human intervention. The difference between the two forms of a computer program has been blurred to such an extent that one can doubt – as noted earlier – whether there is any point in attaching importance to it and drawing further consequences. This seems to be confirmed by the fact that a computer program is subject to copyright protection irrespective of its form of expression, whether as a source code or as an object code.

Computer-related offences

The criminalisation of the following two acts is recommended under Title II: computer-related forgery (Article 7) and computer-related fraud (Article 8). The former consists of the illegal and intentional input, alteration, deletion or suppression of computer data, resulting in the generation of inauthentic data which, as intended by the perpetrator, is to be considered or acted upon for legal purposes as if it were authentic. For this offence to exist, it is irrelevant whether or not the data is directly readable and intelligible. States may require an intent to defraud, or similar dishonest intent before criminal liability is attached. The object of the offence may be a public document or a private document having legal effects. In the light of the discussed provision, creating a forged document takes place as a result of an illegal input of correct or incorrect data, whereas forging an already existing document involves data alteration (modifications), deletion (removal of data) and suppression (holding back or the concealment of data).

The term "for legal purposes" refers also to legal transactions and documents which are legally relevant.[76]

Computer-related fraud (Article 8), in turn, involves an illegal and intentional action of a perpetrator who, by an input, alteration, deletion or suppression of computer data, or by any other interference with the functioning of a computer system, causes a loss of property to another person.[77]

The terms "input, alteration, deletion or suppression" have the same meaning as in the previous articles. The perpetrator's act may be classified as a computer fraud if the perpetrator has acted with a specific fraudulent or other dishonest intent to gain an economic or other benefit for oneself or another.

It should be emphasised that the crime of "computer fraud" differs from "classic" fraud due to its subject matter, that is the subject of the perpetrator's act is computer data and not another person (of course, aggrieved is a natural or legal person, not computer data).

76 Explanatory Report, point 84.
77 Cf. Karpiuk (2023), p. 192.

Examples of conduct representing computer-related fraud may include overloading the server to make the computers from which services are provided inefficient (e.g., DDoS attacks), entering false data into a computer, usually by an authorised user, in order to obtain financial benefit (so-called input manipulation, e.g., opening a bank account in the name of a fictitious account holder, debiting a bank account with an amount relating to someone else), withdrawing money online from bank accounts of bank customers and modifying a computer program to perform additional operations resulting in financial gain (e.g., transferring small amounts with each financial operation performed by the program).[78]

The Cybercrime Convention does not include the crime of identity theft[79] (about this offence see subchapter "Sanctions" of chapter 5). However, one may encounter the view that the Convention defines an offence, a form of which can be deemed to include identity theft, namely the so-called computer related forgery,[80] which was described in this subchapter. But I don't agree with this statement. Article 7 defines *inter alia* acts that could qualify as "identity fraud", but not as a "identity theft". It does not provide for liability for preparing to commit a crime, such as obtaining an identity. The perpetrator may be held accountable if he or she uses this identity to commit a crime.

Content-related offences

Title III – "Content-related offences" (or offences related to the character of contained information) – includes only one article, in which the State Parties were obliged to criminalise offences related to child pornography (Article 9). On a side note, it is worth mentioning the Additional Protocol to the Convention on Cybercrime concerning the criminalisation of acts of a racist and xenophobic nature committed through computer systems, dated 28 January 2003.[81] A decision to include the provisions on offences of this category in a separate protocol, instead of in the Convention itself, was based on the attitude of the delegates of the participating states. Differences between individual states as regards their constitutional standards of freedom of expression made it difficult to adopt a common standpoint. Therefore, in order not

78 See more Adamski (2000), pp. 117–121.

79 The following crimes can be distinguished related to the use of someone else's identity: 1) identity theft – conduct consisting of the concept of obtaining ("acquisition") an existing identity (which is authentic and not fabricated and does not belong to the perpetrator but to a third party); 2) identity fraud – this concept refers to stealing money, goods, services and other benefits by the use of a false identity (as in the instance of identity crime); and 3) identity crime – this term generally defines a crime for the purpose of which the perpetrator makes use of a false identity (in a broad sense, i.e., an identity that either belongs to another person or has been fabricated).

80 Cf. Summer, Schwarzenegger, Ege, Young (2014), p. 246; Kittichaisaree (2017), pp. 276–277.

81 The text is available on http://conventions.coe.int; access on 19 June 2024.

to inhibit the work on the Convention, it was considered advisable to include the provisions concerning them in a separate document.[82]

Here it is worth specifying what pornography is. As the Convention on Cybercrime does not cover the definition issues, this will be limited to mentioning two. According to Jarosław Warylewski, "pornographic content" ("pornography") means

> in the narrow (normative) sense, content that can be identified in an information message (presentation) or its key or properly consistent fragments, in a physical or non-tangible form, stored on any storage medium or not stored, characterised by the presentation of any forms of authentic or imaginary (created) manifestations of sexuality or human sex life, limited (reduced to) physiological functions and technical and biological aspects.[83]

Marek Filar and Maciej Berent define pornography by identifying properties that, when occurring jointly, decide about the pornographic nature of given contents:

1) the essence of a given presentation is to demonstrate manifestations of sexuality and human sex life;
2) the presentation is focused solely on depicting the technical and biological aspects;
3) the presentation includes the image of genital organs in their sex-related functions;
4) the said presentation aspects expressly point to the fact that the author's sole and main intention was to evoke sexual arousal in viewers;
5) an additional criterion may include the aesthetic value of a given presentation; the lower it is, the more likely a given presentation is to be classified as pornographic.[84]

For the purposes of the Convention, the term "child pornography" means material in the form of data stored on a computer or data carrier (e.g., pen drive, DVD-ROM or memory stick) which can be transformed into a visual representation, depicting:

a) a minor engaged in sexually explicit conduct;
b) a person appearing to be a minor engaged in sexually explicit conduct;
c) realistic images representing a minor engaged in sexually explicit conduct.

82 See Adamski (2001), p. 49. Cf. Reed, Angel (2012), p. 580. Explanatory Report to Additional Protocol to the Convention on cybercrime, concerning the criminalisation of acts of a racist and xenophobic nature committed through computer systems, http://conventions.coe.int/Treaty/en/Reports/Html/189.htm, accessed on 19 June 2024.

83 Warylewski (2011), pp. 11–13.

84 Berent, Filar (2016).

The term "minor" means all persons under 18 years of age. A Party may require in its national legislation a lower age limit regarding child pornography, but not lower than 16 years (9 (3)). A "sexually explicit conduct" covers at least real or simulated:

> a) sexual intercourse, including genital-genital, oral-genital, anal-genital or oral-anal, between minors, or between an adult and a minor, of the same or opposite sex; b) bestiality; c) masturbation; d) sadistic or masochistic abuse in a sexual context; or e) lascivious exhibition of the genitals or the pubic area of a minor. It is not relevant whether the conduct depicted is real or simulated.[85]

In Article 9 (2), three types of child pornography were distinguished. Firstly – "ordinary", i.e., with the participation of "real" minors. In the next paragraph – fake pornography, i.e. material which presents a person who looks like a minor engaged in sexually explicit conduct who has reached the legal age for sexual activities as prescribed in internal law. And in the last one – virtual pornography.

The term virtual pornography refers to a range of images, not all of which are actually "virtual". The doctrine distinguishes two types of virtual pornography. Firstly, these are real images (including, of course, moving ones) processed by computer. This will be, for example, the image of an adult modified to look more childlike ("morphing") or when an image is created from fragments of several others (a "photomontage"). "Rendered" images, i.e., the actual image, may also fall into this category – it is manipulated to look like a drawing or to look like a three-dimensional computer generated image. The second group is "entirely" computer-generated images. These are completely "virtual" images. This category also includes images such as drawings and caricatures that depict sexual activity involving children.[86]

Article 9 (2) protects different legal interests. Article 9 (2)(a) focuses more directly on the protection against child abuse. Article 9 (2)(b) and (9) (2)(c) aim at providing protection against behaviour that, while

> not necessarily creating harm to the "child" depicted in the material, as there might not be a real child, might be used to encourage or seduce children into participating in such acts, and hence form part of a subculture favouring child abuse.[87]

85 Explanatory Report, point 100.
86 Clough (2015), pp. 313–314. Sea also Rowland, Kohl, Charlesworth (2016), p. 327.
87 Explanatory Report, point 102.

Article 9 (1) obliges Parties to adopt such legislative and other measures as may be necessary to criminalise, when committed intentionally and without right, the following acts:

a) producing child pornography for the purpose of its distribution through a computer system;
b) offering or making available child pornography through a computer system;
c) distributing or transmitting child pornography through a computer system;
d) procuring child pornography through a computer system for oneself or for another person;
e) possessing child pornography in a computer system or on a computer-data storage medium.

This provision criminalises various acts related to child pornography. Firstly – production of child pornography for distribution via a computer system. The next paragraph criminalises "offering" child pornography through a computer system, which means making it possible for others to obtain child pornography. "Making available" is intended to include posting child pornography on the internet for use by others, for example by creating child pornography sites, hosting, creating or compiling hyperlinks to child pornography sites to facilitate access to child pornography. Article 9 (1)(c) criminalises the distribution or transmission of child pornography via a computer system. Distribution is active dissemination. The transmission would include transmission of child pornography via a computer system to another person. The term "procuring for oneself or for another" means actively obtaining child pornography, especially by downloading it. In Article 9 (1)(e) is criminalised the possession of child pornography in a computer system or on a data carrier, such as a pen-drive or memory card. In the Explanatory Report it is stressed that the possession of child pornography stimulates demand for such material. An effective way to curtail the production of child pornography is to attach criminal consequences to the conduct of each participant in the chain from production to possession.[88]

The use of the term "without right" allows the Party to take into account fundamental rights such as freedom of expression. Furthermore, it allows for the exclusion of responsibility in special circumstances due to, for example, artistic value or scientific or medical merit.

The Convention on Cybercrime obliges Parties to criminalise intentionally acts. The authors of the Convention left the meaning of "intentionally" to national interpretation. An offender cannot be held criminally liable if he has not the required intent. So – for example – the service provider that served as a conduit or hosted the website containing child pornography, without the requisite intention, cannot be held criminally liable under that provision.

88 Explanatory Report, point 98.

Moreover, the service provider is not obliged to monitor the conduct in order to avoid criminal liability.[89]

However, it is not forbidden to adopt strict standards towards service providers. For example, provisions of Directive 2000/31 make the intermediary service provider's liability dependent on knowledge of the nature of the content transmitted or stored. Liability arises when service providers receive information about their illegal nature and do not take appropriate action (e.g., the hosting provider does not remove the website containing illegal content from the server).[90]

But a service provider is not required to monitor conduct to avoid criminal liability.

Each Party may reserve the right not to criminalise procuring child pornography through a computer system or possessing it (Article 9 (1)(d) and 9 (1)(e)).

Moreover, a Party may criminalise only acts related to pornographic materials presenting a "real" minor engaged in sexually explicit conduct (Article 9 (2)(a)) – not images presenting a person pretending to be a minor (fake pornography – Article 9 (2)(b)) and realistic images of a minor (virtual pornography – Article 9 (2)(c)).

The signing of the Convention by such a large number of countries made it possible to take action to combat child pornography on a large scale. For instance, "Operation Daylight" carried out in 2015 by EUROPOL, which led to the initiation of 207 investigations and criminal proceedings involving at least 75 people in the 28 European countries that are States Parties to the Convention.[91]

The Convention of Cybercrime criminalises only child pornography and is silent on other types of "hardcore pornography" – pornography presenting the use of violence (BDSM – bondage, discipline (or domination), sadism and masochism), using animals (zoophilia/animal/bestiality pornography) or corpses (necrophilia pornography).

The Convention on Cybercrime does not address the issue of the use of a technical "gatekeeper" system, in which the state controls access using filtering software to prevent access to illegal content. Currently, countries are adopting various solutions to regulate this issue. First, there is the criminalisation of providing or accessing certain types of content, online or offline, with law enforcement monitoring the internet and prosecuting criminals. Secondly, the combination of the criminalisation system and the "gatekeeper". Thirdly, there is a system of co-regulation – cooperation between the state and

89 Explanatory Report, point 103.

90 "The Notice & Takedown procedure" was first included in the new DMCA (Digital Millennium Copyright Act) and then adopted by the European Union in the Electronic Commerce Directive.

91 Kittichaisaree (2017), pp. 272–272.

internet service providers. This means that service providers establish an applicable "code" for controlling access to online content, and the state regulatory authority steps in only when it considers the solutions of the said code to be insufficient.[92]

Offences related to infringements of copyright and related rights

In Article 10 of the Convention of Cybercrime, constituting the only article under Title IV ("Offences related to infringements of copyright and related rights"), the State Parties were obliged to criminalise conduct constituting the infringement of copyright, as defined under the law of the Party, pursuant to the obligations they have undertaken under the Paris Act revising the Bern Convention for the Protection of Literary and Artistic Works[93] (hereinafter: the Paris Act), the Agreement on Trade-Related Aspects of Intellectual Property Rights[94] (hereinafter: the TRIPS Agreement), and the WIPO[95] Copyright Treaty[96] (the WCT), the International Convention for the Protection of Performers, Producers of Phonograms and Broadcasting Organisations (the Rome Convention),[97] and the WIPO Performances and Phonograms Treaty,[98] except for any moral rights conferred by such conventions, where such acts are committed wilfully, on a commercial scale and utilising a computer system.

Copyright and related rights offences must be committed "wilfully" for criminal liability to apply. In contrast to all the other substantive law provisions of this Convention, the term "wilfully"[99] is used instead of "intentionally" in

92 Kittichaisaree (2017), p. 272.

93 The Paris Act revising the Bern Convention for the Protection of Literary and Artistic Works was signed in Paris on the 24th July 1971.

94 The Agreement on Trade-Related Aspects of Intellectual Property Rights (the so-called TRIPS Agreement), constituting Appendix 1 C to the Agreement Establishing the World Trade Organization (WTO) signed in Marrakesh on the 15th April 1994 r.

95 The World Intellectual Property Organization (WIPO), French: Organisation Mondiale de la Propriété Intelectuelle (OMPI) – an organisation established under the Convention of the World Intellectual Property Organisation signed in Stockholm on 14 July 1967 with its seat in Geneva. It aims to promote the protection of intellectual property across the globe through the interaction of states in cooperation with other international organisations. It deals with drawing up regulations pertaining to this field. Since 1974 it has held the status of a UN-specialised agency. See the official website of WIPO on www.wipo.int, date of entry.

96 The World Intellectual Property Organization (WIPO) Copyright Treaty signed in Geneva on 20 December 1996.

97 The International Convention for the Protection of Performers, Producers of Phonograms and Broadcasting Organizations was signed in Rome on 26 October 1961.

98 The World Intellectual Property Organization (WIPO) Performances and Phonograms Treaty was signed in Geneva on 20 December 1996.

99 An act is conducted "wilfully" if done voluntarily and intentionally and with the specific intent (dolus specialis) to do something the law forbids. It is unnecessary to demonstrate malicious intent on the part of the accused to prove that the act was committed "wilfully".

both Paragraphs 1 and 2 of Article 10 of the Convention on Cybercrime, as this is the term employed in the TRIPS Agreement (Article 61),[100] governing the obligation to criminalise copyright violations.[101]

The Convention on Cybercrime commits to criminalising violations "on a commercial scale" and through a computer system. However, parties may wish to go beyond the threshold of "commercial scale" and criminalise other types of copyright infringement as well.

A Party may reserve the right not to impose criminal liability under Article 10 (1) and (2) in limited circumstances, provided that other effective remedies are available and that such reservation does not derogate from the Party's international obligations set forth in the international instruments referred to in Paragraphs 1 and 2 of this article.

Article 10 (3) allows Parties to reserve the right not to impose criminal liability under Paragraphs 1 and 2 of this article in "limited circumstances" (e.g., parallel imports, rental rights), provided that other effective remedies are available and that such reservation does not derogate from the obligations referred to in Article 61 of the TRIPS Agreement, which is the minimum pre-existing criminalisation requirement.[102]

Accessorial and stadial forms

Article 11 of the Convention on Cybercrime expands the scope of individuals who are subject to penal liability for the crimes set out in this provision. Paragraph 1 requires that the State Parties establish as criminal offences, when committed intentionally, the acts of aiding and abetting the commission of any crimes provided for in the Convention on Cybercrime. In Polish penal law is applied the concept of aiding and abetting, according to which these constructs apply only in the case of aiding and abetting in the commission of a crime by specific persons. Hence facilitating the commission of a crime by non-specific individuals by making available a "hacker" tool or posting a link to a website on which it is available does not represent the act of aiding.[103] A similar situation exists, among others, in German and French criminal law. Those who commit such acts, however, will be held liable under Article 6 of

100 "Members shall provide for criminal procedures and penalties to be applied at least in cases of wilful trademark counterfeiting or copyright piracy on a commercial scale. Remedies available shall include imprisonment and/or monetary fines sufficient to provide a deterrent, consistently with the level of penalties applied for crimes of a corresponding gravity. In appropriate cases, remedies available shall also include the seizure, forfeiture and destruction of the infringing goods and of any materials and implements the predominant use of which has been in the commission of the offence. Members may provide for criminal procedures and penalties to be applied in other cases of infringement of intellectual property rights, in particular where they are committed wilfully and on a commercial scale".

101 Explanatory Report, point 113.

102 Explanatory Report, point 116.

103 Cf. Adamski (2005), p. 60.

the Convention on Cybercrime. As stressed in the Explanatory Report, since the Convention provides for the criminalisation of only intentional conduct without right – which also includes its accessorial forms – it is impossible to consider the internet service provider whose network was used to perpetrate the crime as aiding in the commission of that crime. There is no duty on such a provider to monitor transmitted content (even though such content may contain viruses or be child pornography).[104]

Under Article 11 (2) of the Convention on Cybercrime, attempts to commit certain crimes should be established as criminal offences (with the caveat that the State Parties may refrain from applying the provision, in whole or in part). This applies to the illegal interception of data (Article 3 of the Convention on Cybercrime) and system interference (Article 5 of the Convention on Cybercrime), Title 2 offences (computer-related forgery and fraud), the production of child pornography for the purpose of its distribution through a computer system (Article 9 (1)(a) of the Convention on Cybercrime), distributing or transmitting child pornography through a computer system (Article 9 (1)(c) of the Convention on Cybercrime).

Of course, attempts must be committed intentionally.

Sanctions

In accordance with Article 13 (1) of the Convention on Cybercrime, the State Parties should adopt appropriate sanctions (effective, proportionate and dissuasive) for crimes under the Convention, including deprivation of liberty. As a rule, these should be penal sanctions. State Parties may also apply other penal measures against perpetrators (e.g., forfeiture).

Corporate liability

Article 12 of the Convention provides for the construct of liability of legal persons[105] for the offences established therein.

The authors of the Cybercrime Convention adopted a solution based on the principle of identification, under which acts committed by persons functioning within a corporation are deemed to be actions of that corporation (this solution has been adopted, *inter alia*, in the USA and France). Essentially, this liability is objectified, as it depends solely on the conduct of an individual while the circumstances pertaining to the legal person are irrelevant.

104 Explanatory Report, point 119.

105 The term "legal person" is in this case a kind of "mental shortcut" – its scope includes both legal persons and other organisational units without legal personality; using the terminology of the Polish legal sciences – ułomne osoby prawne (unincorporated entities with legal capacity), i.e., organisational units without legal personality, which are granted legal capacity by law.

The model in question is sometimes referred to by legal commentators as the direct liability model. The reason is that since the behaviour of a natural person is attributed to a legal person, no vicarious (indirect) liability arises in this case. However, in order to hold the legal person liable, it is necessary to identify the natural person being a representative, a body or a member of a body committing the act that might give rise to liability. It is for this reason that the construct of identification liability is criticised – it is often impossible to identify that individual or group of individuals, given the complexity of the organisational structure of some legal persons.

Therefore, the prerequisites for a legal person to be held liable for the offences listed in the decision are as follows: (1) the legal person has gained a "benefit", and (2) this has occurred through the action of a person "having a leading position". Both terms are rather vague and evaluative in nature. As for the "benefit", this concerns the conceptual scope of the term, which seems to include both benefits of a material (financial) nature and benefits of a non-material character. According to Oktawia Górniok, the evaluative character of this term is connected with whether

> the benefit granted or intended to be granted by the perpetrator should be assessed only in objective terms, given the actual interest of the legal person, or whether an intent or motive of the physical action taken by the perpetrator is considered decisive.[106]

The interpretation of the term "leading position" will thus depend on the specific case – on the structure of the legal person and division of powers within that structure. In assessing whether a given person has a leading position, one should take into consideration both the formal aspects and the actual situation. Oktawia Górniok draws attention to a tendency towards "extending the group of individuals whose offences provide grounds for liability of legal persons and including in that group any person who, in the performance of activities of the legal person, has committed an offence for its benefit".[107]

An exception of sorts is a subjective element in the form of "fault in supervision" (culpa in custodiendo). Namely, the legal person is also held liable if the benefit has resulted from the behaviour of an individual who was under the authority of that legal person, due to a lack of supervision or control of those in charge.

There is no clear-cut consensus as regards the nature of liability of a legal person. What there is agreement about is that it is not criminal liability. Currently, the majority of doctrinal representatives are inclined to follow the concept of criminal-administrative liability.

Transferring the aforementioned considerations to the Convention – for a legal person to be held liable, several conditions must be met. For that liability

106 Górniok (2000), p. 274.
107 Górniok (2000), p. 275, Cf., Summers, Schwarzenegger, Ege, Young (2014), pp. 236–237.

to arise, several conditions must be met. First, the offence committed must be stipulated in the Convention. Second, the offence must be committed by a natural person to provide a benefit to that legal person. Third, the perpetrator[108] of the offence must be a natural person in a leading position (either individually or within a body) for that legal person. Fourth, this "leading position" must derive from the power to represent that legal person, an authority to take decisions on their behalf of the legal person or an authority to exercise control within the legal person. This refers to natural persons acting, for example, as directors, members of the management or supervisory board, proxies or commercial representatives. A legal person should also be held liable where the commission of the offence – which resulted in the legal person's obtaining the benefit – was made possible by a lack of supervision or control by the legal person (or, more precisely, by a person having a "leading position" within the legal person, as defined in Article 12 (1) over the perpetrator under its authority).

As indicated in the Explanatory Report, this regulation applies to persons such as employees and agents. Its further consequence is to impose on legal persons the obligation to have in place adequate and effective measures to supervise and control individuals under their authority, and to prevent them from committing offences for their benefit. The type and nature of the measures depend on factors such as, in particular, the size and complexity of the structure of the legal person, or the nature and scope of its activities. Nonetheless, the provisions of Article 12 should not be regarded as a kind of acquiescence to, still less an order for, the employer's surveillance of its employees. Nor is it possible to interpret the content of this article as providing grounds for the possible adoption of a solution of holding the internet service provider liable for the offence that a user has committed through its network. This is because this regulation only applies to natural persons acting within their authority (such as agents or employees of a legal person), which is determined by the use of the term "under its authority" ("its" meaning the legal person's).[109]

Article 12 does not expressly determine the character of liability of legal persons, leaving this matter to the discretion of the State Parties. It merely indicates that this liability may be criminal, civil or administrative (Article 12 (4)) and that it should be without prejudice to the liability of the natural persons who have committed the offence (Article 12 (5)). The latter implies both that the legal person will be held liable in a case where the perpetrator is not (e.g., due to an exculpatory circumstance of insanity), and that holding the legal person liable will not exclude the criminal liability of the perpetrator.[110]

108 In the Explanatory Report (point 124) it was stressed that the term "perpetrator" is also understood as an instigator or an accessory.

109 Explanatory Report, point 125.

110 In Polish law, the issue of liability of legal persons is regulated by the Act of 28 October 2002 on the liability of collective entities for acts prohibited under penalty (consolidated text

In Article 13 (2), it was indicated that legal persons held liable in accordance with Article 12 should be subjected to effective, proportionate and dissuasive criminal or non-criminal sanctions or measures, including monetary sanctions. Along with these, legislators in the State Parties may envisage other measures (e.g., a ban on conducting certain activities by, or even the dissolution of, the legal person).

Procedural measures

Although the subject of this monograph is the provisions of substantive criminal law, I believe that it is worth devoting some space to procedural issues.

Provisions dealing with criminal procedures[111] are contained in the second part of the Convention. They refer to a broader range of offences than those indicated in the first part of the discussed chapter of the Convention – namely, not only to all computer crimes (both the offences envisaged in the Convention, and in particular in Articles 2–12 and other offences that are presumably

---

Polish Journal of Laws of 2023, item 659). The issue of liability of legal persons will be addressed in more detail in the following chapter dealing with EU regulations.

111 A distinction should be made between the procedural measures envisaged in the Convention and the so-called data retention obligation – the obligation imposed on telecommunications operators and providers (e.g., internet service providers) to record and store, for a certain period, all traffic data generated during normal operations in ICT systems (i.e., traffic data). The purpose of this solution is to enable access to the data collected by operators and service providers to law enforcement authorities. This obligation applies to the "potential" evidence of a crime – data generated by all network users (and, therefore, it is not aimed at a specific criminal investigation). In EU law, the issue of data retention is regulated in Directive 2006/24/EC of the European Parliament and the Council of 15 March 2006 on the retention of data generated or processed in connection with the provision of publicly available electronic communications services or of public communications networks and amending Directive 2002/58/EC (the so-called Data Retention Directive – OJ EU 2006 L 105/54). Under its provisions, service providers are obliged to retain data for a period of between six months and two years. There is, however, the possibility for a Member State – under justifiable grounds – to extend that period, of which it is obliged to inform the Commission and the other Member States. It was found invalid as a result of the Judgement of the CJEU of 8 April 2014, *Digital Rights Ireland Ltd v Minister for Communications, Marine and Natural Resources and Others and Kärntner Landesregierung and Others.* Joined Cases C-293/12 and C-594/12. However, this did not lead to the repeal of all provisions adopted in connection with its transposition. The judgement concerned the obligation imposed on Member States to collect information on cases of use of retention data by national authorities and to submit an annual report on this matter to the Commission. The legal basis for data retention at the level of EU law is currently Article 15 (1) of Directive 2002/58/EC of the European Parliament and of the Council of 12 July 2002 concerning the processing of personal data and the protection of privacy in the electronic communications sector (Directive on privacy and electronic communications) (OJ EC 2002 L 201/37). See more Lowe (2020), pp. 38–42. In Poland, the provisions of this Directive were implemented by the Act of 24 April 2009 amending the Telecommunications Act and certain other acts (Polish Journal of Laws of 2009 No. 85, item 716). Pursuant to Article 180a of the Act of 16 July 2004 – Telecommunications Law (consolidated text Polish Journal of Laws of 2024 item 24), the data retention period is 12 months.

"common" but are committed through a computer system, such as the disclosure of state secrets or money laundering) but also to those where only the evidence of their perpetration is in electronic form (e.g., intercepted data transmissions between members of criminal groups). Article 15 emphasises that the incorporation into the national order of the procedures provided for in the Convention, as well as their application, are subject to conditions and safeguards provided for under domestic law, which should provide for the adequate protection of human rights and liberties, including rights arising pursuant to obligations it has undertaken under the ECHR, and the United Nations International Covenant on Civil and Political Rights.[112] The procedural measures adopted by states should comply with the principle of proportionality, and their application should be subject to judicial review.

The Convention (under Titles 2–5) puts the Member States under the obligation to introduce several new procedural measures:[113]

- preservation IT data (including traffic data) – in particular when there is a risk of loss or modification – and partially disclosing traffic data thus secured to the competent authority to identify the service providers and the channels used to transmit the data (Articles 16 and 17);
- a production order (Article 18) addressed to:
  - a person in its territory, with the aim of submitting specified computer data in that person's possession or control, which is stored in a computer system or a computer-data storage medium; and
  - a service provider offering its services in the territory of the Party, to submit subscriber information relating to such services in that service provider's possession or control;[114]
- search and seizure of stored computer data (as well as data in a computer system or part of it) and of a computer-data storage medium in which computer data may be stored (Article 19);
- the real-time collection of traffic data connected with specific transfers implemented in the territory of a State Party (Article 20) and data regarding the content of specific transfers implemented therein (Article 21).

The preceding solutions were instantly criticised by non-governmental organisations concerned with internet issues (whose representatives, as

112 International Covenant on Civil and Political Rights, open to signature in New York, 16 December 1966.

113 See more, e.g. Radoniewicz (2022a), pp. 121–131; Savin (2017), pp. 336–338.

114 Under Article 18 (3) of the Convention, the term "subscriber information" means any information (other than content or traffic data) which enables determining: the type of communication service used, a subscriber's identity, postal or geographic address, telephone and other access numbers, billing and payment information, available based on the service agreement or arrangement, and any other information on the site of the installation of communication equipment.

mentioned earlier, were not invited to participate in the work on the Convention). They pointed out that such solutions might compromise the right to privacy and internet freedom, in general.

Jurisdiction

The third part of Chapter II – as mentioned – is devoted to the issue of jurisdiction. The drafters of the Convention took a classic approach to this subject, assuming that cyberspace does not constitute an autonomous area (similar to outer space; see previous comments) with no frontiers.[115] This results from the fact that both the actions of network users and the effects of those actions take place in the territory of a given state (although not necessarily the same one). In addition, offences committed online (despite its global reach) can be prosecuted under the traditional principles of criminal jurisdiction, namely the territoriality principle and the personal principle.[116]

The provisions regarding jurisdiction were included in one specific article (Article 22 of the Convention), in which State Parties to the Convention were obliged to establish jurisdiction over conventional offences (i.e., those listed in Articles 2–11) for which the application of the territoriality principle, expressed in Article 22 (1)(a), (b) and (c), was envisaged. Under these provisions, each State Party is obliged to determine jurisdiction over any offence established in accordance with Articles 2–11, committed in its territory, onboard a ship flying the flag of that Party, and onboard an aircraft registered under the laws of that Party. In addition, the personal principle was made applicable – where an offence has been committed by one of its nationals, if the offence is punishable under the law of the place where it was committed or if it was committed in a territory under no one's authority (Article 2 (1)(d)).[117]

Most Council of Europe Member States have adopted the so-called ubiquity principle, under which it is sufficient that one of the elements of the criminal act (the perpetrator's behaviour or, in the case of financial offences, the effect of the intended effect) occurs in the territory of the country in question for that act to fall under its jurisdiction. In the case of computer crimes, particularly complex situations may arise against this background. For example, if the perpetrator launches a DDoS (distributed denial of service) attack from country A against a server located in country B, using computers located in countries C and D, and this action will affect countries E and F, then each of these countries has jurisdiction in light of the Convention. Accordingly, Article 22 provides for a procedure for consultation between states in the event of a conflict of jurisdiction between them. However, as Andrzej Adamski points

115 Radziwill (2015), pp. 110–112.
116 Adamski (2001), pp. 102–103. Cf. Akhgar, Staniforth, Bosco (2014), pp. 3–4; Radziwill (2015), pp. 112–120.
117 Cf. Tehrani (2017), pp. 102–103.

out, these consultations are not obligatory, so state authorities may unilaterally choose not to conduct them if they consider them to be contrary to the interests of their justice system[118] or if they obtain information that such consultations are unnecessary (e.g., upon confirmation that the state, which could instigate the proceedings, will not do so).[119] At the same time, states acceding to the Convention were allowed to make reservations resulting in non-application (or application only in strictly defined cases or conditions) of both the territoriality principle in the case of the offences stipulated in the Convention, committed on board a ship flying its flag or on board an aircraft registered under its law, and the personal principle. Consequently, the obligation to exercise jurisdiction when an offence stipulated in the Convention is committed in the territory of a state, in the strict sense of the word, is the only obligation that is absolute. Article 22 (4) once again emphasises the complementary nature of the Convention, this time concerning the rules of national orders, by providing that it does not exclude the jurisdiction exercised by a State Party in accordance with its national law.

In Article 22 (5), the possibility of ad hoc consultations between states, whose jurisdiction a given act is subject to, was adopted in order to determine which of these states will exercise jurisdiction in a given case. These consultations are not necessary and may be unilaterally waived if their conduct would conflict with the interest of the justice.

The Convention on Cybercrime of course demands "double criminality" as a condition of mutual assistance,[120] but it has been limited. Under Article 25 par. 5 the requested Party is permitted to make mutual assistance conditional upon the existence of dual criminality, that condition shall be deemed fulfilled, irrespective of whether its laws place the offence within the same category of offence or denominate the offence by the same terminology as the requesting Party, if the conduct underlying the offence for which assistance is sought is a criminal offence under its laws.

Concluding remarks

Article 46 of the Convention on Cybercrime requires that the State Parties hold periodic consultation. Their primary aim is to facilitate the effective use and implementation of the Convention on Cybercrime, including the exchange of information on significant legal, policy or technological developments pertaining to cybercrime, and the collection of evidence in electronic form, as well as the consideration of possible supplementation or amendment

118 Adamski (2001), p. 104.
119 See Explanatory Report, point 239.
120 Contrary Rustad (2009), p. 258.

of the Convention.[121] The forum for these consultations is provided by the Cybercrime Convention Committee (T – CY), which convenes at least once a year. Its first meeting took place on 20–21 March 2006 in Strasburg. In addition to the State Parties, these meetings are attended by representatives of invited states, other international organisations (both government and non-government), the private sector and the scientific community.

The ratification of the Convention on Cybercrime proceeded much slower than expected.[122] This was due to a number of factors. Firstly, there was a substantial number of complicated procedural measures required under the Convention, forcing governments to work on amending not only substantive but also procedural criminal regulations. Secondly, EU Member States usually made efforts to adopt the provisions of the Convention on Cybercrime while also implementing EU law instruments (especially Framework Decision 2005/222/JHA of 24 February 2005 on attacks against information systems,[123] Directive 2006/24/EC of the European Parliament and of the Council of 15 March 2006 on the retention of data generated or processed in connection with the provision of publicly available electronic communications services or of public communications networks and amending Directive 2002/58/EC[124] or Directive 2013/40/EU of the European Parliament and of the Council of 12 August 2013 on attacks against information systems, and repealing Council Framework Decision 2005/222/JHA).[125] Above all, however, fighting cybercrime was not considered to be of primary concern. This changed in the aftermath of cyber-attacks against Estonia in 2007, and later against other states. EU authorities, which had previously only encouraged governments to sign and ratify the Convention on Cybercrime through the so-called Stockholm Programme, issued a more categorical request that all Member States should do so by the end of 2012.[126]

121 Under Article 46 (3) of the Convention on Cybercrime, the first such meeting would be held, at the latest, three years after the Convention entered into force in order for the CPDC, in cooperation with the State Parties, to conduct a review of all of the Convention's provisions and, if necessary, recommend any appropriate amendments.

122 Poland was one of the first to sign the Convention on Cybercrime (on the day it was opened for signature – 23 November 2001) but did not ratify until 29 June 2015. So far, there have been two amendments to the Penal Code, the purpose of which was to adjust its provisions to the provisions of the Convention on Cybercrime. A similar situation occurred with Sweden, which signed the Convention on 23 November 2001 but ratified it on 28 April 2021. In the UK, there were also problems with ratification – it happened in 2011 (see Rowland, Kohl, Charlesworth 2016). On the other hand, Ireland has not yet ratified it.

123 OJ EU 2005 L 69/67.

124 OJ EU 2006 L 105/54.

125 OJ EU 2013 L 218/8.

126 Seger (2012), pp. 174–175. More about Stockholm Programme, i.e. Radziwill (2015), pp. 694–700.

4 Cybercrime in the law of the Council of Europe (part II)

Protection of services based on, or consisting of, conditional access

The solution provided for in Article 6 (1) Convention on Cybercrime is consistent with regulations on the protection of services based on, or consisting of, conditional access, which prohibit the production, distribution and possession of devices enabling illegal access to such services, and with regulations in the field of copyright and related rights, which provide for technical protection of works.

In the Council of Europe documents, the provisions dealing with the first of the aforementioned issues are found primarily in Convention No. 178 on the Legal Protection of Services based on, or consisting of, Conditional Access[1] (hereinafter Convention No. 178).[2] Article 1 indicates its purpose, which is to make acts that grant unauthorised access to protected services illegal in the laws of the Member States and to make national laws governing this matter more consistent. In the light of Article 2 (a) of Convention No. 178, the "protected services" referred to earlier are understood as including television, radio and information society services if they provided against remuneration and on the basis of conditional access, or the provision of conditional access to the aforementioned services considered as a service in its own right.

1 Convention No. 178 on the Legal Protection of Services based on, or consisting of, Conditional Access of 21 June 2001, www.coe.int/en/web/conventions/-/council-of-europe-european-convention-on-the-legal-protection-of-services-based-on-or-consisting-of-conditional-access-ets-no-178-translations, access 1 June 2024.

2 Previously, the problem was addressed in Recommendation R (91) 14 on the legal protection of encrypted television services of 27 September 1991 (www.coe.int/en/web/freedom-expression/committee-of-ministers-adopted-texts/-/asset_publisher/aDXmrol0vvsU/content/recommendation-no-r-91–14-of-the-committee-of-ministers-to-member-states-on-the-legal-protection-of-encrypted-television-services, access 1 June 2024). Its provisions – as the very name suggests – concerned taking appropriate legal measures, whether criminal, administrative or civil, against the activities consisting of producing, distributing, advertising and possessing for profit (private use was left to the discretion of the State Parties) decoding devices enabling access to encrypted television services, to the detriment of service providers.

DOI: 10.4324/9781003476771-4

Services based on conditional access involve the use of conditional access techniques (including, in particular, service encryption or encoding) by the service provider to secure payment. By extension, these services are rendered by entities that provide access to specific material on the internet for a fee (e.g., "cable" TV operators). In turn, services consisting of conditional access are the services whose purpose is to protect other services provided electronically from access by persons who have not purchased the protected service, i.e., have not gained access to it under an individual authorisation (examples include certification services provided by specialised entities). It follows from the preceding that there is a relationship between such services (i.e., services based on conditional access and services consisting of conditional access), in that services consisting of conditional access are indispensable for the provision of services based on conditional access. Convention No. 178, and more specifically Article 2 (d), identifies the means for gaining unauthorised access to protected services as "illicit devices", understood as any equipment, software and/or arrangement designed or adapted to provide access in an intelligible form (perceptible to humans) to one of the protected services, without the authorisation of the service provider. This term encompasses in particular illegal decoders, pirated smart cards and access passwords.

Article 5 of Convention No. 178 obliges State Parties to introduce effective, dissuasive and proportionate sanctions of a criminal, administrative or of another character for the manufacture or production, import, distribution, sale or rental, as well as for possession, installation and servicing (repair, maintenance, replacement) of the "illicit devices" defined in Article 4 of Convention No. 178 if these are carried out for commercial purposes. In addition, the commercial promotion, marketing and advertising of such devices and services should be punishable.

Technical protection of works

Technical protection of works is another identified issue that needs some attention in the context of the prohibitions arising from Article 6 of the Convention on Cybercrime. The WIPO Treaties were the first to address this issue in international law. In accordance with Article 11 of the WCT,

> Contracting Parties shall provide adequate legal protection and effective legal remedies against the circumvention of effective technological measures that are used by authors in connection with the exercise of their rights under this Treaty or the Berne Convention and that restrict acts, in respect of their works, which are not authorised by the authors concerned or permitted by law.

A similar solution is provided in Article 18 of the WIPO Performances and Phonograms Treaty.

As regards the Council of Europe documents, this issue was addressed in Recommendation Rec (2001) 7 on measures to protect copyright and neighbouring rights and combat piracy, especially in the digital environment.[3] Point 3 of the Recommendation, included in the section on criminal law, recommends that the Council of Europe Member States introduce appropriate anti-piracy procedures and sanction. In the subsequent point, the Recommendation stipulates that the legal regulations should permit searching for the premises of legal or natural persons reasonably suspected of engaging in piracy activities, and for the seizure, confiscation or destruction of pirated copies, their means of production, materials and devices predominantly used in the commission of the offence, as well as devices designed or adapted to circumvent technical measures which protect copyright and neighbouring rights. Piracy offences should be punishable by criminal sanctions including imprisonment and/or fines.

One of the technical measures to protect copyright and neighbouring rights is DRM (Digital Rights Management) systems. They are a sign of the times – a response to technological advancements and the emergence of the internet. Making work publicly available online involves an unprecedented risk of infringement of an author's economic and personal copyright. A work disseminated online is potentially available throughout the world, to all users connected to the internet. At the same time, digital recording techniques mean that copies of the work constitute its faithful representations. This may give rise, *inter alia*, to unrestricted and ideal reproduction of copies of a work without the copyright holder's consent and awareness.[4] The response to this problem is the emergence of DRM systems. They are systems of measures based on cryptographic (and other content-disguising) mechanisms to counteract the use of works in a manner contrary to the copyright holder's intent. They consist of computer-readable information (usually placed in the so-called metadata) about the work, the creator, the copyright holders and the exploitation rules. The scope of activities that a user may undertake (e.g., indicating that there is the possibility to make copies and modifications, or determining how many times it can be launched) is recorded using so-called rights expression languages (e.g., XrML). Technological measures to protect digital works play a major role in this context. A common distinction is between measures to protect access to the work and mechanisms to control the modes of use.[5] Therefore, there are two categories of DRM systems: "technological protection measures" (TPM), which are technical measures used to prevent certain activities (in particular copying), and "rights management information" (RMI), which manages how these works are made available to users. For

3 Recommendation Rec (2001) 7 of the Committee of Ministers to member states on measures to protect copyright and neighbouring rights and combat piracy, especially in the digital environment of 5 September 2001, https://search.coe.int/cm#{%22CoEIdentifier%22:[%220 9000016804deb54%22],%22sort%22:[%22CoEValidationDate%20Descending%22]}, access 1 June 2024.

4 Kleban (2010), passim.

5 Cf. Gienas (2005), pp. 3–4.

example, by limiting the number of copies that may be made from a digital work. Some jurisdictions provide for sanctions in connection with the removal of such safeguards. For example, in the United States, Digital Millennium Copyright Act provides for criminal liability for this, but there are civil remedies available in the UK.[6] This may lead to a specific situation – someone does not infringe copyright because his act meets the conditions of fair use, but at the same time commits a crime, misdemeanour or tort of civil or administrative law (depending on how this issue is regulated in national law) because it violates DRM protection.

Lanzarote Convention

The Convention on the Protection of Children against Sexual Exploitation and Sexual Abuse open to signature on 25 October 2007 in Lanzarote (hereinafter the Lanzarote Convention or the Convention) has a wide scope, the provisions relating to substantive criminal law, including child pornography, are only part of it. Moreover, these provisions do not cover acts committed using means of information and communication technology. However, there is no doubt that currently the main means of disseminating child pornography is the internet. The authors of the draft Lanzarote Convention on issues relating to pornography drew on the solutions adopted in the Convention on Cybercrime. Hence there are many similarities between both acts in this matter.

In the light of Article 3 (a) "child" is any person under the age of 18 years. In addition the Convention uses the term "victim" as any child subject to sexual exploitation or sexual abuse (Article 3 (c)). The term "child pornography" means "any material that visually depicts a child engaged in real or simulated sexually explicit conduct or any depiction of a child's sexual organs for primarily sexual purposes". The scope of this term includes so-called virtual pornography and fake pornography (see subchapter "Content-related offences" of chapter 3).

The term "sexually explicit conduct" covers the same real or simulated acts as in the Convention on Cybercrime (see subchapter "Content-related offences" of chapter 3).

Intentional conducts, committed without right, which Parties are obliged to criminalise as offences concerning child pornography, are stipulated in Article 20 (of the same title). These are the following acts:

a) producing child pornography;
b) offering or making available child pornography;
c) distributing or transmitting child pornography;
d) procuring child pornography for oneself or for another person;

6 Clough (2015), pp. 262–263.

e) possessing child pornography;
f) knowingly obtaining access, through information and communication technologies, to child pornography.

Terms "producing", "offering", "making available", "distributing", "transmitting", "procuring for oneself or for another person" and "possessing" have the same meaning as their counterparts in the Convention on Cybercrime (see subchapter "Content-related offences" of chapter 3). The last act referred to in Article 20 – knowingly obtaining access, through information and communication technologies, to child pornography – is not provided for in the Convention on Cybercrime. It means obtaining access to child pornography without download it, i.e., browsing websites containing such content or streaming.

As in the Convention on Cybercrime, states are obliged to criminalise only intentional and without rights acts. The interpretation of these terms is left to national legislatures (see subchapter "Content-related offences" of chapter 3).

States may reserve the right not to criminalise production or possession of materials which either consist entirely of simulated representations or realistic images of a child who does not exist in reality (virtual pornography), or which involve children who have reached the legal age for sexual activities as prescribed in internal law, where the materials are produced and possessed by them with their consent and solely for their own private use. This means that conduct related to fake pornography (production or possession) should be punishable, and the Party may choose not to do so, but must introduce a requirement to meet the conditions indicated earlier [Article 20(1)(3)]. Each Party may reserve the right not to apply, in whole or in part, Article 20(1)(f), which obliges to criminalise knowingly obtaining access, through information and communication technologies, to child pornography (Article 20(1)(4)).

Article 23 of the Convention defined a type of crime that was not covered by any act of international law existing at the time of its creation – the solicitation of children for sexual purposes, commonly known as "grooming". Grooming[7] includes actions taken to establish an emotional bond with a child for the purpose of sexually exploiting him or her or engaging in the production of child pornography. Article 23 defines grooming as intentionally making proposals, via information and communication technologies, of an adult for the purpose of meeting a child (any person under 18 years of age) with a view to engaging in sexual activity with him or her, where, in accordance with the applicable provisions of national law, he or she has not reached the age of

7 Grooming is not a new phenomenon. The internet has only given it a new form. And it provided criminals with wonderful opportunities to interact with children. In the past, "private access to children" was usually only given to family members or family friends and relatives, teachers or coaches. Now, thanks to the internet, strangers have this opportunity (Clough (2015), p. 378).

consent for sexual activity, or producing child pornography, where this proposal has been followed by material acts leading to such a meeting.

For the purposes of assigning criminal liability, it does not matter whether the meeting took place. It is necessary to prove that the perpetrator intended to exploit the child (engaging in sexual activities or production of child pornography).

Article 24 (1) obliges each Party to criminalise intentionally aiding or abetting to offences provided in the Convention. Attempting to commit a crime should also be punishable, but each Party may reserve the right not to apply, in whole or in part this provision to, *inter alia*, offences established in accordance with Article 20, Paragraphs 1.b., d., e. and f. (offer, make available, distribute, transmit, possess or knowingly access child pornography), and Article 23 (grooming).

Sanctions for natural persons established in accordance with this Convention should be effective, proportionate and dissuasive, taking into account their seriousness. These sanctions shall include deprivation of liberty which can give rise to extradition (Article 27 (1)). Each Party may adopt other measures in relation to perpetrators, such as withdrawal of parental rights or monitoring or supervision of convicted persons (Article 27 (4)).

In Article 26, the principles of liability of legal persons are regulated. These are solutions typical of legal acts of the European Council, the same as, among others, in the Convention on Cybercrime (see subchapter "Corporate liability" of chapter 3). However, in this case – in addition to stating that sanctions should be effective, proportionate and dissuasive – it was indicated that national legislation should provide for criminal or non-criminal monetary fines as well as other measures, in particular:

a) exclusion from entitlement to public benefits or aid;
b) temporary or permanent disqualification from the practice of commercial activities;
c) placing under judicial supervision;
d) judicial winding-up order.

National regulations should enable the seizure and confiscation of goods, documents and other instrumentalities used to commit the offences and proceeds derived from such offences or property the value of which corresponds to such proceeds, and the temporary or permanent closure of any establishment used to carry out offences (Article 27 (3)).

Article 27 (5) allows the proceeds of crime or confiscated property to be allocated to a special fund to finance preventive measures and assistance programs for victims of any of the crimes established in accordance with the Convention.

Article 28 stipulates several aggravating circumstances:

a) the offence seriously damaged the physical or mental health of the victim;
b) the offence was preceded or accompanied by acts of torture or serious violence;

c) the offence was committed against a particularly vulnerable victim;
d) the offence was committed by a member of the family, a person cohabiting with the child or a person having abused his or her authority;
e) the offence was committed by several people acting together;
f) the offence was committed within the framework of a criminal organisation;
g) the perpetrator has previously been convicted of offences of the same nature (Each Party should ensure that final sentences issued by another Party can be taken into account.).

Article 25 contains detailed rules on jurisdiction. Accordingly, these issues are discussed here in the context of the crimes that are the subject of this book – child pornography and grooming.

Each Party shall establish jurisdiction over any offence established in accordance with this Convention, when the offence is committed:

a) in its territory; or
b) on board a ship flying the flag of that Party; or
c) on board an aircraft registered under the laws of that Party; or
d) by one of its nationals; or
e) by a person who has his or her habitual residence in its territory (Each Party has the right to declare that this rule of jurisdiction will not apply or will only apply in certain cases or conditions – Article 25 (3).).

The Convention obliges to establish jurisdiction over any offence established in accordance with this Convention where the offence is committed against one of its nationals or a person who has his or her habitual residence in its territory (Article 25 (2)).

The principle of double criminality has been excluded from the prosecution of most offences specified in this Convention (among others, production of child pornography) in the event that the act was committed by a national of a Party – in the light of Article 25 (4), prosecution cannot be conditional on the condition that the acts be punished at the place where they were committed (Article 25 (4)).

When prosecuting most crimes, including those relating to the production of child pornography, the Convention obliges each Party to ensure that its jurisdiction in relation to Paragraphs 1.d. and e. (i.e., the offence was committed by one of its nationals or by a person having a habitual stay on its territory) is not subject to the condition that prosecution may be initiated only on the basis of a notification from the injured party or a denunciation from the state where the crime was committed (Article 25 (6)).

The Convention obliges each Party to establish jurisdiction in cases where an alleged offender is present in its territory and it does not extradite him or her to another Party, solely on the basis of his or her nationality (Article 25 (7)).

In the event of a conflict of jurisdiction, the Parties shall consult each other to determine the most appropriate jurisdiction to prosecute (Article 25 (8)).

Of course, the Convention does not exclude any criminal jurisdiction exercised by a Party in accordance with its internal law (Article 25 (9)).

By 1 June 2024, the Convention has been ratified by all Council of Europe Member States and two non-Council of Europe Member States – Russian Federation and Tunisia.

Hate crimes

Introductory remarks

The criminal law protection of national and ethnic minorities forms part of a broader issue – that is, countering racism and xenophobia through measures envisaged in criminal law. In consequence, these issues are dealt with jointly in international law instruments (mostly of a non-binding character). The acts that they recommend for criminalisation (or, less frequently, put an obligation to criminalise) are referred to as "hate crimes" (or "bias crimes") and "hate speech", due to the motivation used by perpetrators. Before moving on to the main part of this analysis, it seems advisable to explain basic terminology, i.e., national and ethnic minority, racism and xenophobia.

Racism is understood as

> any action, practice, or belief that reflects the racial worldview – the ideology that humans are divided into separate and exclusive biological entities called "races", that there is a causal link between inherited physical traits and traits of personality, intellect, morality, and other cultural behavioural features, and that some "races" are innately superior to others.[8]

In turn, the term "xenophobia" is defined as "a fear or hatred of strangers or foreigners".[9] In light of the documents drawn up by the European Commission against Racism and Intolerance (ECRI; see further comments), the notion of racism also covers such phenomena as the aforementioned xenophobia as well as anti-Semitism and anti-Gypsyism. Following ECRI General Policy Recommendation No. 7 ("On national legislation to combat racism and racial discrimination"),

> racism shall mean the belief that a ground such as race, colour, language, religion, nationality or national or ethnic origin justifies contempt for a person or a group of persons, or the notion of superiority of a person or a group of persons.

8 The Encyclopædia Britannica, www.britannica.com/summary/racism, access 19 June 2024.
9 The Britannica Dictionary, www.britannica.com/dictionary/xenophobia, access 19 June 2024.

It should be stressed that the use of the phrase "a ground such as" implies that we are dealing with an open-ended list – the "grounds" listed in the definition are of an exemplary nature. In turn, in ECRI General Policy Recommendations No. 9 ("On the fight against antisemitism") and No. 13 ("On combating anti-gypsyism and discrimination against Roma"), it was indicated that anti-Semitism and anti-Gypsyism are specific forms of racism (see further comments).

When defining the concept of a national minority, certain distinctive features of such a community are usually mentioned:

1) it is smaller in number than the rest of the population of the country in which it resides, while not occupying a dominant position in it;
2) it has a relatively homogeneous character;
3) its members are citizens of the state in which they reside;
4) it is of distinct ethnic origin;
5) its members are distinguished from other citizens by such national or cultural characteristics as language, culture, religion and tradition;
6) it strives to cultivate the national or cultural characteristics indicated earlier;
7) it is characterised by self-categorisation; and
8) its interests are represented in relations with state authorities.[10]

In some cases, when drafting legal definitions, legislators set out other prerequisites that a group must meet in order to be recognised as a national minority (e.g., staying for a specified period in the territory of a given state, identifying themselves with another nation constituting that state) or simply list the communities they recognise as minorities.

Grzegorz Janusz is right to note that the term "ethnic minority" is commonly used to describe a group that is "weaker" than a national minority and it usually refers to a community without a mother nation constituting a state. The author rightly emphasises that the introduction of additional categories of ethnic groups (in literature, one can still find other, to some extent "related", concepts such as "national group") is not very useful in the activities of state authorities, so it seems advisable to depart from the division into national and other (ethnic) minorities and to include all categories of minorities under the former concept. This was envisaged in the Framework Convention for the Protection of National Minorities.[11,12]

As regards official documents, the term "hate crime" was first used in the OSCE Ministerial Council Decision made in Maastricht in 1993.[13] The very

10 Janusz (2011), p. 26.
11 Framework Convention for the Protection of National Minorities of 1 June 1995.
12 Janusz (2011), pp. 47–48.
13 OSCE Ministerial Council Decision No. 4/03, "Tolerance and Non-discrimination", Maastricht, 2 December 2003, www.osce.org/mc/19382, access 19 June 2024.

idea, however, appeared a little earlier – at a meeting in Geneva in 1991 during which reference was made to discrimination, prejudice and hatred.[14]

To clarify the term "hate crime", it seems advisable to refer to the working definition which was formulated by ODIHR[15] and included, *inter alia*, in its annual report for 2007 concerning this subject matter. According to that definition, hate crime means

> any criminal offence, including offences against persons or property, where the victim, premises, or target of the offence is selected because of a real or perceived connection, attachment, affiliation, support, or membership of a group defined by a characteristic common to its members, such as real or perceived "race", national or ethnic origin, language, colour, religion, sex, age, mental or physical disability, sexual orientation, or other similar factor.[16]

Accordingly, two components can be distinguished in every hate crime. The first consists of the definitional elements of a common type of crime. If the perpetrator's conduct does not have these elements, there is no hate crime. The second necessary component is a specific motive behind the perpetrator's conduct – one arising from hatred.[17]

This type of crime is also referred to as "bias-motivated crime". Some authors claim that it is a more accurate term, as it better reflects the perpetrator's motives. For example, many homicides are committed out of hatred that is not related to the victim's membership of a particular group (be it racial, national or ethnic).[18] Sometimes the two terms are used interchangeably.

Based on the aforementioned definition of "hate crime", it can be inferred that this category will not include acts which entail inciting racial, national

14 *Hate Crimes in the OSCE Region – Incidents and Responses. Annual Report for 2008*, OSCE/ODIHR 2009, p. 12. www.google.com/url?sa=t&source=web&rct=j&opi=89978449&url=www.osce.org/odihr/40203&ved=2ahUKEwi4p_bhjIOHAxVE7LsIHTcrB7IQFnoECBEQAQ&usg=AOvVaw0v3_Y4fWKLiJfUJZoDRPVO, access 19 June 2024.

15 The Office of Democratic Institutions and Human Rights (ODIHR) – an institution operating within the Organisation for Security and Co-operation in Europe (OSCE) whose task is to assist OSCE Member States in meeting their obligations in the field of human rights and democratic development. It has operated since 1991 (until 1992 as the Office for Free Elections) and is based in Warsaw.

16 *Hate Crimes in the OSCE Region – Incidents and Responses. Annual Report for 2007*, p. 11. www.google.com/url?sa=t&source=web&rct=j&opi=89978449&url=www.osce.org/files/f/documents/9/2/40203.pdf&ved=2ahUKEwiQl4y1iYOHAxVb_rsIHeKHBPgQFnoECA4QAQ&usg=AOvVaw0HSap8Lee2hLAdnAslendB, access 19 June 2024.

17 *Hate Crime Laws: A Practical Guide*, 2nd edition OSCE/ODIHR 2009, pp. 15–17. www.google.com/url?sa=t&source=web&rct=j&opi=89978449&url=www.osce.org/odihr/523940&ved=2ahUKEwibl8OuioOHAxWS_7sIHTlcBAEQFnoECBEQAQ&usg=AOvVaw2Dw4xguCTfUVdCWMdVlByj, access 19 June 2024.

18 *Hate Crime Laws*, pp. 17–19.

or ethnic hatred, denying the Holocaust or glorifying crimes committed by totalitarian systems. This is because there is no element of a common crime underlying it. These acts are classified separately, e.g., as so-called hate speech, as they are closely related to the issue of hate crimes, and – as indicated earlier – they are criminalised alongside them.

Hate speech

Recommendation No. R (97) 20 of the Committee of Ministers to Member States on "hate speech"[19] defines the term "hate speech" as all forms of expression which spread, incite, promote or justify racial hatred, xenophobia, anti-Semitism or other forms of hatred based on intolerance, including: intolerance expressed by aggressive nationalism and ethnocentrism, discrimination and hostility against minorities, migrants and people of immigrant origin.

This definition is undoubtedly too narrow. Its scope does not include, for example, acts directed against people due to their sexual orientation. However, we must remember that this is probably the first definition, created in the previous century – in 1997. The definition contained in ECRI general policy Recommendation no. 15 on combating hate speech adopted on 8 December 2015 has a much broader scope. It defines hate speech as advocacy, promotion or incitement, in any form, of the denigration, hatred or vilification of a person or group of persons, as well as any harassment, insult, negative stereotyping, stigmatisation or threat in respect of such a person or group of persons and the justification of all the preceding types of expression, on the ground of "race", colour, descent, national or ethnic origin, age, disability, language, religion or belief, sex, gender, gender identity, sexual orientation and other personal characteristics or status.

Anti-discrimination acts

When discussing the Council of Europe's regulations on the issue of combating racism and xenophobia, one should start with the ECHR, which stipulates, in Article 14, that

> The enjoyment of the rights and freedoms set forth in this Convention shall be secured without discrimination on any ground such as sex, race, colour, language, religion, political or other opinion, national or social origin, association with a national minority, property, birth or another status.

19 Recommendation No. R (97) 20 of the Committee of Ministers to member states on "hate speech" of 30 October 1997. www.coe.int/en/web/freedom-expression/committee-of-ministers-adopted-texts/-/asset_publisher/aDXmrol0vvsU/content/recommendation-no-r-97-20-of-the-committee-of-ministers-to-member-states-on-hate-speech-, access 1 June 2024.

The applicability scope of that provision was extended[20] in Article 1 of Protocol No. 12 to the ECHR.[21]

Other notable acts adopted by the Council of Europe and dealing with the protection of minorities include the European Social Charter[22] (including its revised version of 1996),[23] the aforementioned Framework Convention for the Protection of National Minorities and the Convention on the Participation of Foreigners in Public Life at Local Level.[24]

As stressed by Sławomir Żółtek, the aforementioned legal acts

> aim to protect human rights and are of an anti-discriminatory character.[25] They are also characterised by the multi-disciplinary legal nature of the regulated issues. To a large extent, it is up to the signatories of individual conventions, or protocols to these conventions, to determine the measures which will be used to combat undesirable phenomena.[26]

In consequence, these acts do not envisage an obligation to introduce criminal law protection of national minorities, thus remaining outside the scope of this publication.

Activities of ECRI

Issues surrounding the criminal law protection of minorities fall within the remit of the ECRI (the European Commission against Racism and Intolerance). Operating within the Council of Europe, this institution is responsible for monitoring the respect for human rights, particularly as regards racism, racial discrimination, xenophobia and anti-Semitism. It was established under

20 This entails extending the prohibition of discrimination to the exercise of "any right established by law" and not only, as provided for in Article 14 of ECHR, the rights and freedoms granted in ECHR. See Wróbel (2010), p. 758; Garlicki (2010), pp. 672–674.

21 Protocol No. 12 to the Convention for the Protection of Human Rights and Fundamental Freedoms of 4 November 2000 (regarding the overall ban on discrimination).

22 The European Social Charter of 18 October 1961.

23 The European Social Charter (revised) of 3 May 1996.

24 The Council of Europe Convention of 5 June 1992 on the Participation of Foreigners in Public Life at Local Level.

25 They regulate the relationship between the state and individuals. Indeed, it should be borne in mind that "human rights" are understood as the essential rights that serve individuals in the light of some philosophical concept (philosophical dimension) concerning his or her position within the state, whether they serve him or her on the basis of certain norms of national, supranational or international law (the legal dimension). Consequently, they operate vertically (state – individual). Only in exceptional cases can one speak of the horizontal operation of human rights (i.e., between the individual and another individual or an entity that is not part of the state apparatus).

26 Żółtek (2012), p. 302.

the Vienna Declaration adopted at the Vienna Summit on 9 October 1993,[27] and its role as an independent monitoring body was significantly strengthened by the new statute (Resolution (2002) 8) adopted by the Committee of Ministers on 14 June 2002.[28] Based on its monitoring activities, the ECRI draws up reports, identifying existing problems and suggesting solutions to them. It also issues – as mentioned earlier – general-policy recommendations addressed to the governments of all Member States. The most important of these are presented here.

1) Recommendation No. 1 (CRI (96) 43):[29] "On combating racism, xenophobia, antisemitism and intolerance" which recommends defining common offences of a racist or xenophobic nature as specific criminal offences and adopting the principle that racist or xenophobic motives behind the perpetrator's actions should be taken into consideration in imposing punishment and also that such offences should be prosecuted *ex officio*.[30]
2) Recommendation No. 6 (CRI (2001) 1): "On combating the dissemination of racist, xenophobic and antisemitic material via the internet", which draws attention to the need to introduce certain legislative changes in national legal systems, enabling the combating of racist, xenophobic and anti-Semitic criminal offences committed via the internet.[31]
3) Recommendation No. 7 (CRI (2003) 8): "On national legislation to combat racism and racial discrimination" which enumerates, in particular, acts of a racist or xenophobic nature that should be penalised if committed intentionally, i.e.:

    a) public incitement to violence, hatred or discrimination;
    b) public insults and defamation;
    c) threats;
    d) the public expression of an ideology which promotes racism and xenophobia;

27 https://search.coe.int/cm/Pages/result_details.aspx?ObjectId=0900001680536c83, access 19 June 2024.

28 Resolution Res(2002)8 on the statute of the European Commission against Racism and Intolerance (Adopted by the Committee of Ministers on 13 June 2002 at the 799th meeting of the Ministers' Deputies, amended by Resolutions CM/Res(2013)12 and CM/Res(2014)2 adopted, respectively, on 9 October 2013 and 19 June 2014 at their 1180th and 1192nd meetings, www.google.com/url?sa=t&source=web&rct=j&opi=89978449&url=https://rm.coe.int/0900001680973356&ved=2ahUKEwj5neqvg4OHAxWZ8rsIHeCXA80QFnoECBAQAQ&usg=AOvVaw0vUfYbiJgQ0jWGyYR7WYV-, access 19 June 2024.

29 ECRI documents are available in a separate section of the Council of Europe website, www.ecri.coe.int, access 19 June 2024.

30 www.coe.int/en/web/european-commission-against-racism-and-intolerance/recommendation-no.1, access 19 June 2024.

31 www.coe.int/en/web/european-commission-against-racism-and-intolerance/recommendation-no.6, access 19 June 2024.

e) the denial of crimes of genocide, crimes against humanity or war crimes;
f) the public dissemination of materials of a racist or xenophobic nature;
g) the creation of a group which promotes racism, support for such a group and participation in its activities to contribute to the offences listed previously;
h) racial discrimination in the exercise of one's public office or occupation.
i) it was further recommended that instigating, aiding, abetting or attempting to commit any of the criminal offences listed should also be punishable. It was remarked that these acts should be subject to effective, proportionate and dissuasive sanctions. And as regards offences other than listed in the Recommendations, racist motivation should constitute an aggravating circumstance.[32]

4) Recommendation No. 9 (CRI (2004) 37): "On preventing and combating antisemitism" stresses that in combating racism criminal law also covers combating anti-Semitism as its specific form. Moreover, attention is drawn to the need to penalise conduct involving the trivialisation, justification or condoning of the Holocaust. Penalisation is also recommended for the desecration of Jewish property and monuments out of anti-Semitic motives.[33]
5) Recommendation No. 12 (CRI (2009) 5): "On combating racism and racial discrimination in the field of sport" in which governments of the Member States are recommended, *inter alia*, to penalise racist acts in sports and to introduce a ban on disseminating racist material using the internet.[34]
6) Recommendation No. 13 (CRI (2011) 37): "On combating anti-gypsyism and discrimination against Roma" which stresses – as mentioned earlier – that "anti-gypsyism is a specific form of racism, an ideology founded on racial superiority, a form of dehumanisation and institutional racism".[35]
7) ECRI General Policy Recommendation N°15 (CRI 2015) 15): "Combating Hate Speech",[36] in which it was recommended to

    a) ratify the Additional Protocol to the Convention on Cybercrime, concerning criminalisation of acts of a racist and xenophobic nature committed through computer systems, the Framework Convention for the

32 www.coe.int/en/web/european-commission-against-racism-and-intolerance/recommendation-no.7, access 19 June 2024.
33 www.coe.int/en/web/european-commission-against-racism-and-intolerance/recommendation-no.9, access 19 June 2024.
34 www.coe.int/en/web/european-commission-against-racism-and-intolerance/recommendation-no.12, access 19 June 2024.
35 www.coe.int/en/web/european-commission-against-racism-and-intolerance/recommendation-no.13, access 19 June 2024.
36 www.coe.int/en/web/european-commission-against-racism-and-intolerance/recommendation-no.15, access 19 June 2024.

Protection of National Minorities and Protocol No. 12 to the European Convention on Human Rights;

b) withdraw any reservations to Article 4 of the International Convention on the Elimination of All Forms of Racial Discrimination and to Article 20 of the International Covenant on Civil and Political Rights and recognise the competence of the Committee on the Elimination of Racial Discrimination to receive and consider communications from individuals or groups of individuals under Article 14;
c) seek to identify the conditions conducive to the use of hate speech as a phenomenon and the different forms it takes, as well as to measure its extent and the harm that it causes, with a view to discouraging and preventing its use and to reducing and remedying the harm caused;
d) clarify the scope and applicability of responsibility under civil and administrative law for the use of hate speech which is intended or can reasonably be expected to incite acts of violence, intimidation, hostility or discrimination against those who are targeted by it while respecting the right to freedom of expression and opinion;
e) take appropriate and effective action against the use, in a public context, of hate speech which is intended or can reasonably be expected to incite acts of violence, intimidation, hostility or discrimination against those targeted by it through the use of the criminal law provided that no other, less restrictive, measure would be effective and the right to freedom of expression and opinion is respected.

8) ECRI General Policy Recommendation No. 17 on preventing and combating intolerance and discrimination against LGBTI persons Adopted on 28 June 2023, which recommends, i.e. to ensure that anti-hate crime and anti-discrimination laws and policies provide effective protection for LGBTI people, and refrain from adopting laws or policies which victimise, discriminate against or legitimise hate against LGBTI people.

ECRI periodically prepares reports on the situation of minorities in individual Member States of the Council of Europe (they are prepared in rounds – so far there have been six of them).

Additional Protocol to the Convention on Cybercrime, concerning the criminalisation of acts of a racist and xenophobic nature committed through computer systems

The decision to include provisions regarding crimes motivated by racism or xenophobia in a separate protocol (as mentioned earlier), and not in the Cybercrime Convention itself, was made by representatives of the countries participating in its creation, and resulted from the awareness of differences in constitutional standards regarding freedom of speech.

Finally, provisions on this sensitive matter were included in Additional Protocol to the Convention on Cybercrime, concerning the criminalisation of acts of a racist and xenophobic nature committed through computer systems, open to signature 28 January 2003 (hereinafter referred to as "the Protocol").[37]

For the purposes of the Protocol, under Article 2 (1), "racist and xenophobic material" means

> any written material, any image or any other representation of ideas or theories which advocates, promotes or incites hatred, discrimination or violence against any individual or a group of individuals, based on race, colour, descent or national or ethnic origin, as well as religion if used as a pretext for any of these factors.

Article 2 (2) of the Protocol stipulates that the terms and expressions used in this Protocol should be interpreted in the same manner as they are interpreted under the Convention on Cybercrime. In addition, Article 8 of the Protocol defines in detail the relations between the Convention and the Protocol, indicating the Articles which have the relevant application.

The Protocol introduces the requirement that the conduct indicated therein must be committed "intentionally and without right" in order to be qualified as an offence. The conduct contained in Protocol is not always punishable per se. It may become legal or justified in cases where classical legal defences are applicable, like consent, self-defence or necessity, or where other principles cause the exclusion of criminal liability (e.g., for law enforcement purposes, for academic or research purposes). The authors of the Protocol – similar as authors of the Convention on Cybercrime – left the exact meaning of "intentionally" to national interpretation. An offender cannot be held criminally liable if he has not the required intent. It follows from the preceding that the service provider that served as a conduit or hosted the website containing such content material, without the requisite intention, cannot be held criminally liable under that provision. Moreover, a service provider is not obliged to monitor the conduct in order to avoid criminal liability.[38]

Disseminating, or otherwise making available to the public, racist and xenophobic material through computer systems is the first act to be criminalised under the Protocol, and more specifically under Article 3 (1). The use of the term "public" eliminates any forms of private communication from the scope of criminalisation. The circumstances of an individual case determine whether an exchange of information is considered public or not. Factors to be taken into consideration in the assessment include the sender's intention, the circumstances under which the exchange occurs, the content of the message, the number of recipients and the nature of the relationship between the recipients

37 See also Walden (2016), p. 152; Savin, Trzaskowski (2014), pp. 495–496.

38 Explanatory Report to the Additional Protocol to the Convention on Cybercrime, concerning the criminalisation of acts of a racist and xenophobic nature committed through computer systems, point 24 and 25.

and the sender, or measures taken to prevent third parties from reading the content. However, there is no doubt that posting racist and xenophobic content on websites, forums or chat rooms should be considered public dissemination (doubts may arise, however, in the case of a limited group of users having access to such a forum or chat room, e.g., when it is only a closed and small group of registered persons). A state may reserve the right not to attach criminal liability to conduct as defined by Paragraph 1 of the said Article, where the conduct defined therein advocates, promotes or incites discrimination that is not associated with hatred or violence, provided that other effective remedies (e.g., administrative) are available. A state may also reserve the right not to apply Paragraph 1 to those cases of discrimination for which, due to established principles in its national legal system concerning freedom of expression, it cannot provide for effective remedies as referred to in the said Paragraph 2 (Article 3 (3)).[39]

Article 4 obliges Parties to criminalise under its domestic law, threatening, through a computer system, with the commission of a serious criminal offence as defined under its domestic law,

1) persons for the reason that they belong to a group, distinguished by race, colour, descent or national or ethnic origin, as well as religion, if used as a pretext for any of these factors; or
2) a group of persons which is distinguished by any of these characteristics.

In this event, there is no possibility to exclude criminalisation or to limit its scope (as can be done, e.g., in the case of acts defined in Article 3).

Article 5 (1) obliges State Parties to attach criminal liability to any conduct which entails insulting publicly, through a computer system,

1) persons for the reason that they belong to a group distinguished by race, colour, descent or national or ethnic origin, as well as religion, if used as a pretext for any of these factors; or
2) a group of persons which is distinguished by any of these characteristics.

The Party may either require that the offence in question has the effect that the individual or a group of individuals referred to in the provision is exposed to hatred, contempt or ridicule; or reserve the right not to apply, in whole or in part, Paragraph 1 of the article in question (Article 5 (2)).

The provision of Article 6 (1) envisages an obligation for State Parties to criminalise the following conduct when committed intentionally or without right: distributing or otherwise making available, through a computer system to the public, material which denies, grossly minimises, approves or justifies acts constituting genocide or crimes against humanity, as defined by

39 Savin (2017), p. 140.

international law and recognised as such by final and binding decisions of the International Military Tribunal, established by the London Agreement of 8 August 1945, or of any other international court established by relevant international instruments and whose jurisdiction is recognised by a given state (e.g., International Criminal Tribunals for the former Yugoslavia or Rwanda, or the ICC – the International Criminal Court in The Hague). A State Party may also require that the offence referred to earlier is committed with the intent to incite hatred, discrimination or violence against any person or a group of people, based on race, colour, descent or national or ethnic origin, as well as religion if used as a pretext to commit acts against a group of persons for any of the aforementioned factors. In addition, a state may reserve the right not to apply, in whole or in part, Paragraph 1 of the said article.

In Article 7, an obligation was placed on State Parties to criminalise aiding and abetting, concerning the offences stipulated in the Convention.

The Protocol entered into force on 1 March 2006.[40] Under Article 9 (1), it is open for signature by the states which have signed the Convention. This means that it is also open for signature by states that are not members of the Council of Europe, both from and outside Europe. They may accede to the Convention on Cyberspace provided that they have participated in its creation (the United States, Canada, Japan) or were invited to accede by the Committee of Ministers and subject to the approval of all State Parties.

40 By 1 June 2024, the Protocol had been signed by 46 countries (including six from outside of Europe (Benin, Canada, Morocco, Paraguay, Senegal, South Africa) and ratified by 36 of them.

5 Cybercrime in European Union Law

Framework Decision 2005/222

Preliminary remarks

The Council Framework Decision 2005/222/JHA of 24 June 2005 on attacks against information systems[1] (hereinafter Framework Decision 2005/222) marked the EU legislators' first attempt at regulating this issue.[2] This was due to both the novel character of the subject matter and the fact that criminal law belonged to the third pillar of the EU, within which the EU legislators could only strive to harmonise law. This offered much leeway to individual Member States and only indicated the objective to be achieved, without dictating the manner in which to attain it.

The work on Framework Decision 2005/222 began as early as 2001, as a response to the Commission Communication on Cybercrime of 2001,[3] which contained some proposals for substantive and procedural provisions to combat computer crime, both at the national and Community levels. The measures taken resulted, *inter alia*, in the presentation of a proposal regarding the draft Framework Decision 2005/222 under discussion.

1 OJ EU 2005 L 69/67.

2 On the EU's previous activities on this issue, see, e.g. Radoniewicz (2021c), pp. 71–74.

3 Communication from the Commission to the Council, the European Parliament, the Economic and Social Committee and the Committee of the Regions COM(2000)890 on Creating a Safer Information Society by Improving the Security of Information Infrastructures and Combating Computer-related Crime of 26 June 2001 (the so-called Communication on Cybercrime), in which attention was drawn to the need for effective measures in the fight against cybercrime, a balanced approach was proposed for addressing problems related to cybercrime, and it was deemed necessary to fully take into account the views of all stakeholders in the fight against this phenomenon, including law enforcement bodies, service providers, network operators, other industry groups, consumer groups, data protection authorities, etc.; in this document, the Commission proposed a number of legislative and non-legislative initiatives.

DOI: 10.4324/9781003476771-5

Recitals

In Recital 1 of Framework Decision 2005/222, it was pointed out that its objective was to improve the cooperation between judicial authorities and law enforcement services of the Member States, through approximating rules on criminal law in the Member States, in the areas of attacks against information systems. Further down the line in Framework Decision 2005/222, the need for legislative action at the level of the EU was justified, pointing out that countering attacks against information systems had become an extremely important issue, due to the potential relationship between these types of offences and organised crime, as well as terrorist attacks against information systems which form part of the critical infrastructure of the Member States.

In the Preamble it was stressed that attacks against information systems are often transnational in nature as they form a network located in the territory of many countries. In view of the preceding, it is necessary to approximate criminal law in the area of attacks against information systems in order to facilitate police and judicial cooperation, so as to be able to effectively counter attacks against information systems and to help in the fight against organised crime and terrorism. In particular, it is necessary to adopt common legal definitions of the relevant concepts, especially those of an "information system" and "computer data", to harmonise the definitional elements of crime consisting of illegal access to an information system, illegal system interference and illegal data interference, and for Member States to establish effective, proportionate and dissuasive penalties for attacks against information systems. It was stressed that penalties should be more severe if the perpetrator was acting within the framework of a criminal organisation, as defined in Joint Action 98/733/JHA of 21 December 1998 on making it a criminal offence to participate in a criminal organisation in the Member States of the European Union,[4] or where such an attack has caused serious damage or has affected essential interests.

It was pointed out that certain acts indicated in Framework Decision 2005/222 should not be excessively punished, especially where minor cases are concerned. This point is very pertinent in view of the specificity of computer network crime, where a number of offences are characterised by low social harm. It is also important to avoid the incrimination of the activities of "rights holders and authorised persons". This term can be understood as, *inter alia*, network administrators or persons involved in the protection of information systems, whose activities can formally violate the law.

It was emphasised that the implementation of Framework Decision 2005/222 cannot neglect the protection of personal data, the processing of which should be protected in accordance with the principles of the Convention

4 OJ EC 1998 L 351/1.

of the Council of Europe for the protection of individuals with regard to automatic processing of personal data.[5]

Terminology

Article 1 of Framework Decision 2005/222 contains definitions of the most crucial terms: "information system", "computer data", "legal person" and "without right".[6]

For the purpose of Framework Decision 2005/222, it was assumed that *information system* means any device or group of inter-connected or related devices, one or more of which, pursuant to a program, performs automatic processing of computer data, as well as computer data stored, processed, retrieved or transmitted by them for the purposes of their operation, use, protection and maintenance. The aforementioned decision is apparently close to the definition of a computer system in Article 1 (a) of Convention on Cybercrime[7] discussed in the previous chapter (where it means a single host – a device connected to a computer network, e.g., a computer, a smartphone, a router or a server), but it has an incomparably broader substantive scope. As indicated in the substantiation to Framework Decision 2005/222, referring to the OECD Recommendation of the Council C (92) 188 concerning Guidelines for the Security of Information Systems of 26 November 1992[8] (hereinafter Recommendation C (92) 188), an "information system" is a technologically neutral term which, at the same time, accurately reflects the idea of connected networks and systems containing data. In light of the aforementioned OECD Guidelines, information systems are understood as "computers, communication facilities, computer and communication networks and data and information that may be stored, processed, retrieved or transmitted by them, including programs, specifications[9] and procedures[10] for their operation, use and maintenance".

5 Convention for the Protection of Individuals with regard to Automatic Processing of Personal Data (ETS No. 108), done at Strasbourg on 28 June 1981, www.coe.int/en/web/data-protection/convention108-and-protocol, access 19 June 2024.

6 In the draft presented by the Commission, the following definitions were additionally included: "electronic communications networks", "computer" and "authorised person" (see further discussion in this section).

7 Convention on Cybercrime (ETS No. 185), opened for signature in Budapest on 23 November 2001, www.coe.int/en/web/conventions/full-list?module=signatures-by-treaty&treatynum=185, access 19 June 2024.

8 OECD Recommendation of the Council C (92) 188 concerning Guidelines for the Security of Information Systems of 26 November 1992, https://legalinstruments.oecd.org/en/instruments/OECD-LEGAL-0271, access 1 June 2024.

9 Work environment and programme feature description.

10 Subprogram (procedure, subroutine, subprogram, method) – a sequence (set) of program instructions that performs specific tasks, may be part of a program or be included in so-called libraries and used by many programs.

Therefore, information systems should be understood as both single data-processing devices and computer networks, including small networks (for instance LAN),[11] covering a few computers, and large-scale structures consisting of interconnected networks (e.g., MAN).[12,13] The thesis about the broad meaning of the notion is confirmed by the fact that EU Member States usually use the term "computer system" in their translations of the Convention and the term "information system" in the Framework Decision 2005/222.[14] Expressions such as "cross-border nature" of information systems[15] or "large-scale information system"[16] can be found in EU documents.

The network was defined then (i.e., at the time of the creation of the Framework Decision) in EU law as "electronic communications network", which meant

> transmission systems and, where applicable, switching or routing equipment and other resources which permit the conveyance of signals by wire, by radio, by optical or by other electromagnetic means, including satellite networks, fixed (circuit- and packet-switched, including Internet) and mobile terrestrial networks, electricity cable systems, to the extent that they are used for the purpose of transmitting signals,

11 LAN – a local area network. See subchapter "The history of computer networks and the internet" of chapter 2.

12 MAN – a metropolitan area network covering numerous interconnected local area networks. Networks of this type are developed by public institutions, universities (university networks) or private entities (enterprises).

13 Due to the volume limits of this study, the issue will not be discussed in detail. For more on the subject, see Radoniewicz (2016), pp. 244–249.

14 First of all, obviously, in the English text of the Convention on Cybercrime (importantly, the authentic text), the term "computer system" appears while the text of Directive 2005/222 uses the term "information system". The second authentic text, in French, does not use the term "computer system", for the simple reason that there is no word for "computer" in this language; the term used is "système informatique", but the Directive, by way of contrast, uses the term "système d'information"; finally, in the German texts, the Convention uses the term "Computersystem", and the Directive uses the term "Informationssystem".

15 For instance, Recital 27 of Directive 2013/40 on attacks against information system: "The transnational and borderless nature of modern information systems means that attacks against such systems have a cross-border dimension".

16 Regulation (EU) 2018/1726 of the European Parliament and of the Council of 14 November 2018 on the European Union Agency for the Operational Management of Large-Scale IT Systems in the Area of Freedom, Security and Justice (eu-LISA), and amending Regulation (EC) No 1987/2006 and Council Decision 2007/533/JHA and repealing Regulation (EU) No. 1077/2011 (OJ EU 2018 L 295/99).

networks used for radio and television broadcasting, and cable television networks, irrespective of the type of information conveyed.

(Article 2 (a) Directive 2002/21/EC of the European Parliament and of the Council of 7 March 2002 on a common regulatory framework for electronic communications networks and services (Framework Directive) (hereinafter Directive 2002/21[17])

These include, for example, satellite networks, fixed networks based on packet switching (a method of data transmission consisting in grouping data into packets, each of which can reach its destination via a different route; the process of transmitting packets is called routing and takes place between several network nodes – routers; in local networks, this function is performed by switches) and circuit switching (connection switching involves establishing, on demand, a "permanent" dedicated connection between two or more network points for their exclusive use for the duration of the communication session; currently unheard of) and television cable networks[18] or power networks enabling signal transmission. Switching devices are devices used for switching circuits (e.g., telephone switchboards) or switching packets (in a local network – LAN), and routing devices (mainly routers) are devices used for routing packets. Switching or routing equipment and other signal-carrying resources are not always required to transmit the signal. There are networks that do not contain them.

Many states, when implementing the provisions of the directives, used the literal definition of the electronic communications network from the

17 OJ EC 2002 L 108/33. It is one of the so-called electronic communications directives, which included, apart from it: the Directive 2002/19/EC of the European Parliament and of the Council of 7 March 2002 on access to, and interconnection of, electronic communications networks and associated facilities (Access Directive), OJ EC 2002 L 108 7, Directive 2002/20/EC of the European Parliament and of the Council of 7 March 2002 on the authorisation of electronic communications networks and services (Authorisation Directive) OJ EC 2002 L 108/21, Directive 2002/22/EC of the European Parliament and of the Council of 7 March 2002 on universal service and users' rights relating to electronic communications networks and services (Universal Service Directive) OJ EC 2002 L 108/51, Directive 2002/58/EC of the European Parliament and of the Council of 12 July 2002 concerning the processing of personal data and the protection of privacy in the electronic communications sector (Directive on privacy and electronic communications) OJ EC 2002 L 201/37, Commission Directive 2002/77/EC of 16 September 2002 on competition in the markets for electronic communications networks and services (Text with EEA relevance) (OJ EC 2002 L 249/21) and Decision No. 676/2002/EC of the European Parliament and of the Council of 7 March 2002 on a regulatory framework for radio spectrum policy in the European Community (Radio Spectrum Decision) OJ EC L 108/1.

18 A method of distributing television programmes to viewers using radio frequency (RF) signals transmitted over coaxial cables or, more recently, fibre optic cables.

Framework Directive, e.g., Germany (Telecommunication Law of June 22, 2004).[19,20]

Article 125 Directive (EU) 2018/1972 of the European Parliament and of the Council of 11 December 2018 establishing the European Electronic Communications Code (Recast)Text with EEA relevance)[21] (hereinafter EECC) provides that Directives 2002/19/EC, 2002/20/EC, 2002/21/EC and 2002/22/EC are repealed with effect from 21 December 2020, without prejudice to the obligations of the Member States relating to the time-limits for the transposition into national law and the dates of application of the directives set out in Annex XII, Part B. Article 5 of Decision No. 243/2012/EU is deleted with effect from 21 December 2020.

In the light of Article 2 (1) EECC

> "electronic communications network" means transmission systems, whether or not based on a permanent infrastructure or centralised administration capacity, and, where applicable, switching or routing equipment and other resources, including network elements which are not active, which permit the conveyance of signals by wire, radio, optical or other electromagnetic means, including satellite networks, fixed (circuit- and packet-switched, including internet) and mobile networks, electricity cable systems, to the extent that they are used for the purpose of transmitting signals, networks used for radio and television broadcasting, and cable television networks, irrespective of the type of information conveyed.

It can be assumed that this definition does not differ from its predecessor from Directive 2002/21.

In accordance with Article 2 (d) Directive 2002/21 (Article 2 (8) EECC) "public electronic communications network" means an electronic communications network used wholly or mainly for the provision of publicly available electronic communications services which support the transfer of information between network termination points.[22] *A contrario*, a non-public (internal, private) network will be a network used by the entity solely for its own needs and purposes (including running a business), regardless of its territorial range (local, nationwide, international) or for the purpose of providing only

19 Repealed Telekommunikationsgesetz vom 22. Juni 2004; BGBl. I S. 1190; https://dejure.org/BGBl/2004/BGBl._I_S._1190; access 9 June 2024).

20 Cf. Scherer (2005), p. 352.

21 OJ EU 2018 L 321/36.

22 "Network termination point" means the physical point at which an end-user is provided with access to a public electronic communications network, and which, in the case of networks involving switching or routing, is identified by means of a specific network address, which may be linked to an end-user's number or name (Article 2 (9) EECC).

non-public telecommunications services (e.g., Wi-Fi networks in hotels, available only for hotel guests).

"Computer data" was defined in Framework Decision 2005/222 in an identical way as in the Convention on Cybercrime. This means any representation of facts, information or concepts in a form suitable for processing in an information system, including a program suitable for causing an information system to perform a function.

The way the definition of an information system is formulated in some languages (including English) may raise doubts as to whether computer data processed by an information system, indicated in the second part of the definition ("computer data stored, processed, retrieved or transmitted by that device or group of devices for the purposes of its or their operation, use, protection and maintenance"), are its element. Of course not. Firstly, this is due to definitions formulated in languages in which the declension occurs. In this languages (i.e., Polish, German, Italian) the term computer data is not in the nominative case but in the genitive this means that the definition clearly states that the information system included its own data (first part of definition – a program suitable for causing an information system to perform a function and data necessary to function it) and processes the data transferred to it which are not part of it.[23]

Secondly, this reasoning is confirmed by the content of the definition of "network and information system" contained in the Article 4 (1) NIS Directive,[24] next repeated in Article 6 (1) of the NIS2 Directive,[25] which states that computer data constitute a separate element from the information system and electronic communications networks. In the light of it:

a) an electronic communications network within the meaning of point (a) of Article 2 of Directive 2002/21/EC (i.e., Article 2 (1) EECC);
b) any device or group of interconnected or related devices, one or more of which, pursuant to a program, perform automatic processing of digital data;[26] or
c) digital data stored, processed, retrieved or transmitted by elements covered under points (a) and (b) for the purposes of their operation, use, protection and maintenance.

23 See subchapter "Computer programs" of chapter 2.

24 Directive (EU) 2016/1148 of the European Parliament and of the Council of 6 July 2016 concerning measures for a high common level of security of network and information systems across the Union (OJ EU 2016 L 194/1).

25 Consolidated text: Directive (EU) 2022/2555 of the European Parliament and of the Council of 14 December 2022 on measures for a high common level of cybersecurity across the Union, amending Regulation (EU) No 910/2014 and Directive (EU) 2018/1972, and repealing Directive (EU) 2016/1148 (NIS 2 Directive) (Text with EEA relevance) (OJ EU 2022 L 333/80).

26 This is of course the definition of computer system/information system.

A "legal person", in line with the definition contained in Framework Decision 2005/222, is any entity having such status under the applicable law, except for states or other public bodies in the exercise of state authority and for public international organisations. As can be seen, the Decision refers to the national law of the Member States and, therefore, some differences should be expected in the substantive scope of the concept in individual Member States.[27]

The last definition refers to the term "without right". Access or interference not authorised by the owner, other right holders of the system or part of it or not permitted under national legislation are considered to have been obtained or made without right. The issue of access rights to the information system resources is, in most cases, regulated by "soft law" regulations – internal network regulations, and it is the system administrator who decides about granting rights to a user and about the scope of these rights. What is at stake here is so-called unauthorised access, i.e., access to the resources of a given system by a person who is not authorised to do so. The EU legislators allowed Member States to regulate this issue in more detail.

The original version of Framework Decision 2005/222 also contained a definition of "authorised person". This was understood as any natural or legal person who is entitled, under a contract or law, or authorised by the aforementioned person, to use, manage, control, investigate, carry out legitimate research or perform any other activity in connection with an information system, and who acts in accordance with that entitlement or authorisation (not exceeding the scope of that entitlement or authorisation). As was stressed in the draft substantiation, it is of the utmost importance that certain types of conduct are not punishable in national legislation, such as: actions by ordinary users, both private and commercial, including encryption of communications and data; decompilation[28] (to the extent as permitted by Council Directive 91/250 of 14 May 1991 on the Protection of Computer Programs);[29] actions by entities such as network administrators, security inspectors, etc.; actions performed by authorised security testers, whether operating within an entity or appointed from outside, who are permitted to test the security of a system; and legitimate scientific research.

27 However, considerations concerning legal persons will be omitted in this study as they are outside the scope of the issue under discussion.

28 For more on the subject, see, for instance: Radoniewicz (2009b), pp. 28–29.

29 OJ EC 1991 L 122/42. Replaced by Directive 2009/24/EC of the European Parliament and of the Council of 23 April 2009 on the legal protection of computer programs. OJ UE 2009 L 111/16.

Types of acts

In Articles 2–4 of Framework Decision 2005/222, Member States were put under obligation to ensure that the following acts are criminalised, at least for cases which are not minor:

1) the intentional access without right to the whole or any part of an information system (Article 2). Article 2 (2) stipulates that Member States can make the incrimination of such conduct dependent on the perpetrator infringing a security system;[30]
2) illegal system interference (Article 3). This implies the intentional and illegal serious hindering or interruption of the functioning of an information system by inputting, transmitting, damaging, deleting, deteriorating, altering, suppressing or rendering inaccessible computer data. This therefore mainly concerns logic activities targeted against the information systems, conducted using computer programs, or aimed at hindering or rendering the system operation impossible by affecting the program responsible for system functioning;
3) illegal data interference involving the intentional and illegal deletion, damaging, deterioration, alteration, suppression or rendering inaccessible computer data in an information system (Article 4).

As can be seen, in all three cases, the requirements for considering the conduct in question as crime is that the conduct is intentional, and that the perpetrator acts without right. The term "intentional" should be interpreted in line with the rules of criminal law binding in Member States regarding the issue of "intent". Framework Decision 2005/222 does not require the punishing of activities performed by the perpetrator with no clear intent, i.e., resulting from recklessness or negligence, but it does not prohibit criminalisation of such acts (about "unintentional cybercrimes" see subchapter "Introductory remarks" of chapter 3). Proof of the perpetrator's intent to illegally access, interfere with or disrupt an information system, or to tamper with computer data, should be

30 In the proposed draft Framework Decision 2005/222, that act was defined differently. Its authors, wishing to avoid, in their opinion, an excessive extension of the scope of criminalisation, made criminal liability conditional on one of three alternative requirements, namely that:

1) the act was directed against a part of the information system protected by safeguards;
2) the perpetrator acted with intent to do harm to a natural or legal person;
3) the perpetrator acted with intent to obtain financial benefit.

Ultimately, it was found that this solution could lead to an excessive limitation of the scope of penalisation and only the possibility to make the punishability dependent on the perpetrator breaking the security of the information system would be left. However, this prerequisite is of an optional nature, as it has been recognised that many users of computers (and other connectable devices) are unaware of the dangers of using the network and do not have adequate safeguards, or their safeguards are of limited effectiveness.

sufficient to hold him/her accountable. It should not be necessary to prove that the intent also included acting against a particular information system. Member States are under obligation to ensure that the activities described in Articles 2, 3 and 4 of Framework Decision 2005/222 are punishable, at least in cases which are not minor[31] (it is left to the Member States to clarify this term).

Accessorial and stadial forms

Framework Decision 2005/222 allows the punishment of all accessorial forms of the acts listed in Articles 2–4. Article 5 puts Member States under obligation to ensure that the instigation, aiding and abetting an offence is punishable as a criminal offence. As regards stadial forms, along with committing an offence, which is obvious, attempts to do so should also be punishable (except for the crime referred to in Article 2, i.e., obtaining illegal access to an information system, as to which Framework Decision 2005/222 gives some leeway to Member States as regards the punishability of such attempts).

It would seem that, based on the provisions of Framework Decision 2005/222, the issue of the requirement to make the activities consisting in the creation of so-called hacker tools punishable is quite problematic. Undoubtedly, when the creator of such a program makes it available to the perpetrator, knowing that the latter will use it to commit a criminal offence, he/she may be regarded as an accessory. However, the question arises as to how a situation should be classified if the creator merely makes the program available online. How was stressed (see subchapter "Accessorial and stadial forms" of chapter 3) the penal law of European countries (e.g., German, Polish and French penal law) usually apply the concept of aiding and abetting, according to which these constructs only apply in the case of aiding and abetting in the commission of an offence by specific offenders so they may not be used in cases where the offences were committed by unspecified persons, for example, who used a programme downloaded from a website.

Sanctions

Article 6 of Framework Decision 2005/222 indicates that the criminal penalties stipulated in national legislation for the criminal offences referred to in Framework Decision 2005/222 should be effective, proportionate and dissuasive. This is a traditional and rather vague formula used in most EU documents, as well as in legal acts of the Council of Europe (e.g., in the Convention on Cybercrime). This wording offers leeway to Member States with regards to the choice of sanctions. However, the subsequent provisions of Framework

31 Cf. remarks in chapter 3 regarding Articles 2–5 of the Convention on Cybercrime which are counterparts of the provisions under discussion.

Decision 2005/222 further clarify this general directive. Under Article 6 (2) of Framework Decision 2005/222, offences of illegal system interference and illegal data interference are punishable by criminal penalties of a maximum of at least between one and three years of imprisonment.

In addition, Article 7 of Framework Decision 2005/222, titled *Aggravating Circumstances*, lists the factors which should, either obligatorily or optionally, make criminal liability more severe. Member States are under an obligation to take measures to ensure that the criminal offences under Article 2 (2) (illegal access to data accompanied by infringing a security measure), Article 3 (illegal system interference) and Article 4 (illegal data interference) are punishable by criminal penalties of a maximum of at least two to five years of imprisonment when committed within the framework of a criminal organisation, as defined in Joint Action 98/733/JHA on making it a criminal offence to participate in a criminal organisation in the Member States of the European Union[32] (hereinafter Joint Action 98/733/JHA). Pursuant to Article 1 of that Act, a criminal organisation is understood as a structured association, established over a period of time, of more than two persons, acting in concert with a view to committing offences which are punishable by deprivation of liberty or a detention order of a maximum of at least four years or a more serious penalty, whether such offences are an end in themselves or a means of obtaining material benefits and, where appropriate, of improperly influencing the operation of public authorities. This definition – for the purpose of Framework Decision 2005/222 is subject to certain modifications – it makes the recognition of a group of persons as a criminal organisation regardless of the amount of penalty for the offences for the commission of which the group was formed. Therefore, for the purpose of Framework Decision 2005/222, a criminal organisation simply means a structured association, established over a period of time, of more than two persons, acting in concert with a view to committing offences.[33]

In turn, Article 7 (2) of Framework Decision 2005/222 envisages the possibility for Member States to consider it an aggravating circumstance when the offence has caused serious damages or has affected essential interests.

The provisions of Article 7 of Framework Decision 2005/222 merely refer to ordinary commission (commission by a single individual or accomplice). As regards directing the commission of a prohibited act and other accessorial forms (instigation of, aiding and abetting), as well as attempts (does not refer

32 This provision was adopted by the Council on the basis of Article K.3 of the Maastricht Treaty on making it a criminal offence to participate in a criminal organisation in the Member States of the European Union. Although it has been replaced by Council Framework Decision 2008/841/JHA of 24 October 2008 on the fight against organised crime (OJ EU 2008L 300/42), the reference in the text of Framework Decision 2005/222 has not been altered.

33 The question arises whether "Anonymous" could be – based on provisions of Joint Action 98/733/JHA – an example of such a group. Definitely not – because Anonymous do not have an organised structure, and as a result – are not established for a certain period of time.

to preparation), the Decision offers unlimited leeway to Member States as to the level of introduced sanctions, only requiring that these forms of commission be made punishable.

Corporate liability

Articles 8 and 9 govern the issue of liability of legal persons, which was regulated similarly to other EU legal acts. Article 8 requires the Member States to take appropriate measures to ensure that legal persons are held liable for offences committed for their benefit.[34] As in other framework decisions, the EU legislator does not use the term "criminal liability" in relation to legal persons as it is not envisaged in the legal systems of all Member States. The benefit must be provided by a person acting either individually or as part of a body of the legal person, and having a leading position within the legal person based on:

- a power of representation of the legal person; or
- an authority to take decisions on behalf of the legal person; or
- an authority to exercise control within the legal person.

The preceding analysis shows that the model of liability of legal persons based on the principle of identification was adopted (see subchapter "Corporate liability" of chapter 3).

Article 8 (2) provided for the liability of legal persons on the basis of *culpa in custodiendo*. This means that liability can be attributed to this legal entity in the event that the lack of supervision or control by the person referred to in Article 8, paragraph 1, item 1, caused the commission of the crimes referred to in Articles 2, 3, 4 and 5 for the benefit of this legal entity.

As indicated in Article 8 (3) of the Framework Decision 2005/222, the liability of legal persons shall not exclude criminal proceedings against natural persons who are involved as perpetrators, instigators or accessories in the offences which bring benefits to legal persons. This provision, therefore, expresses the principle of concurrent liability (the accumulation principle).

Sanctions for legal persons

Article 9 (1) of the Framework Decision 2005/222 provides sanctions for legal persons held liable pursuant to Article 8 (1). These sanctions must be effective, proportionate and dissuasive. Along with fines and financial penalties, they can entail exclusion from entitlement to public benefits or aid, temporary or permanent disqualification from the practice of commercial activities, placing a person under judicial supervision, and judicial winding-up.

34 See also Iougleux, Mitrou, Tatianu-Eleni (2016), p. 26.

This list is exemplary and does not exclude a Member State's application of other sanctions. Agnieszka Grzelak emphasises that, by defining sanctions in such a broad manner, the EU is entering "spheres hitherto reserved for the exclusive competence of Member States".[35] Moreover, "the increasing possibilities of imposing criminal sanctions in EU law have the effect of European institutions' encroaching on the legal sphere of entities and persons that are addressees of the European Union policy".[36]

In the event of liability under Article 8 (2) (*culpa in custodiendo*), Framework Decision 2005/222 merely indicates that there must be sanctions or other measures which are effective, proportionate and dissuasive.

Procedural issues

Articles 10 and 11 of Framework Decision 2005/222 regulate procedural issues concerning jurisdiction, extradition and cooperation between Member States. At the same time, it should be noted that, due to the specific nature of criminal offences involving the use of information networks (they very often have a "cross-border" nature), it is extremely important to create transparent rules of procedure.

Jurisdiction

Article 10 of Framework Decision 2005/222 concerns jurisdiction. It stipulates the obligation to establish jurisdiction by a Member State in the event of committing any of the criminal offences described in Framework Decision 2005/222 within its territory (the principle of territoriality), whether in whole or in part, regardless of the perpetrator's citizenship. Two further prerequisites for establishing jurisdiction make it independent of the place of commission, by referring to the situations where:

1) the element linking the offence to the legal system of the state is the subject – the act was committed by a national of that Member State (the principle of subjective nationality);
2) as a result of committing the offence, an advantage was gained by a legal person established in the territory of that Member State.

Neither of these prerequisites is absolute. Article 10 (5) of Framework Decision 2005/222 left it to the discretion of Member States to establish jurisdiction in these cases. They were allowed to either not establish it at all or to limit its exercise to specific cases or circumstances. They had to inform the General Secretariat of the Council and the Commission that they were making

35 Grzelak (2005), p. 423.
36 Grzelak (2005), p. 423.

use of this possibility, and to indicate the specific cases and circumstances in which they would exercise jurisdiction.

Article 10 (2) of Framework Decision 2005/222 further clarified the prerequisite for the exercise of jurisdiction based on the principle of territoriality. Reference was made to a situation where a criminal offence is committed in the territory of one Member State, and the consequence arises in the territory of another. More specifically, the provision stipulates that the Member State shall exercise jurisdiction both in the event of the offender committing the offence when physically present in its territory against an information system (regardless of the location of that system), and if the offence is against an information system in its territory, whether or not the offender commits the offence when physically present in its territory.

Article 10 (3) of Framework Decision 2005/222 made reference to a situation in which the national law of a given Member State does not envisage a possibility of extraditing or surrendering its own nationals. In such situations, the Decision imposes an obligation on the state to establish jurisdiction where a national of that state commits, outside of its territory, any of the offences provided for in Framework Decision 2005/222. The state is to undertake the prosecution of the offender if necessary.

Article 10 (4) of Framework Decision 2005/222 furthermore settled the matter of colliding jurisdiction, stipulating that where two or more Member States have jurisdiction under the aforementioned principles, they shall cooperate in order to decide which of them will prosecute the offenders. They may either ask for assistance from EU bodies or use existing mechanisms for judicial cooperation within the EU. Practically speaking, there are two such "mechanisms": Eurojust and the European Judicial Network (EJN).

Eurojust, the EU's Judicial Cooperation Unit, was established by way of Council Decision 2002/187/JHA of 28 June 2002 setting up Eurojust with a view to reinforcing the fight against serious crime.[37] It is a body composed of members of the judiciary of the Member States who are competent to conduct criminal investigations. It is an auxiliary body entrusted with coordinating and stimulating cooperation between the competent authorities of the Member States in the field of law enforcement.

The European Judicial Network in criminal matters was created by Council Joint Action 98/428/JHA of 29 June 1998 adopted by the Council on the basis of Article K.3 of the Treaty on European Union, on the creation of a

37 OJ 2002 EC L 63/1. Decision 2002/187/JHA was modified by Council Decision 2009/426/JHA of 16 December 2008 on the strengthening of Eurojust and amending Decision 2002/187/JHA (OJ EU 138 L 138/14). Whereas that decision was replaced by Regulation (EU) 2018/1727 of the European Parliament and of the Council of 14 November 2018 on the European Union Agency for Criminal Justice Cooperation (Eurojust), and replacing and repealing Council Decision 2002/187/JHA (OJ EU 2018 L 295/138).

European Judicial Network.[38] Its focus is to strengthen judicial cooperation between the Member States and to combat serious crime (such as corruption, organised crime, terrorism and drug trafficking).

Article 10 (4) of Framework Decision 2005/222 further indicates the criteria which a Member State should use when determining which of them should exercise jurisdiction. Whenever and wherever possible, proceedings should be centralised in a single Member State, preferably the one where the offence was committed or if this is not possible, in the country of which the perpetrator is a national or, as a last resort, in the country in which the perpetrator has been found.

Article 11 of Framework Decision 2005/222 stipulates that for the purpose of the exchange of information relating to offences, Member States shall make use of the existing network of operational points of contact available 24 hours a day, seven days a week. Member States shall inform the General Secretariat of the Council and the Commission of their appointed points of contact for the purpose of exchanging information on offences relating to attacks against information systems, and the General Secretariat shall forward that information to the other Member States.

Special 24-hour points of contact to combat high-tech crime were also established within the framework of the G8 Lyon/Rome Group and the Council of Europe. In the case of the Council of Europe, the creation of such points of contact is envisaged in the Convention on Cybercrime (the so-called 24/7 network). Their purpose is to advise on technical matters, to secure data, to collect evidence, to provide legal information and to locate suspects.

Directive 2013/40/EU

Preliminary remarks

The report on the implementation of Framework Decision 2005/222,[39] published by the European Commission on 14 July 2008, revealed that in most Member States[40] appropriate steps had been taken to implement its provisions, but that process had not been completed by all of them. An assessment of the exactness of the solutions adopted by the Member States is hindered by their

38 OJ EC 1998 L 19/4. Replaced by Council Decision 2008/976/JHA of 16 December 2008 on the European Judicial Network (OJ EU 2008 L 348/130).

39 Report from the Commission to the Council under Article 12 of the Council Framework Decision of 24 June 2005 on attacks against information systems, COM(2008)448.

40 Not all Member States complied with the obligation imposed by Article 12 of Framework Decision 2005/222 to submit to the Commission, by 16 March 2007, the text of any provisions transposing the provisions of that Framework Decision into their national law. As only Sweden (though partially, as its report was incomplete) had complied with this deadline, the Commission asked Member States to send in their reports by 1 June 2008. However, it did not receive replies from Spain, Malta, Slovakia and Poland – this country eventually sent its report, but it did so on 1 July 2008, so its content could not be taken into account in the preparation of this Commission report.

considerable diversity. At the same time, the report focused its attention on a number of threats to the security of data and information systems which had increased in strength in the period since the adoption of Framework Decision 2005/222. These were not the focus of attention of the creators of this Act so consequently were not included in it. This concerns, first and foremost, the phenomenon of large-scale botnet attacks and the creation of malicious software. A limited number of offences referred to in Framework Decision 2005/222, the need to incorporate new threats and the wish to adapt existing legal regulations to new European Union initiatives in the field of cybersecurity, as well as to supplement them in order to regulate the matter comprehensively, led to a decision on commencing work on a new legal instrument addressing the issue of cybercrime. Work on the new regulation coincided with the adoption of the Lisbon Treaty,[41] which made it possible to use the directive to regulate cybercrime. A wide range of experts was consulted before the decision was made on this course of action. A range of meetings was held with the representatives of governments, the private sector, law enforcement agencies, international organisations, European agencies and expert bodies. Among other things, they confirmed the conclusions included in the Commission's report on the implementation of Framework Decision 2005/222 (in particular the need to make the new forms of offences punishable), and their outcome was used to formulate five strategic variants for further action in the fight against cybercrime. The first of them assumed refraining from any new measures and instead relying on existing solutions. The second involved the use of soft law instruments (non-legislative measures) and the development of a programme for protecting critical infrastructure, with cross-border law enforcement and public-private cooperation. The third variant proposed updating the provisions of Framework Decision 2005/222 by adopting a directive. The fourth variant envisaged a comprehensive regulation of cybercrime issues (a combination of non-legislative measures from the second variant and an update of Framework Decision 2005/222 as foreseen under the third one, complemented by legal instruments addressing other issues related to internet security – primarily financial issues and the distribution of illegal content). The fifth variant – the solution that was ultimately adopted – is a combination of the second (using non-legislative measures) and third (adopting a directive) variants. The outcome was the enactment of Directive 2013/40/EU of the European Parliament and of the Council of 12 August 2013 on attacks against information systems, and repealing Council Framework Decision 2005/222/JHA[42] (hereinafter Directive 2013/40).[43]

41 Treaty of Lisbon amending the Treaty on European Union and the Treaty establishing the European Community, signed at Lisbon, 13 December 2007 (OJ EU 2007 C 306/1).

42 OJ EU 2013 L 218/8.

43 Radoniewicz (2021c), p. 46, Cf. Summers, Schwarzenegger, Ege, Young (2014), pp. 238–239; see also Savin (2017), pp. 330–331.

The text of Directive 2013/40/EU of the European Parliament and of the Council of 12 August 2013 on attacks against information systems, and repealing Council Framework Decision 2005/222/JHA,[44] fundamentally reproduced the provisions from Framework Decision 2005/222, while supplementing them with a number of new solutions. Firstly, new types of prohibited acts were defined (illegal interception of computer data and offences related to the use of hacker tools). Secondly, the crime of illegal access to information systems has been modified. Thirdly, new aggravating circumstances (use of botnets, committing against a critical infrastructure information system, use by the perpetrator of the offence of using the real identity of another person and exposing that person to suspicion) were stipulated in addition to the offence of being committed in the framework of a criminal organisation and – optional – causing serious damages or affecting essential interests by the offence.

Recitals

In the recitals to Directive 2013/40, it was stressed that attacks against information systems, especially due to being linked to organised crime and having the potential for terrorist or politically motivated attacks against information systems, are a growing menace. They can pose a real threat to information systems forming part of critical infrastructures of Member States and the European Union (Recital 3 to Directive 2013/40). Moreover, the transnational nature of modern information systems means that attacks against such systems have cross-border dimension, thus underlining the urgent need for further action to approximate criminal law in this area (Recital 27 to Directive 2013/40). Since individual Member States are unable to independently ensure that attacks against information systems in all Member States are subject to effective, proportionate and dissuasive criminal penalties, or to improve and encourage cooperation between judicial and other competent authorities, it is necessary to adopt a directive as it is the only way to lay down common and consistent provisions, which can only be achieved at the EU level (Recital 33 to Directive 2013/40).

Types of acts

As stated earlier, Directive 2013/40 essentially repeated the provisions of Framework Decision 2005/222. Article 2 of Directive 2013/40 reproduces the provisions of Article 1 of Framework Decision 2005/222 containing definitions. Recital 4 of Directive 2013/40 indicates, in turn, that the adoption of common definitions in the field of regulations concerning attacks against information systems (in particular against an information system and computer data) is important to ensure that Member States adopt a consistent approach to the application of the provisions of Directive 2013/40. The provisions

44 OJ EU 2013 L 218/8.

regarding the offences consisting in illegal system interference (Article 3 of Framework Decision 2005/222, Article 4 of Directive 2013/40) and illegal data interference (Article 4 of Framework Decision 2005/222, Article 5 of Directive 2013/40) have remained unchanged. However, the provision regarding the offence consisting in illegal access to information systems has been modified. Currently, infringing security measures is the condition for being punished (Article 2 of Framework Decision 2005/222, Article 3 of Directive 2013/40). Notably, draft Directive 2013/40 envisaged abandoning the condition for punishment in the form of a requirement to infringe upon security measures at all (even as an option, as provided for in Article 2 of Framework Decision 2005/222), but in the course of the legislative work that followed and its submission to the European Parliament, a completely different approach was finally selected. As in Framework Decision 2005/222, the aforementioned acts should be incriminated in legal orders, at least in cases that are not minor. In Recitals to Directive 2013/40 (and more specifically in Recital 11), it was indicated that a case may be considered minor if, for example, the damage caused by the offence and/or the risk to public or private interests, such as to the integrity of a computer system, or to computer data, or to the integrity, rights or other interests of a person, is insignificant or is of such a nature that the imposition of criminal penalties within the legal threshold or the imposition of criminal liability is not necessary. In contrast, the explanatory memorandum to draft Directive 2013/40 indicates that the purpose of this reservation is to make it possible to avoid overextension of incrimination by leaving outside its scope those cases in which the perpetrator's conduct meets the definitional elements of the crime but should not be considered as such, as this would be contrary to the *ratio legis* of the regulation, in view of the fact that it does not threaten the values protected thereunder. Acts committed by young people who try to demonstrate their specialist IT skills were given as an example. At the same time, it was emphasised that the effect of limitation upon the scope of incrimination should not be to supplement the types of offences set out in Directive 2013/40 with definitional elements of the crime (such as the specific intention to obtain illegal proceeds of crime or the occurrence of an effect such as causing considerable damage) in addition to those already introduced in its content. According to the authors of Directive 2013/40, the effect of such legislative procedure would be that offences where the aggravating circumstances stipulated in Directive 2013/40 were present would be deemed punishable.

The first "new" prohibited act (in relation to Framework Decision 2005/222) is the offence of illegal interception, set out in Article 6 of Directive 2013/40, which consists in intercepting, by technical means, non-public transmissions of computer data to, from or within an information system, including electromagnetic emissions from an information system carrying such computer data, intentionally and without right. In relation to this prohibited act, there was initially no provision for waiving incrimination in the event where it was a minor case, as is now done for the offences under Articles

3–5 of Directive 2013/40. A clause enabling this was added during the drafting process, already at the stage of the legislative procedure. This provision reproduces almost word for word the content of Article 3 of the Convention on Cybercrime (see subchapter "Access to a computer system" of chapter 3). However, there is no such clause – as was included in the Convention on Cybercrime – that would allow Member States to make punishment conditional on the perpetrator's dishonest intent, or the requirement that the attacked system (bearing in mind that for the purposes of the Convention, "computer system" means a single host) is connected to another one within the network. Just as in the case of Convention on Cybercrime, Directive 2013/40 does not contain any definition of "interception". A question may be posed whether this action refers to both the contents of communication and traffic data. One should assume that as the reference is to the interception of data transmission, the object of the offence is, by analogy to the Convention on Cybercrime, the content data.

Another novel solution under substantive criminal law, which appears in Directive 2013/40, is the fact that Article 7 considers certain conduct punishable which precedes the commission of prohibited acts stipulated in Directive 2013/40 by introducing a type of criminal offence consisting in illegal and intentional production, sale, procurement for use, import, distribution or otherwise making available – so long as these activities are performed with intention that it be used to commit any of the offences referred to in Articles 3 to 6 – "hacker tools", for instance,

1) a computer program, designed or adapted primarily for the purpose of committing any of the offences referred to in Articles 3–6;
2) a computer password, access code or similar data by which the whole or any part of an information system is capable of being accessed.

Article 7 of Directive 2013/40 is a counterpart of Article 6 of the Convention on Cybercrime. However, it does not provide for the possibility, existing under that Convention, of making criminal liability for the possession of hacker tools conditional on the number of such "items" (see Article 6 (1)(b) of the Convention on Cybercrime). At the same time, as for the other acts that require punishment through Directive 2013/40, this obligation is limited to non-minor cases. It seems that a Member State, when implementing Directive 2013/40, may assume that possession of, for example, one "item" constitutes a minor case. Nonetheless, I believe that such a solution would not be possible in the case of their manufacture and dissemination due to the higher social harm of such conduct, especially since no provision is made for the possibility of such significant reduction in the punishability of conduct involving "hacker tools" as in Convention on Cybercrime (cf. Article 6 (3) of the Convention on Cybercrime). What apparently distinguishes the solution envisaged in Directive 2013/40 from that adopted in the Convention on Cybercrime is the absence of a provision which would explicitly exclude criminal liability in the event of the definitional elements of the crime, as set out in Directive 2013/40, being fulfilled by the conduct of a person who has acted for the legitimate purpose of testing or protecting an information system. At the same time, one should not neglect the fact that the perpetrator must act "without right" and, according to the definition of "without right" contained in Article 2 of Directive 2013/40, this concept means access or interference which is not authorised by the owner or other right holder of the system (or of part of it) or which is not permitted under national law, and where the acts concerning "hacker tools" are carried out with a view to them being used to commit any of the offences set out in the Directive. In addition, Recital 10 to Directive 2013/40 indicates that implementation of the provisions of this Directive should not lead to establishing criminal liability for acts committed for non-criminal purposes, such as the aforementioned authorised testing or protecting of an information system.

There is a further, extremely important, difference between the draft and the final version of Directive 2013/40 as regards the provision of Article 7. Namely, the draft provided for the punishability of activities relating to "device, including a computer program", but in the course of work on Directive 2013/40, the provision was narrowed down to cover only computer programs. As a result, Member States are not obliged to incriminate conduct relating to computer eavesdropping tools, such as hardware keyloggers or devices that can be used to obtain access to a telecommunications network (wired or wireless), in order to intercept data transmitted over it, and to analyse the electromagnetic field emissions generated by equipment during data transmission. Obviously, an indispensable element of each of these devices is a computer program (the so-called firmware). So, theoretically speaking, it would be possible to use an interpretation assuming that activities relating to firmware could be punishable. The only question is whether such an expansive interpretation would not be considered a violation of the *nullum crimen sine lege* principle. However, it is not the provisions of Directive 2013/40, but the specific provisions of national law implementing them, that should be assessed from this angle. As in the course of work on Article 6 of the Convention on Cybercrime, numerous objections as to this provision, given, *inter alia*, the dual character of certain software, were raised by the public, as well as by independent experts and NGOs,[45] including the Electronic Frontier Foundation

45 NGO (non-profit organisation) – it is generally accepted that it is a voluntary organisation independent of public authorities in terms of membership, not-for-profit (non-profit – running a business economic, but the profits from it are used exclusively for statutory purposes, and not for profit – not conducting any gainful activity) and not striving for power, which distinguishes it from political parties (Kuźniar 2004, p. 261). NGOs create the so-called third sector of society (next to public authorities constituting the first sector – state, and entities conducting business activities aimed at profit, i.e., for profit, constituting the second sector – market). NGOs conduct socially useful activities (charity, activities for national minorities, educational, ecological, etc.), to some extent "relieving" the state authorities.

(EFF).[46] Its representatives criticised the solutions adopted in draft Directive 2013/40, and in particular those included in Article 7.[47]

Accessorial and stadial forms

Directive 2013/40 stipulates that the incitement, or aiding and abetting, to commit all offences referred to therein should be punishable (Article 8 (1)). However, the punishing of attempts to commit such offences was limited to offences listed in Articles 4 and 5 of Directive 2013/40 (i.e., illegal system interference and illegal data interference). Importantly, no reference was made (either in the final Directive or in its draft) to directing the commission of a prohibited act.

In the context of aiding and abetting, this issue was raised in the aforementioned EFF Comments. As indicated in that document, it is possible to hold "active" users of p2p networks, such as Tor, criminally liable. The use of the Tor network is currently one of the most effective ways of ensuring one's anonymity while using the internet and not – as is the case with other p2p systems (such as ANts P2P,[48] Freenet,[49] GNUnet[50] or MUTE)[51] – intended to ensure anonymity on the internet mainly in connection with file-sharing. As emphasised by its creators and supporters, its purpose is to provide defence against all forms of network surveillance which pose a threat to general freedom, privacy or freedom of doing business. They point to the positive aspects of the use of Tor in non-democratic countries (especially in China and Iran), where it allows the opposition and journalists to freely exchange information via the internet. Not surprisingly, Tor immediately began to serve illegal purposes, including the dissemination of illegal content (such as child pornography).

46 Electronic Frontier Foundation (EFF) – a non-profit organisation established in the United States in 1990, which aims to protect human rights and freedoms in the digital world, sometimes referred to as digital rights, i.e., primarily such "traditional" human rights as the right to privacy, the right to freedom of expression through the use of new technologies, including in particular the internet, as well as other freedoms, such as the right of access to the internet (recognised as one of the human rights in France). The EFF's activities consist in organising political campaigns against initiatives which may restrict freedom (such as ACTA, for example), appearing in court cases as friends of the court (*amicus curiae*) or providing defence for individuals who have exposed themselves to legal proceedings through their actions in trying to defend freedom on the internet (or, in a broader sense, in the digital world). EFF's official website: www.eff.org/, access 1 June 2024.

47 See, for example: *EFF Comments on the Draft Directive on Attacks against Computer Systems,* www.eff.org/files/filenode/Submission-Parliament-Hacking-Tools-vf.pdf, access 1 June 2023.

48 ANts 2P2 project website, http://antsp2p.sourceforge.net, access 1 June 2024.

49 Freenet project website, http://freenetproject.org, access 1 June 2024.

50 GNUnet project website, https://gnunet.org, access 1 June 2024.

51 MUTE project website, http://mute-net.sourceforge.net, access 1 June 2024.

The name Tor[52] comes from the phrase onion routing.[53] The Tor network uses the so-called second-generation onion routing, which prevents the analysis of network traffic. This technique consists in conducting multiple multilayer (hence the association with an onion) encryption of transmitted data, and then transmitting them one by one through network nodes – onion routers.[54] Each router "removes" the encryption layer intended only for it, obtaining information about the next node to which the data should go. In this way, intermediary routers only obtain information about the nodes directly connected to them, and not about the entire route the data is taking. From the recipient's point of view, the data comes to him/her from the last onion router and not from the real source. With a view to using Tor, a client program must be installed and a connection to a network node (i.e., an onion router) must simply be made.[55] As stated in the EFF Comments, the Tor network user whose computer becomes such an onion router could be held liable as an accessory to a crime if the perpetrator of that crime used a connection involving that onion router. It should be noted that this problem does not concern the Polish legal system. As noted on the occasion of discussing the regulation of accessorial forms in the provisions of the Convention on Cybercrime, Polish penal law (and – *inter alia* – German and French) apply the concept of aiding and abetting, according to which these constructs apply only in the case of inciting or assisting in the commission of a crime by specific persons. Therefore, it would not be considered aiding and abetting to facilitate the commission of a crime by unspecified persons by making such an anonymous connection.[56]

52 Tor project website, www.torproject.org, access 1 June 2024.

53 This solution is based on *the mix-net concept* introduced by D. Chaum in 1981, in which data is encrypted in multiple layers, sent through multiple proxy servers, each of which "pulls" only the layer intended for it, to gain information about where further data should be directed. The network got its name from the "mixing" of messages – they are sent in a random order to make them harder to track.

54 The computer of any network user who wants to participate in the creation and development of Tor can become such a router.

55 Radoniewicz (2011), pp. 259–260; Radoniewicz (2016), pp. 264–265.

56 The Ip2 network, which has been developed since 2003, offers similar opportunities as Tor does. What's more, it enables a fully anonymous use of services similar to internet services: WWW servers with the possibility of uploading websites (so-called *epsites*), mail servers, IRC servers, etc. Like Tor and Freenet, Ip2 has its own top-level pseudo-domain – .ip2. Data transmission within the Ip2 network is based on *garlic routing*, which is a variant of onion routing – encryption is done in multiple layers (similar to onion routing), and data is sent through multiple nodes, in portions called messages which can be combined into packets which resemble garlic heads, and in which messages are the metaphorical "cloves" of garlic. The transfer takes place through "temporary" (created for a short period of time and only for the purpose of a given transfer) one-way receiving and transmitting tunnels. ip2 project website: www.i2p2.de, access 1 June 2024.

Sanctions

With regard to the choice of punishment, Directive 2013/40 (like Framework Decision 2005/222) offers leeway to Member States. Whereas it was generally indicated that all offences set out therein should be punishable by effective, proportionate and dissuasive criminal penalties, it also requires that the offences set out in Articles 3–7 of Directive 2013/40 (meaning that it does not apply to their attempt, incitement and aiding and abetting) be punishable by a maximum term of imprisonment of at least two years, at least for cases which are not minor.

Under Article 8 (2) of Directive 2013/40, attempting to commit an offence referred to in Articles 4 and 5 should be punishable as a criminal offence.

Under Article 9 of Directive 2013/40, a number of aggravating circumstances were listed, yet only with respect to the act defined in Articles 4 and 5 (i.e., illegal system interference and illegal data interference). The first aggravating circumstance, stipulated in Article 9 (3) of Directive 2013/40, includes a situation where a significant number of information systems have been affected through the use of a tool, referred to in Article 7 of Directive 2013/40, designed or adapted primarily for that purpose. In such an event, the perpetrator should be sentenced to a maximum term of imprisonment of at least three years.[57] Under Article 9 (4) of Directive 2013/40, aggravating circumstances, resulting in the possibility to sentence the perpetrator to a maximum sentence of imprisonment of at least five years, include the commitment of offences within the framework of a criminal organisation, as defined in Council Framework Decision 2008/841/JHA of 24 October 2008 on the fight against organised crime[58] (hereinafter Framework Decision 2008/841), causing serious damage, and commitment of an offence against a critical infrastructure information system.

Pursuant to Article 1 (1) of Framework Decision 2008/841, "criminal organisation" means a structured association, established over a period of time, of more than two persons acting in concert with a view to committing offences which are punishable by deprivation of liberty or a detention order of a maximum of at least four years or a more serious penalty, to obtain, directly or indirectly, financial or other material benefit, while "structured association" means an association that is not randomly formed for the immediate commission of an offence, nor does it need to have formally defined roles for its

57 The draft directive provided for a stricter solution. According to its authors, a sentence of imprisonment of at least five years should be permitted for perpetrators of the offences specified in Articles 3–6, if committed with the use of a tool designed to launch attacks affecting a significant number of information systems or attacks causing considerable damage, such as the disruption of system services, financial loss, or a loss of personal data, or committed by the perpetrator using someone else's identity. However, in the case of all acts, the aggravating circumstance affecting criminal liability was that the perpetrator has acted within a criminal organisation.

58 OJ EU 2008 L 300/42.

members, continuity of its membership or a developed structure (Article 1 (2) of Framework Decision 2008/841). There is significant difference between the definition in Joint Action 98/733 and the definition in Framework Decision 2008/841 concerning the purpose for which the group is to be created. In the case of Joint Action 98/733 it is "only" committing crimes ("whether such offences are an end in themselves or a means of obtaining material benefits and, where appropriate, of improperly influencing the operation of public authorities"), while in the case of Framework Decision 2008/841 it is committing crimes for the purpose – to obtain, directly or indirectly, financial or other material benefit.

A solution similar to the one stipulated in Framework Decision 2005/222 was adopted in Directive 2013/40, under which the amount of penalty provided in Framework Decision 2008/841 for the offences for the commission of which the group was formed is not taken into consideration when establishing whether a given structured association can be considered a criminal organisation.

Without a doubt, hacker groups like Anonymous do not meet the definition of a "criminal organisation". They are not an organised association and, most importantly, their "members" act for ideological reasons, not to obtain direct or indirect financial or other material benefit.[59]

In the draft Directive 2013/40, the concept of damage as an aggravating circumstance has been slightly clarified, indicating the disruption of system services, financial loss or a loss of personal data as examples. This catalog was not included in the final version of Directive 2013/40, but a similar list was included in Recital 5 (disrupting system services of significant public importance, or causing major financial cost or loss of personal data or sensitive information) as an example of events covered by this concept, thus giving the national legislator freedom to specify this term more precisely. This solution is intended to enable the provisions aimed at transposing the provisions of Directive 2013/40 into the national legal order to be shaped in such a way that they are compliant with it. As indicated earlier, this circumstance is not optional under Directive 2013/40.

Pursuant to Article 2 (4) of Directive (EU) 2022/2557 of the European Parliament and of the Council of 14 December 2022 on the resilience of critical entities and repealing Council Directive 2008/114/EC (Text with EEA relevance),[60] "critical infrastructure" means an asset, a facility, equipment, a network or a system, or a part of an asset, a facility, equipment, a network or a system, which is necessary for the provision of an essential service whereas "essential service" pursuant to Article 2 (5) of that Directive should be interpreted as a service which is crucial for the maintenance of vital societal functions, economic activities, public health and safety or the environment.

59 Iougleux, Mitrou, Tatianu-Eleni (2016), p. 27.
60 OJ EU 2022 L 333/164.

In provision used the term "critical infrastructure information system" (German. "ein Informationssystem einer kritischen Infrastruktur"). It means any information system that is an element of any critical infrastructure system (e.g., the information system of a military unit, a state body, a hospital), and not just an information system that is critical infrastructure per se (e.g., an element of a telecommunications network), as is evident, for example, from the Polish version of Directive 2013/40, where the term "system informatyczny o charakterze infrastruktury krytycznej" is used, which means: "an information system of a critical infrastructure nature".

A novel solution is the aggravation of criminal liability where the perpetrator, in order to commit an offence referred to in Article 4 or 5 of Directive 2013/40, has concealed his/her true identity by assuming the identity of a third party (so-called identity theft).

The crime of identity theft is becoming an increasingly frequent and dangerous phenomenon. This is due to technological progress in information processing and communication. Services offered over data communication networks use identification methods characterised by the lack of direct contact between the person who provides his or her personal data for identification purposes and who receives it. Thus, the entity in principle has no chance to verify its authenticity.[61] Legal doctrine (especially in US, Australian and English law) distinguishes three categories of acts of using someone else's identity. A report prepared by the Australian Centre for Policing Research suggests the following understanding of these concepts:[62]

1) identity crime – this term generally defines a crime for the purpose of which the perpetrator makes use of a false identity (in a broad sense, i.e., an identity that either belongs to another person or has been fabricated). The concept has the widest of the indicated scopes, including equally serious crimes such as money laundering or terrorism and also the use of a parent's credit card by a minor to buy alcohol online;
2) identity fraud – this concept refers to stealing money, goods, services and other benefits by the use of a false identity (as in the instance of identity crime);
3) identity theft – conduct consisting of the concept of obtaining ("acquisition") an existing identity (which is authentic and not fabricated and does not belong to the perpetrator but to a third party). This conduct is treated as a crime per se, then, to prevent a wider criminalisation, some additional attributes are introduced, such as the perpetrator's intent to use obtained data to commit another crime or have it committed by a third party.

61 Lach (2012), pp. 29–30. Cf. Murray (2016), pp. 429–430.

62 Australian Centre for Policing Research and the Australian Transaction Reports and Analysis Centre, Standardisation of Definitions of Identity Crime Terms: A Step Towards Consistency, Report Series No. 145.3, Australian Centre for Policing Research 2006, pp. 9–10.

An alternative – in relation to criminalising identity crime or identity fraud (but not identity theft – it must be a separate crime – as is clear from its construction), which would be alternative to classifying it as an offence, is to consider the use of stolen personal data as "an aggravating circumstance",[63] i.e., one that increases criminal liability, and thus, applying Polish terminology, creating an aggravated type of offence in which an aggravating attribute would be the perpetrator's use of a false identity during its commission.

Directive 2013/40 adopted the first of the solutions described (identity crime). Pursuant to Article 9 (5), Member States shall take the necessary measures to ensure that when the offences referred to in Articles 4 and 5 of Directive 2013/40 are committed by misusing the personal data of another person, with the aim of gaining trust of a third party, thereby causing prejudice to the rightful identity owner, this may, in accordance with national law, be regarded as aggravating circumstances unless those circumstances are already covered by another offence, punishable under national law.[64]

The provisions regarding the level of penalties set out in Directive 2013/40 were criticised in an opinion adopted by the European Economic and Social Committee (EESC),[65] which proposed much stricter penalties. They gave examples of the UK which allows sentences of up to 10 years in prison for perpetrators of large-scale attacks on information systems, and Estonia which allows sentences of up to 25 years (in the case of a terrorist motive).

Concluding remarks

The issue of liability of legal persons is addressed in Articles 11 and 12 of Directive 2013/40, essentially reiterating the provisions regarding this matter included in Framework Decision 222/2005, and merely supplementing a list of sanctions with the possibility of a temporary or permanent closing of the facilities of legal persons used for committing an offence (Article 12 (1)(e) of Directive 2013/40).

Directive 2013/40 contains less extensive provisions regarding jurisdiction than Framework Decision 2005/222. This is due to the fact that Council Framework Decision 2009/948/JHA of 30 November 2009 on the prevention and settlement of conflicts of exercise of jurisdiction in criminal proceedings, which contains detailed provisions on the settlement of such conflicts, was adopted in 2009.[66] Accordingly, the content of Article 12 of Directive 2013/40 was limited only to imposing an obligation on Member States to establish jurisdiction over the offences specified therein (equivalent to Article

63 For more details see Clough (2015), pp. 218–219, 238–239; Walden (2016), pp. 114–115.

64 See more, e.g. Iougleux, Mitrou, Tatianu-Eleni (2016), pp. 28–29.

65 Opinion of the European Economic and Social Committee on the Proposal for a Directive of the European Parliament and of the Council on attacks against information systems and repealing Council Framework Decision 2005/222/JHA, COM(2010)517.

66 OJ EU 2009 L 328/42.

10 (1) and (2) of Framework Decision 2005/222) in accordance with the principle of territoriality or principle of subjective nationality.

A provision regarding the 24/7 operation of the network of contact points under Framework Decision 222/2005 for the exchange of information relating to the offences defined in the Directive stipulates that Member States are to ensure procedures are in place to respond to urgent requests within a maximum of eight hours. This response should at least consist of an indication as to whether the request will be answered, in what form and by what deadline.

To conclude the discussion on Directive 2013/40, it should be emphasised once again that the provisions contained therein constitute minimum standards. This means that when implementing the Directive, Member States may broaden the scope of incrimination, for instance, by introducing aggravated or mitigated types (e.g., unintentional),[67] or by making attempts to also commit the acts specified in the Directive, other than those indicated by the EU legislators, punishable. However, it is not possible to narrow this scope.

Directive 2019/713/EU on combating fraud and counterfeiting of non-cash means of payment

The aim of Directive 2019/713/EU of the European Parliament and of the Council of 17 April 2019 on combating fraud and counterfeiting of non-cash means of payment and replacing Council Framework Decision 2001/413/JHA[68] (hereinafter Directive 2019/713) is to establish minimum rules concerning the definition of criminal offences and sanctions in the areas of fraud and counterfeiting of non-cash means of payment.

Article 6 of Directive 2019/713 obliged Member States to stipulate offence "Fraud related to information systems".

The stipulated conduct consists in the perpetrator illegally causing, in order to make an unlawful gain for the himself or a third party, the hindrance or interference with the functioning of an information system or introduction, alteration, deletion, transmission or suppression of computer data, resulting in performing or causing a transfer of money, monetary value or virtual currency and thereby causing an unlawful loss of property for another person.

This is similar to the act under Article 8 of the Convention on Cybercrime, so the remarks made when discussing it can be recalled here.

This offence should be punishable by a maximum term of imprisonment of at least three years. But if it is committed within the framework of a criminal organisation, as defined in Framework Decision 2008/841/JHA, regardless of the penalty provided therein, the sanction should be imprisonment for maximum term of at least five years. Incitement, aiding and abetting and attempting to do so should also be punishable and penalties should be

67 See subchapter "Introductory remarks" of chapter 3.
68 OJ UE 2019L 123/1.

effective, proportionate and dissuasive. Their determination was left to the Member States.

Article 7 of Directive 2019/713 is provided criminalisation producing, procurement for oneself or another, including the import, export, sale, transport or distribution, or making available a device or an instrument, computer data or any other means primarily designed or specifically adapted for the purpose of committing offences referred to in Directive 2019/713, *inter alia* information fraud, at least when committed with the intention that these means be used. The term "computer data or any other means" includes computer programs, scripts, access codes and other such computer data.

A Member State establishes its jurisdiction over the offences provided in Directive 2019/713 if the offence is committed in whole or in part on its territory or the offender is one of its nationals. For the purposes of the Directive, it is assumed that an offence is deemed to have been committed in whole or in part within the territory of a Member State where the offender commits the offence when physically present on that territory and irrespective of whether the offence is committed using an information system on that territory.

Directive 98/84/EC of 20 November 1998 on the legal protection of services based on, or consisting of, conditional access

The aim of Directive 98/84/EC of the European Parliament and of the Council of 20 November 1998 on the legal protection of services based on, or consisting of, conditional access[69] (hereinafter Directive 98/84) is the legal protection of services based on conditional access (i.e., access in return for a subscription, *inter alia* pay-television and pay-radio services, on-demand video and audio services, electronic publishing and a large range of online services that are available to the public on a subscription or pay-per-view basis

It prohibits all commercial activities related to illicit devices – any equipment (cards with built-in microprocessors or microchips) or software designed or adapted to give access to a protected service in an intelligible form without the authorisation of the service provider (Article 2 (e) of Directive 98/84), such as:

a) the production, import, sale, rental or possession for commercial profit of illegal equipment or software enabling the unauthorised access to a protected service;
b) installing, servicing or replacing illegal equipment for commercial profit;
c) advertising that promotes illegal equipment or software (Article 4 of Directive 98/84).

69 OJ EC 1998 L 320/54.

Each EU country is obliged to establish sanctions which are effective, dissuasive and proportional to the potential impact of the unlawful behaviour (Article 5 of Directive 98/84);

Directive 2001/29/EC of 22 May 2001 on the harmonisation of certain aspects of copyright and related rights in the information society

The Directive 2001/29/EC of the European Parliament and of the Council of 22 May 2001 on the harmonisation of certain aspects of copyright and related rights in the information society.[70] The Directive concerns the legal protection of copyright and related rights in the framework of the internal market, with particular emphasis on the information society.

The aim of the Directive is harmonisation rights granted to authors and neighbouring rightholders (the reproduction right, the right of communication to the public and the distribution right). It also harmonises the protection of technological measures and of rights management information, sanctions and remedies.

On the latter matter it obliges Member States to provide adequate legal protection against the circumvention of any effective technological measures,[71] which the person concerned carries out in the knowledge, or with reasonable grounds to know, that he or she is pursuing that objective.

Member States shall provide adequate legal protection against the manufacture, import, distribution, sale, rental, advertisement for sale or rental, or possession for commercial purposes of devices, products or components or the provision of services which:

a) are promoted, advertised or marketed for the purpose of circumvention of; or
b) have only a limited commercially significant purpose or use other than to circumvent; or
c) are primarily designed, produced, adapted or performed for the purpose of enabling or facilitating the circumvention of, any effective technological measures.

70 OJ EC 2001 L 167/10.

71 "Technological measures" means any technology, device or component that, in the normal course of its operation, is designed to prevent or restrict acts, in respect of works or other subject matter, which are not authorised by the rightholder of any copyright or any right related to copyright as provided for by law or the sui generis right to the databases. Technological measures shall be deemed "effective" where the use of a protected work or other subject matter is controlled by the rightholders through application of an access control or protection process, such as encryption, scrambling or other transformation of the work or other subject matter or a copy control mechanism, which achieves the protection objective (Article 6 (6) of Directive 2001/29).

Member States must provide for appropriate sanctions and remedies in case of infringements of the rights harmonised in the Directive.

Directive 2011/93/EU on Combating the Sexual Abuse and Sexual Exploitation of Children and Child Pornography

Directive 2011/93/EU of the European Parliament and of the Council of 13 December 2011 on Combating the Sexual Abuse and Sexual Exploitation of Children and Child Pornography, and replacing Council Framework Decision 2004/68/JHA[72] (hereinafter Directive 2011/93) obliges to criminalise various acts related to child pornography. In the light of Article 2 (c) "child pornography" means:

i) any material that visually depicts a child engaged in real or simulated sexually explicit conduct;
ii) any depiction of the sexual organs of a child for primarily sexual purposes;
iii) any material that visually depicts any person appearing to be a child engaged in real or simulated sexually explicit conduct or any depiction of the sexual organs of any person appearing to be a child, for primarily sexual purposes (so-called fake pornography); or
iv) realistic images of a child engaged in sexually explicit conduct or realistic images of the sexual organs of a child, for primarily sexual purposes (so-called virtual pornography – see subchapter "Content-related offences" of chapter 3).

According to Article 2 (a) of Directive 2011/93 a child is "any person under the age of eighteen years". The term "sexually explicit conduct" has the same meaning as in the Cybercrime Convention.

Article 5 (2)–(6) of Directive 2011/93 imposes an obligation on Member States to penalise the intentional and without right:

a) acquisition or possession of child pornography (punishable by a maximum term of imprisonment of at least one year);
b) knowingly obtaining access, by means of information and communication technology, to child pornography (punishable by a maximum term of imprisonment of at least one year);
c) distribution, dissemination or transmission of child pornography (punishable by a maximum term of imprisonment of at least two years);
d) offering, supplying or making available child pornography (punishable by a maximum term of imprisonment of at least two years);
e) production of child pornography (punishable by a maximum term of imprisonment of at least three years).

72 OJ EU 2011 L 335/1.

The term acquisition means “the act of getting or acquiring something”. The meaning of terms “without right”, “possession”, “distribution”, “dissemination”, “transmission”. “obtaining”, “offering” and “making available” have the same meaning as in Convention on Cybercrime (see subchapter “Content-related offences” of chapter 3). The term “supplying” should be understood as to provide someone with what the person wants or needs.

Member States have the right to decide whether this article applies to cases where any person appearing to be a child engaged in the production of child pornography was in fact 18 years of age or older at the time of production (Article 5 (7) of Directive 2011/93).

In cases where pornographic material presenting realistic images of a child engaged in sexually explicit conduct or realistic images of the sexual organs of a child, for primarily sexual purposes has been produced for the offender’s own use without the use of “real” pornographic material (as referred to in Article 2 (c)(i), (ii) or (iii) of Directive 2011/93) and there is no risk of dissemination, the Member States may decide not to criminalise the act (Article 5 (8) of Directive 2011/93).

In Article 6 Member States were obliged to criminalise acts commonly known as grooming. In Article 6 this offence is defined as the proposal, by means of information and communication technology, by an adult to meet a child who has not reached the age of sexual consent, for the purpose of engaging in sexual activities or production of child pornography, where that proposal was followed by material acts leading to such a meeting. This offence shall be punishable by a maximum term of imprisonment of at least one year.

Of course, like the provisions of the Lanzarote Convention which provide for this crime, for the purposes of attributing criminal liability it is irrelevant whether the meeting took place. It is necessary to prove that the perpetrator intended to exploit the child (by subjecting him to sexual activity or producing child pornography).

In the next section, the UE legislator obliged Member States to ensure that an attempt, by means of information and communication technology, to commit the offences of acquisition or possession of child pornography or knowingly obtaining access, by means of information and communication technology, to child pornography by an adult soliciting a child who has not reached the age of sexual consent to provide child pornography depicting that child is punishable.

Member States may decide not to criminalise the production, acquisition or possession of material involving children who have reached the age of sexual consent (the age below which, in accordance with national law, it is prohibited to engage in sexual activities with a child) where that material is produced and possessed with the consent of those children and only for the private use of the persons involved, in so far as the acts did not involve any abuse (8 (3) of Directive 2011/93).

In Article 9 of Directive 2011/93, titled *Aggravating circumstances*, are listed the factors which should make criminal liability more severe:

a) the offence was committed against a child in a particularly vulnerable situation, such as a child with a mental or physical disability, in a situation of dependence or in a state of physical or mental incapacity;
b) the offence was committed by a member of the child's family, a person cohabiting with the child or a person who has abused a recognised position of trust or authority;
c) the offence was committed by several persons acting together;
d) the offence was committed within the framework of a criminal organisation within the meaning of Council Framework Decision 2008/841/JHA on the fight against organised crime;
e) the offender has previously been convicted of offences of the same nature;
f) the offender has deliberately or recklessly endangered the life of the child; or
g) the offence involved serious violence or caused serious harm to the child.

In the light of Article 7 (1) of Directive 2011/93 acts of inciting or aiding and abetting in the commission of any of the offences provided for in the Directive should be criminalised.

Under Article 7 (2) of Directive 2011/93 attempts to commit the offences of distribution, dissemination or transmission of child pornography; offering, supplying or making available child pornography; and production of child pornography should be established as criminal offences.

In order to prevent a person convicted of any of the offences in the Directive from running the risk of re-offending, that person may be temporarily or permanently prevented from exercising at least professional activities involving direct and regular contact with children (Article 10 (1) of Directive 2011/93).

Member States shall ensure that information concerning the existence of criminal convictions for any of the offences referred to in Articles 3 to 7 of Directive 2011/93, or of any disqualification from exercising activities involving direct and regular contacts with children arising from those criminal convictions, is transmitted in accordance with the procedures set out in Council Framework Decision 2009/315/JHA of 26 June 2009 on the organisation and content of the exchange of information extracted from the criminal record between Member States.[73]

Member States should ensure that national provisions can be applied to the seizure and confiscation by the competent authorities of instrumentalities and proceeds from the offences referred to in Articles 3, 4 and 5 of Directive 2011/93.

73 OJ EU 2009 L 93/23.

Articles 12 and 13 of Directive 2011/93 relating to the liability of legal persons are analogous to the provisions of Directive 2013/40.

In the light of Article 14 of Directive 2011/93, competent national authorities should be empowered not to prosecute or impose penalties on child victims of sexual abuse and sexual exploitation for their involvement in criminal activities which they have been compelled to commit as a direct consequence of being subjected to any of the acts referred to in Article 4 (2), (3), (5) and (6) of Directive 2011/93 and in Article 5 (6) of Directive 2011/93.

Under Article 17 (1) of Directive 2011/93 Member States shall establish their jurisdiction over the offences specified therein in accordance with the principle of territoriality and principle of subjective nationality.

A Member State may decide to establish further jurisdiction over an offence criminalised in Directive 2011/93 committed outside its territory, *inter alia*, where:

a) the offence is committed against one of its nationals or a person who is a habitual resident in its territory;
b) the offence is committed for the benefit of a legal person established in its territory; or
c) the offender is a habitual resident in its territory.

Member States shall ensure that their jurisdiction covers situations where the offences relating to child pornography (Article 5 of Directive 2011/93) and grooming (Article 6 of Directive 2011/93) (and inciting or aiding and abetting the commission of any of them and attempting to offer, supply or make available and the production of child pornography) are committed by means of information and communication technologies accessed from their territory, whether or not it is located in their territory.

Like the Lanzarote Convention, the Directive 2011/93 excludes the principle of double criminality for most crimes, including – inter alia – production of child pornography (Article 17 (4) of Directive 2011/93).

However, for the prosecution of any of the offences referred in Directive 2011/93 committed outside the territory of the Member State, by a national of that state, the Member State shall ensure that its jurisdiction is not subordinated to the condition that the prosecution can only be initiated following a report made by the victim in the place where the offence was committed, or a denunciation from the state of the place where the offence was committed (Article 17 (5) of Directive 2011/93).

Directive 2011/93/EU obliges Member States to create measures for removing websites containing or disseminating child pornography hosted in their territory and to take steps aimed at ensuring the removal of such websites hosted outside of their territory.

It is one of two cases when the European Union obliges Member States to block or remove in an institutionalised manner, directly by the state, illegal content on the internet. The second situation is related to so-called terrorist content (see next chapter). This solution is due to the high social noxiousness of both kinds of contents.

Furthermore, Article 25 (2) of Directive 2011/93/EU allows Member States to take measures to block access to websites containing or disseminating child pornography on the internet within their territory, stipulating that such measures must be set following transparent procedures and provide adequate safeguards, in particular to ensure that the restriction is limited to what is necessary and proportionate to the intended purpose; the regulation is to require state authorities to inform users of the reason for any restriction. Those safeguards shall also include the possibility of judicial redress (Article 25 (2) of Directive 2011/93).[74] The provisions of the Directive on safeguards refer only to measures aimed at blocking access to websites. However, in the light of Recital 47, they should refer to both the blocking and the removal of websites.[75]

Liability of intermediary service providers

As indicated earlier, the group of Internet Service Providers – Intermediary Services Providers (i.e., providers of mere conduit, caching and hosting services) is covered by regulations in the EU Member States as a result of the implementation of the provisions of Directive 2000/31/EC of the European Parliament and of the Council of 8 June 2000 on certain legal aspects of information society services, in particular electronic commerce, in the Internal Market ("Directive on electronic commerce")[76] (hereinafter Directive 2000/31) providing – in the event of the conditions specified in in the Directive – exclusion of administrative, civil and criminal liability[77] (so-called Notice & Takedown procedure).

Under Article 12 of Directive 2000/31, service provider of services consist of the transmission in a communication network of information provided by a recipient of the service, or the provision of access to a communication network (mere conduit), is not liable for the information transmitted, on condition that the provider:

a) does not initiate the transmission;
a) does not select the receiver of the transmission; and
b) does not select or modify the information contained in the transmission.

74 Cf. Summers, Schwarzenegger, Ege, Young (2014), p. 182.
75 Radoniewicz (2022b), p. 168.
76 OJ EC 2000 L 178/1.
77 Currently, the scope of exclusion of administrative liability (e.g., liability of legal persons) and civil liability has been limited due to the entry into force of the Directive (EU) 2019/790 of the European Parliament and of the Council of 17 April 2019 on copyright and related rights in the Digital Single Market and amending Directives 96/9/EC and 2001/29/EC (Text with EEA relevance) (OJ EU 2019 L 130/92). However, its provisions do not affect the scope of exclusion of criminal liability.

In the light Article 13 of Directive 2000/31, if the service involves caching, its provider is not responsible for the content of the processed data if it meets the following conditions:

a) the provider does not modify the information;
b) the provider complies with conditions on access to the information;
c) the provider complies with rules regarding the updating of the information, specified in a manner widely recognised and used by industry;
d) the provider does not interfere with the lawful use of technology, widely recognised and used by industry, to obtain data on the use of the information; and
e) the provider acts expeditiously to remove or to disable access to the information it has stored upon obtaining actual knowledge of the fact that the information at the initial source of the transmission has been removed from the network, or access to it has been disabled, or that a court or an administrative authority has ordered such removal or disablement.

To be exempt from liability for the content stored by its service recipients, a hosting service provider must meet at least one of two conditions. The first is the lack of reliable information about the illegal nature of the activity of the service recipient or data coming from him/her, and in relation to claims for damages – the lack of knowledge about the facts or circumstances that clearly prove this illegality. The second one, provided for in Article 14 of Directive 2000/31 condition of the exclusion of liability, is that the hosting provider shall immediately take appropriate action to remove or disable access to the information when it receives such messages or is notified of them. Of course, the exclusion of liability will not apply if the service recipient acts under the authority or is under the control of the service provider.

Articles 12, 13 and 14 of Directive 2000/31 cannot constitute a basis for Member States to impose filtering obligations on processed data ("general obligation actively to seek facts or circumstances indicating illegal activity") (Article 15 of Directive 2000/31).

Restrictive measures

Sanctions (restrictive measures) are directed against individual entities (both natural and legal persons) in connection with conducted cyber-attacks.

The legal basis for the European Union's application of economic sanctions, as an instrument aimed at fulfilling the objectives of the Union's external actions, is Article 215 of the Treaty on the Functioning of the European Union[78] (TFEU).

78 Consolidated versions of the Treaty on European Union and the Treaty on the Functioning of the European Union – Consolidated version of the Treaty on the Functioning of the

Article 215 TFEU consists of three paragraphs. Article 215 (1) TFEU specifies the form and procedure for adopting restrictive measures against one or more third countries. Article 215 (2) TFEU specifies the form and procedure for adopting restrictive measures against natural or legal persons, groups or non-state entities. Finally, Article 215 (3) lays down the obligation to include necessary provisions on legal safeguards to the measures adopted under Article 215 (1) or (2).

The objectives of the Common Foreign and Security Policy (CFSP) were specified for all EU external actions and include, i.e., the need to safeguard its values, fundamental interests, security, independence and integrity; to consolidate and support democracy, the rule of law, human rights and the principles of international law; to preserve peace, prevent conflicts and strengthen international security in line with the purposes and principles of the United Nations Charter, the principles of the Helsinki Final Act and the aims of the Charter of Paris, including those relating to external borders (Article 21 (2) points (a) to (c) TEU).

The sanctions applied by the EU can be divided into autonomous sanctions and UN-transposed sanctions, imposed under UN resolutions which are adopted by the Security Council under the provisions of Chapter VII of the United Nations Charter in the event of a threat to, or breach of, international peace and security. Autonomous sanctions are related to EU actions on the global stage and are the EU's independent response to violations of international law (including the provisions of international agreements).

Smart sanctions (targeted sanctions; in German: Intelligente Sanktionen) are special economic sanctions applied in UN and EU practice. General economic sanctions, i.e., measures targeting a given state, inevitably affect civilian populations and third countries, whereas targeted sanctions, being more precise, are directed against specified entities (individuals, enterprises or organisations) or affect specific products of key significance to a given state. They are intended to be more precise than the general ones due to their targeted nature. Thanks to this, the risk of a negative impact of imposing the sanctions on entities which are not the target of such measures is mitigated.[79]

The procedure for imposing economic sanctions as part of the CFSP consists of two stages. The first is laid down in Articles 29–31 of the Treaty on European Union (TEU), and the second in Article 215 TFEU (as regards general sanctions), and in Article 215 (1) TFEU, in conjunction with Article 215 (2) TFEU (concerning restrictive measures against natural or legal persons, groups or non-state entities).

As per Article 29 TEU, "the Council shall adopt decisions which shall define the approach of the Union to a particular matter of a geographical

---

European Union which adopted the Treaty of Lisbon, signed on 13 December 2007 (OJ EU 2012 C 326/1).

79 Niedźwiedź (2012), art. 215.

or thematic nature" (as there is no legal definition of the term, "matters of a geographical or thematic nature" must be construed according to its common meaning). Decisions shall be taken by the Council unanimously (Article 31 of the TEU). However, it is possible to apply constructive abstention (the second subparagraph of Article 31 (1) TEU). Such abstention will not result in waiving the obligation to apply a given decision in the Member State whose representative in the Council has abstained, and it is only when a member of the Council makes a formal declaration to qualify their abstention that the Member State they represent will not be obliged to apply the decision. They shall accept, however, the fact that the decision commits the Union and, in a spirit of mutual solidarity, the Member State concerned shall refrain from any action likely to conflict with or impede Union action based on that decision. At the same time, other Member States must respect their position. If Council members qualifying their abstention in this manner represent at least one-third of the Member States and comprise at least one-third of the population of the Union, then the decision shall not be adopted (the second subparagraph of Article 31 (1) TEU).[80]

As part of the second stage of the sanction procedure, the Council, acting on a joint proposal from the High Representative of the Union for Foreign Affairs and Security Policy and the Commission, shall adopt the necessary measures of a general nature (acting under Article 215 (1) TFEU) or measures against natural or legal persons, groups or non-state entities (acting under Article 215 (1) TFEU, in conjunction with Article 215 (2) TFEU). In such an event, the Council makes decisions by a qualified majority. The categorical wording of the provisions ("the Council shall adopt") means that the adoption of necessary measures is obligatory. Afterwards, the measures are specified in secondary non-legislative acts of law. In practice, they most often assume the form of a regulation as it is binding and directly applicable. This contributes to the uniform application of the sanctions by all Member States.

Targeted sanctions can assume various forms depending on the circumstances in which they are adopted, e.g.:

1) freezing of funds and other financial resources – e.g., Regulation No. 881/2002 imposing certain specific restrictive measures directed against certain persons and entities associated with Usama bin Laden, the Al-Qaida network and the Taliban, and repealing Council Regulation No. 467/2001 prohibiting the export of certain goods and services to Afghanistan, strengthening the flight ban, and extending the freezing of funds and other financial resources in respect of the Taliban of Afghanistan;[81]

80 Niedźwiedź (2012), art. 215.
81 OJ EC 2002 L 139/9.

2) ban on equipment which might be used for internal repression – e.g., Regulation No. 174/2005 imposing restrictions on the supply of assistance related to military activities to Côte d'Ivoire;[82]
3) restrictions on exports or imports of specified products – e.g., Council Regulation No. 1210/2003 concerning certain specific restrictions on economic and financial relations with Iraq and repealing Regulation (EC) No. 2465/96;[83]
4) prohibition of financial services – e.g., Council Regulation No. 2580/2001 on specific restrictive measures directed against certain persons and entities to combat terrorism.[84]

The characteristic feature of regulations issued to adopt targeted sanctions is an annex including a list of entities covered by such sanctions or a list describing products subject to sanctions, depending on the type of targeted sanctions. In the event of individuals covered by targeted sanctions, they are identified through the provision of first name, surname, gender, date and place of birth, nationality, address, passport number, sometimes the indication of functions; as for enterprises, the full name, place of business activities, registered office, as well as the place and date of registration are provided. Regulations concerning targeted sanctions are adopted in line with the procedure set out under Article 215 (2) TFEU.

Examples of legal acts that include sanctions imposed in relation to cyber-attacks:

1) Council Decision (CFSP) 2020/1127 of 30 July 2020 amending Decision (CFSP) 2019/797 concerning restrictive measures against cyber-attacks threatening the Union or its Member States[85] and Council Implementing Regulation (EU) 2020/1125 of 30 July 2020 implementing Regulation (EU) 2019/796 concerning restrictive measures against cyber-attacks threatening the Union or its Member States ST/9568/2020/INIT[86] (the matter of "WannaCry" and "NotPetya" cyber-attacks, and "Operation Cloud Hopper");
2) Council Decision (CFSP) 2020/1537 amending Decision (CFSP) 2019/797 concerning restrictive measures against cyber-attacks threatening the Union or its Member States,[87] and Council Implementing Regulation (EU) 2020/1536 implementing Regulation (EU) 2019/796 concerning restrictive measures against cyber-attacks threatening the

82 OJ UE2005 L 29/5.
83 OJ EC1996 L 169/6.
84 OJ EC2001 L 344/70.
85 OJ EU 2020 L 246/12.
86 OJ EU 2020 L 246/4.
87 OJ EU 2020 L 351/5.

Union or its Member States[88] (the matter of a cyber-attack directed against the federal German parliament – Deutscher Bundestag).

The characteristic feature of regulations issued to adopt targeted sanctions is an annex including a list of entities covered by such sanctions or a list describing products subject to sanctions, depending on the type of targeted sanctions.

Under Article 215 (3), the measures referred to in Article 215 must include necessary provisions on legal safeguards. This means that the legal measures adopted under Article 215 TFEU cannot infringe on human rights, expressed in, i.e., the Charter of Fundamental Rights of the European Union,[89] and the European Convention on Human Rights.[90]

The TFEU includes Declaration No. 25 on Articles 75 and 215 TFEU. It was noted in the declaration that "the respect for fundamental rights and freedoms implies, in particular, that proper attention is given to the protection and observance of the due process rights of the individuals or entities concerned". It was stressed that decisions subjecting an individual or entity to sanctions must be based on clear and distinct criteria and a clear legal basis for imposing individual sanctions to guarantee a thorough judicial review of decisions.

Activities of the European Union and the Convention on Cybercrime

In 1999, the European Council expressed its full support for the draft Convention on Cybercrime, which took the form of a common position adopted on 27 May 1999,[91] recommending that Member States also support work on this project. Within the European Union, no comprehensive regulation to counter high-tech crime had been established up to that date, so it was recommended that Member States should accede to the Convention on Cybercrime.[92] In addition, the possibility was envisaged to make it a global regulation,[93] with accession of the European Union being also considered. However, there were still announcements of the creation of an EU legal instrument.[94]

88 OJ EU 2020L 351/1.

89 OJ EU 2012 C 326/2.

90 Convention for the Protection of Human Rights and Fundamental Freedoms, done at Rome on 4 November 1950, amended by Protocols Nos. 3, 5 and 8 as well as supplemented by Protocol No. 2.

91 Common Position of 27 May 1999 adopted by the Council on the basis of Article 34 of the Treaty on European Union, on negotiations relating to the Draft Convention on Cybercrime held in the Council of Europe (OJ 1999 EU L 142/1).

92 All EU Member States acceded to the Convention on Cybercrime. By 15 June 2024 almost all (without Ireland) ratified it.

93 As was already remarked, the Stockholm Programme, on the one hand, recommended that Member States adopt the Convention on Cybercrime and, on the other hand, pointed to the need to work on the general EU regulation.

94 Cf. Schjølberg (2020), p. 112.

Ultimately, the concept of EU accession to the Cybercrime Convention was abandoned. This was due to new opportunities for a comprehensive EU regulation to counter cybercrime that appeared with the entry into force of the Lisbon Treaty, due to the abolition of the third pillar and the harmonisation of legal instruments within the EU. The use of directives provides a range of advantages. Firstly, there are the solutions they envisage entering into force more promptly (compared to conventions) due to the implementation deadline indicated therein. Secondly, there is the enforceability of implementation of these legal instruments by Member States. Thirdly, there is the ease with which directives can be amended (compared to conventions which make it more difficult and incomparably more time-consuming); this, in view of the subject matter being regulated, i.e., computer crime, is extremely important. And fourthly, the Convention on Cybercrime – as has been noted many a time – is partially outdated and fails to take into account a number of new developments, having been drawn up at the end of the previous century.[95]

95 Cf. Gercke (2011), p. 219. See also Summers, Schwarzenegger, Ege, Young (2014), p. 237.

6 Cyberterrorism in European Union law

Cyberterrorism

Terrorism

In the vernacular, terrorism is understood as the use of terror and, in particular, as the activities of certain extremist groups which attempt, by means of political assassinations, hostage-takings, hijacking of aircraft and similar measures, to draw the attention of the public to their own slogans or to extract certain concessions or benefits from governments. There are many definitions of terrorism in the literature. Marian Flemming's definition of terrorism is extremely synthetic and useful for the purposes of this publication. He defined terrorism as "intentional acts in violation of criminal law, which aim, by means of violent acts or the threat of such acts, to intimidate state organs or significant sections of society and to compel certain behaviour".[1]

Accordingly, a "terrorist act" fulfils the elements of a common offence (e.g., murder, unlawful deprivation of liberty, e.g., "taking hostages", causing a disaster or interference with the operation of an information and communication network), but at the same time it is accompanied by the intention to cause a specific effect in the form of, for example, disruption of public order, the creation of a state of insecurity in society or a specific reaction on the part of state authorities.[2]

Directive 2017/541 of the 15th of March 2017 on combating terrorism

The first EU legal instrument to counteracting terrorism was the Council Framework Decision 2002/475/JHA of the 13th of June 2002 on combating terrorism[3] (hereinafter the Framework Decision 2002/475). It was replaced by Directive (EU) 2017/541 of the European Parliament and of the

1 Flemming (1996), p. 31.
2 This is why the actions of groups such as Anonymous cannot be classified as terrorist acts. The purpose of carrying out the attacks is not of a "terrorist nature", e.g., disturbing public order or forcing any action on state authorities. See also Hill, Marion (2016), pp. 154–155.
3 OJ EU 2002 L 164/3.

DOI: 10.4324/9781003476771-6

Council of the 15th of March 2017 on combating terrorism and replacing Council Framework Decision 2002/475/JHA and amending Council Decision 2005/671/JHA[4] (hereinafter Directive 2017/541), which is based on the Framework Decision, and substantially replicates its solutions (this refers to, e.g., the definition of a terrorist offence), at the same time clarifying some solutions and adding new ones.

Most of all, Directive 2017/541 established the minimum rules concerning the definition of criminal offences and sanctions in the field of terrorist offences, offences related to a terrorist group and offences related to terrorist activities, as well as measures for the protection of, support for and assistance to victims of terrorism. The definition of a terrorist offence laid down in Article 3 of Directive 2017/541 (similar to the one included in Framework Decision 2002/475) is composed of two elements, i.e., objective (*actus reus*) and subjective (*mens rea*) elements. For a prohibited act to be considered a terrorist offence, first of all, it must meet an objective criterion, i.e., it must be one of the acts listed in an exhaustive schedule included in Article 3 (1)(a) to (i)[5] or the threat to commit any of the acts (Article 3 (1)(j)). Second, a terrorist offence must meet at least one of the subjective premises listed in the second part of the definition, i.e., it must be committed with one of the aims listed in Paragraph 2, including:

1) seriously intimidating a population;
2) unduly compelling a government or an international organisation to perform or abstain from performing any act;
3) seriously destabilising or destroying the fundamental political, constitutional, economic or social structures of a country or an international organisation.[6]

4 OJ EU 2017 L 88/6.

5 The following acts were listed in Article 3 (1): a) attacks on a person's life which can cause death; b) attacks on the physical integrity of a person; c) kidnapping or hostage-taking; d) causing extensive destruction to a government or public facility, a transport system, an infrastructure facility (including an information system), a fixed platform located on the continental shelf, a public place or private property, likely to endanger human life or result in major economic loss; e) seizing aircraft, ships, or other means of public or goods transport; f) the manufacture, possession, acquisition, transporting, supply or use of explosives or weapons, including chemical, biological, and radiological or nuclear weapons, as well as research into, and development of, chemical, biological, radiological or nuclear weapons; g) releasing dangerous substances or causing fires, floods or explosions, the effect of which is to endanger human life; h) interfering with or disrupting the supply of water, power or any other fundamental natural resource, the effect of which is to endanger human life; i) illegal system interference, as referred to in Article 4 of Directive 2013/40/EU of the European Parliament and of the Council of 12 August 2013 on attacks against information systems and replacing Council Framework Decision 2005/222/JHA, in cases in which Article 9 (3) or points (b) or (c) of Article 9 (4) of that Directive apply, and illegal data interference, as referred to in Article 5 of that Directive in cases in which point (c) of Article 9 (4) of that Directive applies (see further remarks).

6 Radoniewicz (2021a), pp. 43–44; Summers, Schwarzenegger, Ege, Young (2014), pp. 57–59.

Article 4 of Directive 2017/541 obliges Member States to ensure that directing a terrorist group,[7] and participating in the activities of a terrorist group, are acts punishable as criminal offences. It has been pointed out that the latter should also be understood as including supplying information or material resources, or by funding its activities in any way, in the knowledge of the fact that such participation will contribute to the criminal activities of the terrorist group.

In the following Articles of Directive 2017/541, Member States are obliged to criminalise "offences related to terrorist activities", involving certain activities, which are not terrorists acts per se, but might constitute the preparation to commit terrorist acts.[8]

In the light of Article 15 (1) of Directive 2017/541, the offences referred to in the Directive should be punishable by effective, proportionate and dissuasive criminal penalties, which may entail surrender or extradition.

The terrorist offences referred to in Article 3 of Directive 2017/541 and its Article 14 (aiding, abetting and attempting to commit the offences set out in the Directive),[9] should be punishable by custodial sentences more severe than those imposed under national law for such offences, which do not contain an element of "terrorist intent" (Article 15 (2)).

The offences listed in Article 4 of Directive 2017/541 (offences relating to a terrorist group) should be punishable by custodial sentences, with a maximum sentence of not less than 15 years for the offence referred to in point (a) of Article 4 (directing a terrorist group), and a maximum sentence of not less than eight years for the offences listed in point (b) of Article 4 (participating in the activities of a terrorist group) (Article 15 (3)).

7 According to the definition laid down in Article 2 (3) of Directive 2017/541, the terms should be understood as "a structured group of more than two persons, established for a period of time and acting in concert to commit terrorist offences". According to the definition included in the second part of the cited provision, "structured group" means a group which is not randomly formed for the immediate commission of an offence, and that does not need to have formally defined roles for its members, continuity of membership or a developed structure".

8 They include the following offences: public provocation to commit a terrorist offence (Article 5); recruitment for terrorism (Article 6); providing training for terrorism (Article 7); receiving training for terrorism (Article 8); travelling for the purpose of terrorism (Article 9); organising or otherwise facilitating travelling for the purpose of terrorism (Article 10); terrorist financing (Article 11) and other offences related to terrorist activities, listed in Article 12: (a) aggravated theft with a view to committing one of the offences listed in Article 3; (b) extortion with a view to committing one of the offences listed in Article 3; (c) drawing up or using false administrative documents with a view to committing one of the offences listed in points (a) to (i) of Article 3 (1), point (b) of Article 4, and Article 9.

9 Aiding and abetting the offences referred to in Articles 3 to 8, 11 and 12 (and Article 14 (1)), inciting the offences referred to in Articles 3 to 12 (and Article 14 (2)), and attempting to commit the offences referred to in Articles 3, 6, 7, Article 9 (1), point (a) of Article 9 (2), and Articles 11 and 12, with the exception of possession as provided for in point (f) of Article 3 (1), and the offences referred to in point (j) of Article 3 (1) (and Article 14 (3)), should be punishable by law.

Article 16 listed mitigating circumstances (no aggravating circumstances were stipulated). Under this provision Member States may decide that the penalty may be reduced if two conditions are met: the perpetrator renounces terrorist activity and he/she provides the administrative or judicial authorities with information which they would not otherwise have been able to obtain, helping them to:

1) prevent or mitigate the effects of the offence;
2) identify or bring to justice the other offenders;
3) find evidence; or
4) prevent further offences referred to in Articles 3 to 12 and 14.

Article 19 concerns jurisdiction. It stipulates the obligation to establish jurisdiction by a Member State in the following cases:

a) the offence is committed in whole or in part in its territory;
b) the offence is committed on board a vessel flying its flag or an aircraft registered there;
c) the offender is one of its nationals or residents;
d) the offence is committed for the benefit of a legal person established in its territory;
e) the offence is committed against the institutions or people of the Member State in question or against an institution, body, office or agency of the Union based in that Member State.

Moreover, Each Member State may extend its jurisdiction if the offence is committed in the territory of another Member State (Article 19 (1) in fine)).

Article 19 (3) of the Directive furthermore settled the matter of colliding jurisdiction, stipulating that where two or more Member States have jurisdiction and when any of the Member States concerned can validly prosecute on the basis of the same facts, the Member States concerned shall cooperate in order to decide which of them will prosecute the offenders with the aim, if possible, of centralising proceedings in a single Member State. To this end, the Member States may have recourse to Eurojust in order to facilitate cooperation between their judicial authorities and the coordination of their action. Account shall be taken of the following factors:

a) the Member State shall be that in the territory of which the offence was committed;
b) the Member State shall be that of which the offender is a national or resident;
c) the Member State shall be the country of origin of the victims;
d) the Member State shall be that in the territory of which the offender was found.

In light of Article 19 (4), each Member State shall take the necessary measures also to establish its jurisdiction over the offences referred to in Articles 3 to 12 and 14 in cases where it refuses to surrender or extradite a person suspected or convicted of such an offence to another Member State or to a third country.

Of course Article 19 does not exclude possibility of the exercise of jurisdiction in criminal matters as laid down by a Member State in accordance with its national law (Article 19 (6)).

"Cyber terrorist crime"

Like terrorism, cyberterrorism has a large number of definitions in the literature.[10] I will limit myself to two. The first one (which has already been cited) is extremely concise and therefore general and synthetic, and it was formulated by Susan Brenner. This author makes a precise distinction between computer crime and the phenomena of cyber terrorism and cyber warfare, treating them as notions separate from cybercrime. She defines the former term, making the assumption that it includes terrorist attacks which are carried out via computers and computer networks, and differs from cybercrime in the intent of the perpetrator, which is to advance a political or social agenda.[11]

The second definition of cyberterrorism I want to cite, proposed by Dorothy Denning, is more detailed. In accordance with this author, cyberterrorism is the convergence of terrorism and cyberspace. It is generally understood to mean unlawful attacks and threats of attack against computers, networks and the information stored therein when done to intimidate or coerce a government or its people in furtherance of political or social objectives. Further, to qualify as cyberterrorism, an attack should result in violence against persons or property, or at least cause enough harm to generate fear. Attacks that lead to death or bodily injury, explosions, plane crashes, water contamination or severe economic loss would be examples. Serious attacks against critical infrastructures could be acts of cyberterrorism, depending on their impact. Attacks that disrupt nonessential services or that are mainly a costly nuisance would not.[12]

We will not find in any legal act a definition of cyberterrorism or a type of prohibited act so called. But we can assume that there is a "cyber terrorist crime". Pursuant to point (i) of Article 3 (1), in conjunction with Article 3 (2) of the Directive 2017/541 (see remarks earlier), illegal system interference as referred to in Article 4 of the Directive in cases in which Article 9 (3) or points (b) or (c) of Article 9 (4) of that Directive applies, and illegal data interference as referred to in Article 5 of that Directive, in cases in which point (c) of Article

10 Radziwill (2015), pp. 334–337; Hill, Marion (2016), pp. 154–157.

11 Brenner (2011), p. 16. See also Brenner (2014), pp. 1–9.

12 Denning (2000b); Cf, Chen, Jarvis, Macdonald (eds.) (2014), pp. 20–23.

9 (4) of that Directive applies, constitute a terrorist offence. This means that terrorist offences should include acts involving illegal system interference committed with one of the aims listed in Article 3 (2) of Directive 2017/541, with the use of one of the tools referred to in Article 7 of Directive 2013/40, designed or adapted primarily for that purpose, in which a significant number of information systems have been intentionally affected, or in which substantial damage has been inflicted. In addition, an unlawful act under Article 5 should be considered a terrorist offence if it has been directed against a critical infrastructure information system.[13]

"Terrorist content"

Directive 2017/541/EU

As mentioned, European Union provisions stipulate that two categories of illegal content on the internet, due to their significant social harm, should be neutralised (i.e., blocked or removed) in an institutionalised manner, directly by state authorities. These are, of course – discussed earlier – child pornography and so-called terrorist content.

Directive 2017/541/EU contains provisions similar to those of Directive 2011/93/EU on combating the sexual abuse and sexual exploitation of children and child pornography with regard to "online content" constituting a public provocation to commit a terrorist offence. Member States are required to develop regulations to ensure the prompt removal of "terrorist content" hosted in their territory, obliging them to take measures and actions to ensure that such content hosted outside their territory is removed. It also provides, similarly to Directive 2011/93, that Member States may, when removal of the content constituting a public provocation to commit a terrorist offence at its source is not feasible, take measures to block access to such content towards internet users within their territory. Removal and blocking measures must be set following transparent procedures and provide adequate safeguards, in particular to ensure that those measures are limited to what is necessary and proportionate and that users are informed of the reason for those measures. Safeguards relating to removal or blocking shall also include the possibility of judicial redress.[14]

Regulation of the European Parliament and of the Council on Preventing the Dissemination of Terrorist Content Online (the so-called TERREG)

The EU legislators considered the requirement for Member States to regulate the subject of making terrorist content available on the internet by means of

13 Radoniewicz (2021a), p. 49.
14 Radoniewicz (2022b), p. 169.

Directive 2017/541 to be insufficient, since, even during the period of its implementation (its provisions had to be transposed into national law by 8 September 2018), work was initiated on a regulation intended to regulate only this matter.

As stated in the Explanatory Memorandum of the Proposal for a Regulation of the European Parliament and of the Council on Preventing the Dissemination of Terrorist Content Online (the so-called TERREG – from "terrorism" and "regulation"), hosting service providers have put in place certain measures to tackle terrorist content on their services. Progress has been made through voluntary frameworks and partnerships including the EU Internet Forum which was launched in December 2015 under the European Agenda on Security promoting Member States' and hosting service providers' voluntary cooperation and actions to reduce accessibility to terrorist content online. However, these measures were considered insufficient. However, there is – in the Commission's view – a clear need to intensify the European Union's measures against terrorist content online. On 1 March 2018, the Commission adopted – based on Communication from the Commission of 28 September 2017 on Tackling Illegal Content Online and towards the enhanced responsibility of online platforms[15] – Recommendation 2018/334 of 1 March 2018 on the effective fight against illegal content online.[16] The Commission, indicating serious terrorist attacks in the EU and the fact that terrorist content is still easily accessible, found it necessary to establish a clear and harmonised legal framework for the purpose of preventing and addressing the dissemination of terrorist content online, and that the best way to do this would be to issue a Regulation. This proposal was prepared as a contribution from the European Commission to the Leaders' meeting in Salzburg on 19–20 September 2018.[17]

In the light of Article 1 (2) of Regulation (EU) 2021/784 of the European Parliament and of the Council of 29 April 2021 on addressing the dissemination of terrorist content online[18] (TERREG), its provisions apply to hosting service providers offering services to the society in the Union, irrespective of where their main establishment may be placed.

Under Article 2 (1) of the Regulation in conjunction with point (b) of Article 1 of Directive (EU) 2015/1535, of the European Parliament and of the Council of 9 September 2015 laying down a procedure for the provision of information in the field of technical regulations and of rules on information society services (codification) (Text with EEA relevance),[19] the term "hosting service provider" (HSP) means a provider of information society services

15 COM(2017)555 final.
16 OJ UE 2018 L 63/50.
17 Radoniewicz (2021h), pp. 164–165.
18 OJ EU 2021 L 172/79.
19 OJ EU 2015 L 241/1.

consisting of the storage of information provided by and at the request of a content provider. Information society service means any service normally provided for remuneration, at a distance, by electronic means and at the individual request of a recipient of services.

For the purposes of this definition:

a) "at a distance" means that the service is provided without the parties being simultaneously present;
b) "by electronic means" means that the service is sent initially and received at its destination by means of electronic equipment for the processing (including digital compression) and storage of data, and entirely transmitted, conveyed and received by wire, by radio, by optical means or by other electromagnetic means;
c) "at the individual request of a recipient of services" means that the service is provided through the transmission of data on individual request.

"Content provider" means a user that has provided information that is, or that has been, stored and disseminated to the public by an HSP. "Dissemination to the public" means the making available of information, at the request of a content provider, to a potentially unlimited number of persons. "Offering services in the Union" means enabling natural or legal persons in one or more Member States to use the services of a hosting service provider which has a substantial connection to that Member State or those Member States. "Terrorist content" means one or more of the following types of material, namely material that:

a) incites the commission of one of the offences referred to in points (a) to (i) of Article 3 (1) of Directive (EU) 2017/541,[20] where such material, directly or indirectly, such as by the glorification of terrorist acts, advocates the commission of terrorist offences, thereby causing a danger that one or more such offences may be committed; soliciting a person or a group of persons to commit or contribute to the commission of one of the offences referred to in points (a) to (i) of Article 3 (1) of Directive (EU) 2017/541, thereby causing danger that one or more such offences may be committed;
b) solicits a person or a group of persons to commit or contribute to the commission of one of the offences referred to in points (a) to (i) of Article 3 (1) of Directive (EU) 2017/541;
c) solicits a person or a group of persons to participate in the activities of a terrorist group, within the meaning of point (b) of Article 4 of Directive (EU) 2017/541; posing a threat to commit one of the offences referred to in points (a) to (i) of Article 3 (1) of Directive (EU) 2017/541, thereby causing danger that one or more such offences may be committed;

20 See the previous subchapter.

d) provides instruction on the making or use of explosives, firearms or other weapons or noxious or hazardous substances, or on other specific methods or techniques for the purpose of committing or contributing to the commission of one of the terrorist offences referred to in points (a) to (i) of Article 3 (1) of Directive (EU) 2017/541;
e) constitutes a threat to commit one of the offences referred to in points (a) to (i) of Article 3 (1) of Directive (EU) 2017/541.

"Competent authority" shall mean a single judicial or independent administrative authority designated in a Member State for the purposes listed in Article 12 (1) of the Regulation, i.e.:

1) issuing removal orders pursuant to Article 3;
2) scrutinising removal orders pursuant to Article 4;
3) overseeing the implementation of specific measures pursuant to Article 5;
4) imposing penalties pursuant to Article 18.

The regulation establishes security measures to combat the public dissemination of terrorist content:

1) removal order issued by the competent authority requiring hosting providers to remove terrorist content or to disable access to terrorist content in all Member States as soon as possible and in any event within one hour of receipt of the removal order (Article 3);
2) procedure for cross-border removal orders – which applies when the hosting provider does not have a main establishment or legal representative in the Member State of the competent authority (Article 4);
3) specific measures that are applied when a hosting service provider is exposed to terrorist content which include in their terms and conditions and apply provisions to address the misuse of its services for the dissemination to the public of terrorist content (Article 5);
4) preservation of content and related data – hosting service providers shall preserve terrorist content as well as any related data removed with it, which are necessary for administrative or judicial review proceedings or complaint-handling under Article 10 and for the prevention, detection, investigation and prosecution of terrorist offences.

The regulation provides several legal safeguards:

1) transparency obligations for HSPs;
2) transparency reports by national authorities;
3) legal remedies for hosting providers and content providers;
4) complaints mechanisms;
5) information to content providers.

In addition, Member States, in order to ensure that HSPs fulfil their obligations, are required to establish effective, proportionate and dissuasive penalties. However a "systematic or persistent" failure to comply with obligations pursuant to Article 3 (3) (removing terrorist content or blocking access) shall be punishable with financial penalties of up to 4% of the hosting service provider's global turnover of the preceding business year.

Conclusion – what the future may bring

As stressed on multiple occasions, the only binding and widely applicable international legal act governing cybercrime against computer data, information systems and ICT networks is the Council of Europe's Convention on Cybercrime of 23 November 2001. While countries from outside Europe also acceded to the Convention, and numerous countries that have not done so have modelled their regulations on the document, the Convention continues to be a legal act of regional reach. This is unfortunate, since only global legal solutions can effectively target cybercrime, which knows no boundaries and reaches every part of the world. This situation and the fact that the Convention itself is now outdated (it was drafted over 20 years ago)[1] has prompted the UN to commence work on a worldwide convention concerning measures against cybercrime – the International Convention on Countering the Use of Information and Communications Technologies for Criminal Purposes. Similarly to the Council of Europe's Convention on Cybercrime, it is intended as a comprehensive regulation containing both substantive and procedural law provisions.

It is worth stressing that the most difficult task entrusted to the draft authors is to create appropriate procedural law regulations (evidence law, legal assistance and cooperation between individual states or, more specifically, between their justice authorities). I believe that substantive-law issues will be less challenging, in particular those discussed in this publication, including provisions concerning offences against computer data and information systems. "Hackers' havens", states where computer crimes are not prosecuted, were common at the time when works on the Convention on Cybercrime commenced, but are not likely to be found nowadays in any part of the world. The principle of dual criminality, a prerequisite for a perpetrator's penal liability, is thus effective in most cases. Regulations specifying the constituents of offences are similar,

1 Directive 2013/40/EU on attacks against information systems is a much more up-to-date legal act covering substantive law. Obviously, it is applicable only in European Union Member States.

DOI: 10.4324/9781003476771-7

differing mostly in the level of detail and the severity of sanctions. This does not mean, however, that these differences can be regarded as insignificant.

The open-ended Ad Hoc Committee to Elaborate a Comprehensive International Convention on Countering the Use of Information and Communications Technologies for Criminal Purposes was established by the General Assembly in its resolution 74/247 in 2020. Due to the Covid-19 pandemic, work on the Convention began in 2022. Negotiations between Member States lasted two years and ended in failure – at the concluding session of the Ad Hoc Committee in New York from 29 January to 9 February 2024 the draft treaty was not implemented because Member States failed to reach consensus on several important issues (i.e., preventive measures, collection of electronic evidence, protection of human rights).

The Ad Hoc Committee decided to suspend its work and recommended to the General Assembly that it set a date of concluding session of the Committee in a later date. It will be held in accordance with Decision 78/549 of the General Assembly from July 29 to August 9 2024.

Bibliography

Literature

Adamski, A. "Prawo karne komputerowe" (2000) C.H. Beck, Warsaw

Adamski, A. "Przestępczość w cyberprzestrzeni. Prawne środki przeciwdziałania zjawisku w Polsce na tle projektu konwencji Rady Europy" (2001) Dom Organizatora, Toruń

Adamski, A. "Cyberprzestępczość – aspekty prawne i kryminologiczne" (2005) *Studia Prawnicze* 4

Adamski, A. "Botnety jako zagadnienie prawno-kryminologiczne na tle doświadczeń amerykańskich" (2013) *Prokuratura i Prawo* 11

Ahn, G.J., Doupe, A., Zhao, Z., Liao, K. "Ransomware and cryptocurrency: Partners in crime" in: Holt, T.J. (ed.) "Cybercrime Through on Interdisciplinary Lens" (2019) Routledge

Akhgar, B., Staniforth, A., Bosco, F. "Cyber Crime and Cyber Terrorism Investigator's Handbook" (2014) Elsevier, Amsterdam – Boston

Amoroso, E.G. "Cyber Attacks: Protecting National Infrastructure" (2013) Elsevier, Amsterdam

Armstrong, D., Hyde, D., Thomas, S. "Cyber Security: Law and Practice" (2017) Jordan Publishing Limited

Barta, J., Markiewicz, R. "Główne problemy prawa komputerowego" (1993) Wydawnictwo Naukowo-Techniczne, Warsaw

Barta, J., Markiewicz, R. "Prawo autorskie" (2010) Wolters Kluwer, Warsaw

Bell, R., Ray, N. "EU Electronic Communications Law" (2004) Oxford University Press

Berent, M., Filar, M. In: Bojarski, J., Bojarski, M., Czarnecki, P., Filipkowski, W., et al. "Kodeks karny. Komentarz" Rozdział XXVPrzestępstwa przeciwko wolności seksualnej i obyczajności (2016) Wolters Kluwer, Warsaw

Bilski, T., Pankowski, T., Stokłosa, J. "Bezpieczeństwo danych w systemach informatycznych" (2001) Wydawnictwo Naukowe PWN, Warsaw – Poznań

Brenner, S.W. In: Clifford, R.D. (ed.) "Cybercrime. The Investigation, Prosecution and Defense of a Computer-Related Crime" Chapter Two: Defining Cybercrime: A Review of Federal and State Law (2011) Carolina Academic Press, Durham

Brenner, S.W. "Cybercrime and the Law. Challenges. Issues, and Outcomes" (2012) Northeastern University Press, Boston

Brenner, S.W. "Cyberthreats and the Decline of the Nation-State" (2014) Routledge

Brunst, P.W., Gecrke, M. "Praxishandbuch Internetstrafrecht" (2009) Kohlhammer, Stuttgart

Casey, E., Daywalt, C. "Computer intrusions" in: Casey, E. (ed.) "Digital Evidence and Computer Crime. Forensic Science, Computers and the Internet" (2011) Waltham – San Diego – London

Chałubińska-Jentkiewicz, K. "Cyberspace as an area of legal regulation" in: Chałubińska-Jentkiewicz, K., Radoniewicz, F., Zieliński, T. (eds.) "Cybersecurity in Poland – Legal Aspects" (2021) Springer

Chauhan, V., Saini, P. "ICMP flood attacks: A vulnerability analysis" in: Bokhari, M.U., Agrawal, N., Saini, D. (eds.) "Cyber Security: Proceedings of CSI 2015" (2018) Springer, Singapore

Chen, T., Jarvis, L.E., Macdonald, S. (eds.) "Cyberterrorism: Understanding, Assessment, and Response" (2014) Springer, New York

Clough, J. "Principles of Cybercrime" (2015) Cambridge University Press, New York

Cole, D. "Preserving privacy in a digital age lessons of comparative constitutionalism" in: Davis, F., McGarrity, N., Williams, G. (eds.) "Surveillance, Counter-Terrorism and Comparative Constitutionalism" (2017) Routledge

Comer, D.E. "Computer Networks and Internets: Global Edition" (2015) Pearson

De Arimateia da Ruz, J. "The Legislative Framework of the European Union (EU) convention on cybercrime" in: Holt, T.J., Bossler, A.M. (eds.) "The Palgrave Handbook of International Cybercrime and Cyberdeviance, Vol. 1" (2020) Palgrave

de Loiola, R.R.G. "A Convenciao de Budapeste e a Problematica da Competencia Para o Julgamento de Cybercrimes" in: Scriptore, V., Almeida, F., Almeida, D.F.E. (eds.) "OS Cybercrimes Internacionais E a Convenção de Budapeste – Rumo a Um Direito Global Para a Internet Capa comum por" (2019) Lawinter Editions

Denning, D.E. "Reflections on cyberweapons controls" (2000a) *Computer Security Journal* XVI, No. 4, http://faculty.nps.edu/dedennin/publications/reflections_on_cyberweapons_controls.pdf, access 1 June 2024

Denning, D.E. "Statement Made at a Congressional Hearing, May 23, 2000 – House Special Oversight Panel on Terrorism" (2000b), https://irp.fas.org/congress/2000_hr/index.html, access 1 June 2024

Easttom, C., Taylor, J. "Computer Crime, Investigation, and the Law, 1st Edition" (2010) Cengage Learning PTR

Erickson, J. "Hacking: The Art of Exploitation, 2nd Edition. Kindle Edition" (2008) No Starch Press

"Explanatory Report to Additional Protocol to the Convention on Cybercrime, Concerning the Criminalisation of Acts of a Racist and Xenophobic Nature Committed through Computer Systems", http://conventions.coe.int/Treaty/en/Reports/Html/189.htm, access 19 June 2024

"Explanatory Report to the Convention on Cybercrime", http://conventions.coe.int/Treaty/en/Reports/Html/185.htm, access 19 June 2024

Flemming, M. "Terroryzm polityczny w międzynarodowym prawodawstwie" (1996) *Wojskowy Przegląd Prawniczy* 3–4

Garlicki, L. In: Garlicki, L. (ed.) Hofmański, P., Wróbel, A. "Konwencja o Ochronie Praw Człowieka i Podstawowych Wolności. Komentarz do art. 1–18. Vol. 1" Artykuł 8 [Prawo do poszanowania życia prywatnego i rodzinnego] (2010) C.H. Beck, Warsaw

Gates, B. "The Road Ahead" (1995) Viking

Gearty, C. "State surveillance in an age of security" in: Davis, F., McGarrity, N., Williams, G. (eds.) "Surveillance, Counter-Terrorism and Comparative Constitutionalism" (2017) Routledge

Gercke, M., "Understanding Cybercrime: A Guide for Developing Countries", www.itu.int/ITU-D/cyb/cybersecurity/docs/ITU_Guide_A5_12072011.pdf, access 1 June 2024

Ghernaouti, S. "Cyber Power: Crime, Conflict and Security in Cyberspace" (2013) EPFL Press, Lausanne

Gibson, W. "Neuromancer" (1984) Ace Books, New York

Gienas, K. "Digital Rights Management – nowa era prawa autorskiego?" (2005) *Monitor Prawniczy – addendum: Prawo Mediów Elektronicznych* 2

Gienas, K. "Prawnokarne aspekty >>narzędzi hakerskich<<" (2006) *Monitor Prawniczy addendum: Prawo Mediów Elektronicznych* 2

Gillespie, A.A. "Cybercrime: Key Issues and Debates" (2016) Routledge, London – New York

Goban-Klas, T., Sienkiewicz, P. "Społeczeństwo informacyjne: Szanse, zagrożenia, wyzwania" (1999) Wydawnictwo Fundacji Postepu Telekomunikacji, Kraków

Górniok, O. "Komentarz do Konwencji w sprawie ochrony interesów finansowych Wspólnot Europejskich i innych aktów" in: Zielińska, E. (ed.) "Prawo Wspólnot Europejskich a prawo karne, Vol.3: Dokumenty karne" (2000) Oficyna Naukowa, Warsaw

Grabosky, P. "Electronic Crime" (2006) Hoboken, NJ

Grabosky, P. "Cybercrime" (2016) Oxford University Press, New York – Oxford

Grabosky, P., Smith, R. "Crime in the Digital Age: Controlling Telecommunications and Cyberspace Illegalities" (1998) Routledge, Sydney

Graham, R.S., Smith, S.K. "Cybercrime and Digital Deviance" (2020) Routledge, New York – London

Grzelak, A. "Komentarz do decyzji ramowej w sprawie zwalczania fałszowania i oszustw związanych z bezgotówkowymi środkami płatniczymi" in: Zielińska, E. (ed.) "Prawo Wspólnot Europejskich a prawo karne, Part II, Vol. 6: Dokumenty karne" (2005) Oficyna Naukowa, Warsaw

"Hate Crime Laws: A Practical Guide, 2nd Edition, OSCE/ODIHR 2009", www.google.com/url?sa=t&source=web&rct=j&opi=89978449&url=www.osce.org/odihr/523940&ved=2ahUKEwibl8OuioOHAxWS_7sIHTlcBAEQFnoECBEQAQ&usg=AOvVaw2Dw4xguCTfUVdCWMdVlByj, access 19 June 2024.

"Hate Crimes in the OSCE Region – Incidents and Responses. Annual Report for 2007", www.google.com/url?sa=t&source=web&rct=j&opi=89978449&url=www.osce.org/files/f/documents/9/2/40203.pdf&ved=2ahUKEwiQl4y1iYOHAxVb_rsIHeKHBPgQFnoECA4QAQ&usg=AOvVaw0HSap8Lee2hLAdnAslendB, access 19 June 2024

Hill, J.B., Marion, N.E. "Introduction to cybercrime: Computer Crimes, Laws, and Policing in the 21st Century" (2016) ABC-CLIO

Hollinger, R.C. In: Hollinger, R.C. (ed.) "Crime, Deviance and the Computer (International Library of Criminology, Criminal Justice & Penology)" Introduction (1997) Ashgate Publishing Limited, Dartmouth

Holt, T.J., Bossler, A.M. (eds.) "The Palgrave Handbook of International Cybercrime and Cyberdeviance" (2020) Palgrave

Holt, T.J., Bossler, A.M., Seigfried-Spellar, K.C. "Cybercrime and Digital Forensics: An Introduction, 2nd Edition" (2017) Routledge

Hołyst, B. "Internet jako miejsce popełnienia przestępstwa" (2009) *Prokuratura i Prawo* 4

Hubbard, A.M., Schjølberg, S. "Harmonizing National Legal Approaches on Cybercrime" (2005), www.itu.int/osg/spu/cybersecurity//docs/Background_Paper_Harmonizing_National_and_Legal_Approaches_on_Cybercrime.pdf, access 1 June 2024

Huber, E. "Cybercrime: Eine Einführung (German)" (2019) Springer

"Implementation of Recommendation N° R (89) 9 on Computer-Related Crime", Report prepared by Professor Dr. H.W.K. Kaspersen [doc. CDPC (97) 5 and PC-CY (97) 5], www.google.com/url?sa=t&source=web&rct=j&opi=89978449&url=www.oas.org/juridico/english/89-9%26final%2520Report.pdf&ved=2ahUKEwjtq5-IsKuHAxXtQvEDHdMoDngQFnoECBEQAQ&usg=AOvVaw0_cCGOSaJvfDiYrZt-jJbR, access 1 June 2024

Inc. Cisco Systems. "Network Basics Companion Guide, 1st Edition" (2014) Cisco Networking Academy

Iougleux, P., Mitrou, L., Tatianu-Eleni, S. "Chapter 2. Criminalization of attacks against information systems" in: Iglezakis, I. (ed.) "The Legal Regulation of Cyber Attacks" (2016) Wolters Kluwer

Izdebski, H. "Rada Europy. Organizacja demokratycznych państw Europy i jej znaczenie dla Polski" (1996) Wydawnictwo Naukowe Scholar, Warsaw

Jajodia, S., Shakarian, P., Subrahmanian, V.S., Swarup, V., Wang, C. (eds.) "Cyber Warfare: Building the Scientific Foundation" (2015) Springer

Janczewski, L., Colarik, M. (eds.) "Cyber Warfare and Cyber Terrorism" (2008) Information Science Reference, Hershey
Janusz, G. "Ochrona praw mniejszości narodowych w Europie" (2011) Wydawnictwo UMCS, Lublin
Johnson, M. "Cyber Crime, Security and Digital Intelligence" (2013) Routledge
Karpiuk, M. "Computer Fraud" (2023) *Cybersecurity and Law* 2
Khurana, M., Yadav, R.F., Kumari, M. "Buffer overflow and SQL injection: To remotely attack and access information" in: Bokhari, MU., Agrawal, N., Saini, D. (eds.) "Cyber Security: Proceedings of CSI 2015" (2018) Springer, Singapore
Kilian, W. In: Gołaczyński, J. (ed.) "Prawne i ekonomiczne aspekty komunikacji elektronicznej" Wprowadzenie (2003) LexisNexis Warsaw
Kittichaisaree, K. "Public International Law of Cyberspace (Law, Governance and Technology Series Book 32)" (2017) Springer
Kleban, B. "Rozdział IV. Digital Rights Management Systems (Systemy elektronicznego zarządzania prawami do utworów utrwalonych techniką cyfrową)" in: Kępiński, W.K. (ed.) "Granice prawa autorskiego" (2010) C.H. Beck, Warsaw
Koops, B.J., Robinson, T. "Cybercrime law: A European perspective" in: Casey, E. (ed.) "Digital Evidence and Computer Crime" (2011) Elsevier Science Publishing
Kosiński, J. "Paradygmaty cyberprzestępczości" (2015) Difin Warsaw
Krysiak, K. "Sieci komputerowe" (2005) Kompendium, Helion, Gliwice
Krzysztofek, K., Szczepański, M. "Zrozumieć rozwój. Od społeczeństw tradycyjnych do informacyjnych" (2002) Wydawnictwo Uniwersytetu Śląskiego, Katowice
Kuźniar, R. "Prawa człowieka: prawo, instytucje, stosunki międzynarodowe" (2004) Wydawnictwo Naukowe Scholar, Warsaw
Lach, A. "Kradzież tożsamości" (2012) *Prokuratura i Prawo* 3
Latoszek, E. "Organizacja Współpracy Gospodarczej i Rozwoju – geneza, mechanizm funkcjonowania, struktura, działalność" in: Latoszek, E., Proczek, M. (eds.) "Organizacje międzynarodowe. Założenia, cele, działalność. Podręcznik akademicki" (2001) Elipsa, Warsaw
Lavorgna, A. "Cybercrimes: Critical Issues in a Global Context" (2020) Macmillan International Higher Education, Red Globe Press, London
Lloyd, J. "Information Technology Law" (2017) Oxford University Press, Oxford
Loundy, D.J. "Computer Crime, Information Warfare, and Economic Espionage" (2003) Carolina Academic Press, Durham
Lowe, D. "UE data protection law: Is it fettering police ability to investigate terrorist activity and organized crime?" in: Hale-Ross, S., Lowe, D. (eds.) "Terrorism and State Surveillance of Communication" (2020) Routledge
Middleton, B. "A History of Cyber Security Attacks: 1980 to Present" (2017) CRC Press, Boca Raton – London – New York
Mitrou, L. "Chapter 1. Attacks against information systems: Technical definitions" in: Iglezakis, I. (ed.) "The Legal Regulation of Cyber Attacks" (2016) Wolters Kluwer
Morreale, S.P., Spitzberg, B.H., Barge, J.K. "Komunikacja między ludźmi. Motywacja, wiedza i umiejętności" (2007) Wydawnictwo Naukowe PWN, Warsaw
Murphy, M.H. "Survillance and the Law. Language, Power and Privacy" (2020) Routledge
Murray, A. "Information Technology Law: The Law and Society" (2016) Oxford University Press, Oxford
Muszyński, J. In: Janoś, T. (ed.) "Vademecum teleinformatyka III" Rozdział 26. Strefa bezpieczeństwa sieci. (2004) Wydawnictwo IDG, Warsaw
Niedźwiedź, M. In: Kowalik-Bańczyk, K., Szwarc-Kuczer, M., Wróbel, A. (eds.) "Traktat o funkcjonowaniu Unii Europejskiej. Komentarz. Tom II (art. 90–222)" TYTUŁ IV Środki ograniczające (2012) Wolters Kluwer, Warsaw
Nowak, J.S. "Społeczeństwo informacyjne – geneza i definicje" in: Sienkiewicz, P., Nowak, J.S. (eds.) "Społeczeństwo informacyjne. Krok naprzód, dwa kroki wstecz" (2008) Polskie Towarzystwo Informatyczne, Katowice

Nowicka, A. "Prawnoautorska i prawnopatentowa ochrona programów komputerowych" (1995) Dom Wydawniczy ABC, Warsaw

Nowicki, M.A. "Wokół Konwencji Europejskiej" (2010) Wolters Kluwer, Warsaw

Payne, B.K. "Defining cybercrime" in: Holt, T.J., Bossler, A.M. (eds.) "The Palgrave Handbook of International Cybercrime and Cyberdeviance, Vol. 1" (2020) Palgrave

Pehlivan, O.P. "Confronting Cyberespionage under International Law" (2018) Routledge

Pisarek, W. "Wstęp do nauki o komunikowaniu" (2008) Wydawnictwo WAiP, Warsaw

Radoniewicz, F. "Ochrona programów komputerowych w prawie UE (cz. I)" (2009a) *Europejski Przegląd Sądowy* 3

Radoniewicz, F. "Ochrona programów komputerowych w prawie UE (cz. II)" (2009b) *Europejski Przegląd Sądowy* 5

Radoniewicz, F. "Pornografia w Internecie – zagadnienia wybrane" in: Mozgawa, M. (ed.) "Pornografia" (2011) Wolters Kluwer, Warsaw

Radoniewicz, F. "Odpowiedzialność karna za hacking i inne przestępstwa przeciwko bezpieczeństwu danych komputerowych i systemów informatycznych" (2016) Wolters Kluwer, Warszawa

Radoniewicz, F. "Cyberspace, cybercrime, cyberterrorism" in: Chałubińska-Jentkiewicz, K., Radoniewicz, F., Zieliński, T. (eds.) "Cybersecurity in Poland – Legal Aspects" (2021a) Springer

Radoniewicz, F. "International Regulations of Cybersecurity" in: Chałubińska-Jentkiewicz, K., Radoniewicz, F., Zieliński, T. (eds.) "Cybersecurity in Poland – Legal Aspects" (2021b) Springer

Radoniewicz, F. "Cybersecurity in the European Union law" in: Chałubińska-Jentkiewicz, K., Radoniewicz, F., Zieliński, T. (eds.) "Cybersecurity in Poland – Legal Aspects" (2021c) Springer

Radoniewicz, F. "Cybercrime in selected European countries" in: Chałubińska-Jentkiewicz, K., Radoniewicz, F., Zieliński, T. (eds.) "Cybersecurity in Poland – Legal Aspects" (2021d) Springer

Radoniewicz, F. "Strategic monitoring in the judicial decisions of the European Court of Human Rights" (2021e) *Cybersecurity and Law* 2

Radoniewicz, F. "The issue of surveillance carried out by technical means within the jurisprudence of the European Court of Human Rights and the Constitutional Tribunal". (2021f) *Przegląd Prawa Konstytucyjnego* 6

Radoniewicz, F. "The surveillance of ICT networks – selected issues" in: Żarna, K. (ed.) Bezpieczeństwo – Prawa człowieka – Stosunki międzynarodowe, tom III" (2021g) Wydawnictwo Uniwersytetu Rzeszowskiego, Rzeszów

Radoniewicz, F. "Zwalczanie nielegalnych treści w Internecie – aspekty wybrane" in: Chałubińska-Jentkiewicz, K., Nowikowska, M., Wąsowski, K. (eds.) Media w erze cyfrowej. Wyzwania i zagrożenia" (2021h) Wolters Kluwer, Warsaw

Radoniewicz, F. "Procedural provisions in the convention on cybercrime" in: Karpiuk, M., Kostrubiec, J. (eds.) "The Public Dimension of Cybersecurity" (2022a) LexLocalis, Maribor

Radoniewicz, F. "Solutions on blocking access to and removing illegal content on the internet under EU regulations and Polish law" in: Chałubińska-Jentkiewicz, K., Hoffman, I. (eds.) "The Role of Cybersecurity in the Public Sphere – The European Dimension" (2022b) LexLocalis, Maribor

Radoniewicz, F. "Cyberprzestępstwa przeciwko danym komputerowym i systemom informatycznym w kodeksie karnym – propozycje zmian" (2024) C.H. Beck, Warszawa

Radziwill, Y. "Cyber-Attacks and the Exploitable Imperfection of International Law" (2015) Brill Nijhoff, Leiden – Boston

Reed, C., Angel, J. (eds.) "Computer Law. The Law and Regulation of Information Technology" (2012) Oxford University Press

Richardson, M. "Cyber Crime. Law and Practice" (2019) Wildy, Simmonds & Hill Publishing

Rowland, D., Kohl, U., Charlesworth, A. "Information Technology Law" (2016) Routledge, London – New York.

Russell, R. (ed.) "Hack Proofing Your Network, 2nd Edition. Kindle Edition" (2002) Syngress.

Rustad, M.L. "Internet Law in a Nutshell (Nutshell Series)" (2009) West Academic Press

Savin., A. "EU Internet Law, 2nd Edition" (2017) Edward Elgar Publishin – Cheltenham, UK – Northampton, MA

Savin, A., Trzaskowski, J. (eds.) "Research Handbook on EU Internet Law" (2014) Edward Elgar, Cheltenham, UK – Northampton, MA

Scherer, J. (ed.) "Telecommunication Laws in Europe" (2005) Tottel Publishing

Schjølberg, S. "The History of Global Harmonization on Cybercrime Legislation – The Road to Geneva" (2008), www.cybercrimelaw.net, access 1 June 2024

Schjølberg, S. "The History of Cybercrime" (2020) Books on Demand

Seger, A. "The Budapest Convention 10 years on: Lessons learnt" in: Manacorda, S. (ed.) "Cybercriminality: Finding a Balance Between Freedom and Security. Proceedings of the International Conference on "Cybercrime: Global Phenomenon and Its Challenges", 2–4 December 2011" (2012) Milan

Shackelford, J. "Managing Cyber Attacks in International Law, Business, and Relations in" Search of Cyber Peace" (2015) Scott. Cambridge University Press, New York

Shinder, D.L., Tittel, E. "Scene of the Cybercrime: Computer Forensics Handbook, 1st Edition. Kindle Edition" (2002) Syngress

Sieber, U. "Legal Aspects of Computer-Related Crime in the Information Society – Comcrime-Study" (1998) Würzburg

Sobczak, J. "Swoboda wypowiedzi w orzecznictwie Trybunału Praw Człowieka w Strasburgu (część I)" (2007a) *Ius Novum* 2–3

Sobczak, J. "Swoboda wypowiedzi w orzecznictwie Trybunału Praw Człowieka w Strasburgu (część II)" (2007b) *Ius Novum* 4

"Standardisation of Definitions of Identity Crime Terms: A Step towards Consistency", Australian Centre for Policing Research and the Australian Transaction Reports and Analysis Centre, Report Series No. 145.3, www.google.com/url?sa=t&source=web&rct=j&opi=89978449&url=https://catalogue.nla.gov.au/catalog/3769040&ved=2ahUKEwjYt-u4oayGAxViJhAIHeT1C4IQFnoECA4QAQ&usg=AOvVaw3gKDjY1y2inruIGdVn8w7C, access 1 June 2024

Summers, S., Schwarzenegger, C., Ege, G., Young, F. "The Emergence of EU Criminal Law: Cybercrime and the Regulation of the Information Society" (2014) Hart Publishing, Oxford – Portland

Teach, E. "The Big Black Book of Electronic Surveillance" (2020) Independently Published

Tehrani, P.M. "Cyberterrorism: The Legal and Enforcement Issues" (2017) World Scientific Publishing Europe, Hackensack, NJ

Walczak-Żochowska, A. "Internet a seksualne wykorzystywanie dzieci" in: Girdwoyń, P. (ed.) "Prawo wobec nowoczesnych technologii" (2008) Wydawnictwo Liber, Warsaw

Walden, I. "Computer Crimes and Digital Investigations" (2016) Oxford University Press, Oxford

Wall, D. "Cybercrime. The Transformation of Crime in the Information Age" (2013) Malden

Warylewski, J.K. "Pornografia – próba definicji" in: Mozgawa, M. (ed.) "Pornografia" (2011) Wolters Kluwer, Warsaw

Wiener, N. "Cybernetics: Or Control and Communication in the Animal and the Machine" (1985) MIT Press

Willems, E. "Cyberdanger: Understanding and Guarding Against Cybercrime" (2019) Springer
Wojnicki, Z. "Zagadnienia ogólne" in: Wróblewski, J. (ed.) "Wstęp do informatyki prawniczej" Wydawnictwo PWN (1985) Warsaw
Wróbel, A. In: Garlicki, L., Hofmański, P., Wróbel, A. (eds.) "Konwencja o Ochronie Praw Człowieka i Podstawowych Wolności. Komentarz. Vol. I" Artykuł 14 [Zakaz dyskryminacji] (2010) C.H. Beck, Warsaw
Wróblewski, J. "Prawo a cybernetyka (Zarys problemów)" (1968) *Państwo i Prawo* 12
Zieliński, T. "Introduction" in: Chałubińska-Jentkiewicz, K., Radoniewicz, F., Zieliński, T. (eds.) "Cybersecurity in Poland – Legal Aspects" (2021) Springer
Żółtek, S. "Rozdział VIII. Współpraca w zaresie prawa karnego materialnego w ramach Rady Europy i Unii Europejskiej" in: Grzelak, A., Królikowski, M., Sakowicz, A. (eds.) "Europejskie Prawo Karne" (2012) C.H. Beck, Warsaw

Legal acts

International law

Council of Europe

Additional Protocol to the Convention on Cybercrime, concerning the criminalisation of acts of a racist and xenophobic nature committed through computer systems of 28 June 2003 (Polish Journal of Laws of 2015, item 2015, item 730)
Convention No. 108 for the Protection of Individuals with regard to Automatic Processing of Personal Data, done at Strasbourg on 28 June 1981, OJ EU 2003 No. 3, item 25, as amended
Convention No. 178 on the Legal Protection of Services based on, or consisting of, Conditional Access of 21 June 2001, www.coe.int/en/web/conventions/-/council-of-europe-european-convention-on-the-legal-protection-of-services-based-on-or-consisting-of-conditional-access-ets-no-178-translations, access 1 June 2024
Convention No. 201 on the Protection of Children against Sexual Exploitation and Sexual Abuse, done at Lanzarote on 25 October 2007, OJ EU of 2015, item 608.
Convention on Cybercrime of the Council of Europe of 23 November 2001
OSCE Ministerial Council Decision No. 4/03, "Tolerance and Non-discrimination", Maastricht, 2.12.2003, www.osce.org/mc/19382, access 19 June 2024
OSCE – Organization for Security and Co-operation in Europe/ECRI – European Commission against Racism and Intolerance
Recommendation CM/Rec (2021) 8 of the Committee of Ministers to member States on the protection of individuals with regard to automatic processing of personal data in the context of profiling of 3 November 2021, https://search.coe.int/cm?i=0900001680a46147, access 1 June 2024
Recommendation No. 1 (CRI (96) 43) "On Combating Racism, Xenophobia, Antisemitism and Intolerance", www.coe.int/en/web/european-commission-against-racism-and-intolerance/recommendation-no.1, access 19 June 2024
Recommendation No. 6 (CRI (2001) 1): "On Combating the Dissemination of Racist, Xenophobic and Antisemitic Material Via the Internet", www.coe.int/en/web/european-commission-against-racism-and-intolerance/recommendation-no.6, access 19 June 2024
Recommendation No. 7 (CRI (2003) 8) "On National Legislation to Combat Racism and Racial Discrimination", www.coe.int/en/web/european-commission-against-racism-and-intolerance/recommendation-no.7, access 19 June 2024
Recommendation No. 9 (CRI (2004) 37) "On Preventing and Combating Antisemitism", www.coe.int/en/web/european-commission-against-racism-and-intolerance/recommendation-no.9, access 19 June 2024

Recommendation No. 12 (CRI (2009) 5) "On Combating Racism and Racial Discrimination in the Field of Sport", www.coe.int/en/web/european-commission-against-racism-and-intolerance/recommendation-no.12, access 19 June 2024
Recommendation No. 13 (CRI (2011) 37) "On Combating Anti-gypsyism and Discrimination against Roma", www.coe.int/en/web/european-commission-against-racism-and-intolerance/recommendation-no.13, access 19 June 2024
Recommendation No. 15 (CRI (2015) 15) "Combating Hate Speech", www.coe.int/en/web/european-commission-against-racism-and-intolerance/recommendation-no.15, access 19 June 2024
Recommendation No. R (89) 9 on computer-related crime and final report of the European Committee on Crime Problems, Council of Europe, Publishing and Documentation Service, Strasburg 1990. The text of Recommendation R (89) 9 is available online at: https://wcd.coe.int/wcd/com.instranet.InstraServlet?command=com.instranet.CmdBlobGet&InstranetImage=610660&SecMode=1&DocId=702280&Usage=2, access 1 June 2024
Recommendation No. R (91) 14 on the legal protection of encrypted television services of 27 September 1991, www.coe.int/en/web/freedom-expression/committee-of-ministers-adopted-texts/-/asset_publisher/aDXmrol0vvsU/content/recommendation-no-r-91–14-of-the-committee-of-ministers-to-member-states-on-the-legal-protection-of-encrypted-television-services, access 1 June 2024
Recommendation No. R (97) 20 of the Committee of Ministers to member states on "hate speech" of 30 October 1997, www.coe.int/en/web/freedom-expression/committee-of-ministers-adopted-texts/-/asset_publisher/aDXmrol0vvsU/content/recommendation-no-r-97–20-of-the-committee-of-ministers-to-member-states-on-hate-speech-, access 1 June 2024
Recommendation No. R (99) 5 on the protection of privacy on the internet of 23 June 1999, https://search.coe.int/cm#{%22CoEIdentifier%22:[%2209000016804f4429%22],%22sort%22:[%22CoEValidationDate%20Descending%22]}, access 1 June 2024
Recommendation Rec (2001) 7 of the Committee of Ministers to member states on measures to protect copyright and neighbouring rights and combat piracy, especially in the digital environment of 5 September 2001, https://search.coe.int/cm#{%22CoEIdentifier%22:[%2209000016804deb54%22],%22sort%22:[%22CoEValidationDate%20Descending%22]}, access 1 June 2024
The European Convention for the Protection of Human Rights and Fundamental Freedoms signed in Rome on 4 November 1950, amended by Protocols Nos. 3, 5, and 8, and supplemented by Protocol No. 2, Polish Journal of Laws of 1993, No. 61, item 284
Vienna Declaration adopted at the Vienna Summit on 9 October 1993, https://www.ohchr.org/en/about-us/history/vienna-declaration, access 19 June 2024

OECD – Organization for Economic Co-operation and Development

Recommendation of the Council Concerning Guidelines for the Security of Information Systems of 26 November 1992 (C(92)188/FINAL)
Recommendation of the Council Concerning Guidelines for the Security of Information Systems and Networks – Towards a Culture of Security of 25 July 2002 (C(2002)131)
Recommendation of the Council on Cross-Border Co-operation in the Enforcement of Laws against Spam of 13 April 2006 (C(2006)57)
Recommendation of the Council on Cross-border Co-operation in the Enforcement of Laws Protecting Privacy of 12 December 2007 (C(2007)67(final)

Recommendation of the Council on Digital Risk Management for Economic and Social Prosperity of 17 September 2015 (C(2015)115)
Recommendation of the Council on Protection of Critical Information Infrastructures of 30 April 2008 (C(2008)35)

Others

International Covenant on Civil and Political Rights, open to signature in New York, 16 December 1966
OECD Model Provisions on the Protection of Computer Software, adopted in 1978
Paris Act Relating to the Berne Convention for the Protection of Literary and Artistic Works of 9 September 1886, concluded on 24 June 1971
The Agreement on Trade-Related Aspects of Intellectual Property Rights (the so-called TRIPS Agreement), constituting Appendix 1 C to the Agreement Establishing the World Trade Organization (WTO) signed in Marrakesh on the 15 April 1994
The International Convention for the Protection of Performers, Producers of Phonograms and Broadcasting Organizations was signed in Rome on 26 October 1961
"Vienna Declaration on Crime and Justice: Meeting the Challenges of the Twenty-first century" adopted by the Tenth United Nations Congress on the Prevention of Crime and the Treatment of Offenders in Vienna (10–17 April 2000 r.) annex to General Assembly Resolution nr 45/121of 4 December 2000
WIPO (World Intellectual Property Organization) Copyright Treaty adopted in Geneva on 23 December 1996

European Union

Bengemann Report entitled "Europe and the Global Information Society – Recommendations to the European Council", published in Brussels on 26 May 1994
Commission Directive 2002/77/EC of 16 September 2002 on competition in the markets for electronic communications networks and services (Text with EEA relevance) (OJ EC 2002 L 249/21)
Common Position of 27 May 1999 adopted by the Council on the basis of Article 34 of the Treaty on European Union, on negotiations relating to the Draft Convention on Cybercrime held in the Council of Europe (OJ 1999 EU L 142/1)
Communication from the Commission of 28 September 2017 on Tackling Illegal Content Online and towards the enhanced responsibility of online platforms COM(2017)555 final
Communication from the Commission to the Council, the European Parliament, the Economic and Social Committee and the Committee of the Regions COM(2000)890 on Creating a Safer Information Society by Improving the Security of Information Infrastructures and Combating Computer-related Crime of 26 June 2001 (the so-called Communication on Cybercrime)
Consolidated versions of the Treaty on European Union and the Treaty on the Functioning of the European Union – Consolidated version of the Treaty on the Functioning of the European Union which adopted the Treaty of Lisbon, signed on 13 December 2007 (OJ EU 2012 C 326/1)
Council Decision 2002/187/JHA of 28 June 2002 setting up Eurojust with a view to reinforcing the fight against serious crime (OJ 2002 EC L 63/1)
Council Decision 2008/976/JHA of 16 December 2008 on the European Judicial Network (OJ EU 2008 L 348/138)
Council Decision 2009/426/JHA of 16 December 2008 on the strengthening of Eurojust and amending Decision 2002/187/JHA (OJ EU 138 L 138/14)

Council Decision (CFSP) 2020/1127 of 30 July 2020 amending Decision (CFSP) 2019/797 concerning restrictive measures against cyber-attacks threatening the Union or its Member States (OJ EU 2020 L 246/12) and Council Implementing Regulation (EU) 2020/1125 of 30 July 2020 implementing Regulation (EU) 2019/796 concerning restrictive measures against cyber-attacks threatening the Union or its Member States ST/9568/2020/INIT (OJ EU 2020 L 246/4) (the matter of “WannaCry” and “NotPetya” cyber-attacks, and “Operation Cloud Hopper”)

Council Decision (CFSP) 2020/1537 amending Decision (CFSP) 2019/797 concerning restrictive measures against cyber-attacks threatening the Union or its Member States (OJ EU 2020 L 351/5), and Council Implementing Regulation (EU) 2020/1536 implementing Regulation (EU) 2019/796 concerning restrictive measures against cyber-attacks threatening the Union or its Member States (OJ EU 2020L 351/1) (the matter of a cyber-attack directed against the federal German parliament – Deutscher Bundestag)

Council Directive 2008/114/EC of 8 December 2008 on the identification and designation of European critical infrastructures and the assessment of the need to improve their protection (OJ EU 2008 L 345/75)

Council Framework Decision 2002/475/JHA of the 13th of June 2002 on combating terrorism (OJ EU 2002 L 164/3)

Council Framework Decision 2005/222/JHA of 24 June 2005 on attacks against information systems (OJ EU 2005 L 69/67)

Council Framework Decision 2008/841/JHA of 24 October 2008 on the fight against organised crime (OJ EU 2008 L 300/42)

Council Framework Decision 2009/948/JHA of 30 November 2009 on the prevention and settlement of conflicts of exercise of jurisdiction in criminal proceedings (OJ EU 2009 L 328/42)

Council Regulation No. 174/2005 imposing restrictions on the supply of assistance related to military activities to Côte d’Ivoire (OJ UE 2005 L 29/5)

Council Regulation No. 881/2002 imposing certain specific restrictive measures directed against certain persons and entities associated with Usama bin Laden, the Al-Qaida network and the Taliban, and repealing Council Regulation No. 467/2001 prohibiting the export of certain goods and services to Afghanistan, strengthening the flight ban, and extending the freezing of funds and other financial resources in respect of the Taliban of Afghanistan (OJ EC 2002 L 139/9)

Council Regulation No. 1210/2003 concerning certain specific restrictions on economic and financial relations with Iraq and repealing Regulation (EC) No. 2465/96 (OJ EC1996 L 169/6)

Council Regulation No. 2580/2001 on specific restrictive measures directed against certain persons and entities to combat terrorism (OJ EC2001 L 344/70)

Decision No. 676/2002/EC of the European Parliament and of the Council of 7 March 2002 on a regulatory framework for radio spectrum policy in the European Community (Radio Spectrum Decision) (OJ EC L 108/1)

Directive 91/250 of 14 May 1991 on the Protection of Computer Programs (OJ EC 1991 L 122/42)

Directive 2000/31/EC of the European Parliament and of the Council of 8 June 2000 on Certain Legal Aspects of Information Society Services, in Particular Electronic Commerce in the Internal Market (the e-Commerce Directive) (OJ EC 2000 L 178/1)

Directive 2002/19/EC of the European Parliament and of the Council of 7 March 2002 on access to, and interconnection of, electronic communications networks and associated facilities (Access Directive), (OJ EC 2002 L 108/7)

Directive 2002/20/EC of the European Parliament and of the Council of 7 March 2002 on the authorisation of electronic communications networks and services (Authorisation Directive) (OJ EC 2002 L 108/21)

Directive 2002/21/EC of the European Parliament and of the Council of 7 March 2002 on a common regulatory framework for electronic communications networks and services (Framework Directive) (OJ EC 2002 L 108/33)
Directive 2002/22/EC of the European Parliament and of the Council of 7 March 2002 on universal service and users' rights relating to electronic communications networks and services (Universal Service Directive) (OJ EC 2002 L 108/51)
Directive 2002/58/EC of the European Parliament and of the Council of 12 July 2002 concerning the processing of personal data and the protection of privacy in the electronic communications sector (Directive on privacy and electronic communications) (OJ EC 2002 L 201/37)
Directive 2006/24/EC of the European Parliament and of the Council of 15 March 2006 on the retention of data generated or processed in connection with the provision of publicly available electronic communications services or of public communications networks and amending Directive 2002/58/EC (OJ EU 2006 L 105/54)
Directive 2009/24/EC of the European Parliament and of the Council of 23 April 2009 on the legal protection of computer programs (OJ UE 2009 L 111/16)
Directive 2011/93/EU of the European Parliament and of the Council of 13 December 2011 on Combating the Sexual Abuse and Sexual Exploitation of Children and Child Pornography, and replacing Council Framework Decision 2004/68/JHA (OJ EU 2011 L 335/1)
Directive 2013/40/EU of the European Parliament and of the Council of 12 August 2013 on attacks against information systems, and repealing Council Framework Decision 2005/222/JHA (OJ EU 2013 L 218/8)
Directive (EU) 2015/1535, of the European Parliament and of the Council of 9 September 2015 laying down a procedure for the provision of information in the field of technical regulations and of rules on Information Society services (codification) (Text with EEA relevance) (OJ EU 2015 L 241/1)
Directive (EU) 2016/1148 of the European Parliament and of the Council of 6 July 2016 concerning measures for a high common level of security of network and information systems across the Union (OJ EU 2016 L 194/1)
Directive (EU) 2017/541 of the European Parliament and of the Council of the 15th of March 2017 on combating terrorism and replacing Council Framework Decision 2002/475/JHA and amending Council Decision 2005/671/JHA (OJ EU 2017 L 88/6)
Directive (EU) 2018/1972 of the European Parliament and of the Council of 11 December 2018 establishing the European Electronic Communications Code (Recast)Text with EEA relevance
Directive (EU) 2019/713 of the European Parliament and of the Council of 17 April 2019 on combating fraud and counterfeiting of non-cash means of payment and replacing Council Framework Decision 2001/413/JHA (OJ UE 2019L 123/1)
Directive (EU) 2019/790 of the European Parliament and of the Council of 17 April 2019 on copyright and related rights in the Digital Single Market and amending Directives 96/9/EC and 2001/29/EC (Text with EEA relevance) (OJ EU 2019 L 130/92)
Directive (EU) 2022/2557 of the European Parliament and of the Council of 14 December 2022 on the resilience of critical entities and repealing Council Directive 2008/114/EC (Text with EEA relevance) OJ EU 2022 L 333/164.
Joint Action 98/428/JHA of 29 June 1998 adopted by the Council on the basis of Article K.3 of the Treaty on European Union, on the creation of a European Judicial Network (OJ EC 1998 L 19/4)
Joint Action 98/733/JHA of 21 December 1998 adopted by the Council on the basis of Article K.3 of the Treaty on European Union, on making it a criminal offence to

participate in a criminal organisation in the Member States of the European Union (OJ EC 1998 L 351/1)

Opinion of the European Economic and Social Committee on the Proposal for a Directive of the European Parliament and of the Council on attacks against information systems and repealing Council Framework Decision 2005/222/JHA, COM(2010)517

Recommendation 2018/334 of 1 March 2018 on the effective fight against illegal content online (OJ UE 2018 L 63/50)

Recommendation of the Council concerning Guidelines for the Security of Information Systems of 26 November 1992 [C(92)188/FINAL]

Regulation (EC) No. 460/2004 of the European Parliament and of the Council of 10 March 2004 establishing the European Network and Information Security Agency (OJ EU 2004 L 77/1)

Regulation (EU) No. 2018/1726 of the European Parliament and of the Council of 14 November 2018 on the European Union Agency for the Operational Management of Large-Scale IT Systems in the Area of Freedom, Security and Justice (eu-LISA), and amending Regulation (EC) No. 1987/2006 and Council Decision 2007/533/JHA and repealing Regulation (EU) No. 1077/2011 (OJ EU 2018 L 295/99)

Regulation (EU) No. 2018/1727 of the European Parliament and of the Council of 14 November 2018 on the European Union Agency for Criminal Justice Cooperation (Eurojust), and replacing and repealing Council Decision 2002/187/JHA (OJ EU 2018 L 295/138)

Regulation (EU) No. 2019/881 of the European Parliament and of the Council of 17 April 2019 on ENISA (the European Union Agency for Cybersecurity) and on information and communications technology cybersecurity certification and repealing Regulation (EU) No. 526/2013 (Cybersecurity Act) (Text with EEA relevance) (OJ UE 2019 L 15115)

Regulation (EU) No. 2021/784 of the European Parliament and of the Council of 29 April 2021 on addressing the dissemination of terrorist content online (OJ EU 2021 L 172/79)

Report from the Commission to the Council under Article 12 of the Council Framework Decision of 24 June 2005 on attacks against information systems, COM(2008)44

The Lisbon Strategy – a socio-economic development plan for the European Union adopted by the European Council on 23–24 March 2000, whose objective was to make Europe the most dynamic and competitive economic region in the world through the development of knowledge-based economies

Treaty of Lisbon amending the Treaty on European Union and the Treaty establishing the European Community, signed at Lisbon, 13 December 2007 (OJ EU 2007 C 306/1)

National law

Act of 6 June 1997 – Penal Code (consolidated text Polish Journal of Laws of 2024, item 17 as amended)

Act of 18 April 2002 on the Natural Disasters (consolidated text Polish Journal of Laws of 2017, item 1897)

Act of 21 June 2002 on the State of Emergency (consolidated text Polish Journal of Laws of 2017, item 1928)

Act of 18 July 2002 on the Provision of Services by Electronic Means (consolidated text Polish Journal of Laws of 2020, item 344)

Act of 29 August 2002 Martial Law and the Competences of the Commander-in-Chief of the Army and the Rules of the Commander-in-Chief's Subordination to the Constitutional Authorities of the Republic of Poland (consolidated text Polish Journal of Laws of 2022, item 2001)

Act of 28 October 2002 on the liability of collective entities for acts prohibited under penalty (consolidated text Polish Journal of Laws of 2023, item 659)

Act of 16 July 2004 – Telecommunications Law (consolidated text Polish Journal of Laws of 2024, item 24 as amended)

Act of 17 June 2005 on the computerisation of the operations of entities carrying out public-service task (consolidated text Polish Journal of Laws of 2024, item 307)

Act of 24 April 2009 amending the Act of 16 July 2004 – Telecommunications Law and certain other acts (Polish Journal of Laws of 2009 No. 85, item 716)

American Copyright Act of 1976, Telekommunikationsgesetz vom 22. Juni 2004; BGBl. I S. 1190, United States Code (USC)

An Act to make provision for securing computer material against unauthorised access or modification; and for connected purposes (Computer Misuse Act – CMA) c. 18)

Civil Code of the Russian Federation of 2006 [Part Four of the Civil Code of the Russian Federation, adopted by the State Duma on 24 November 2006 approved by the Federation Council on 8 December 2006 (№ 230-ФЗ от 18.12.2006)]

Czech Penal Code of 8 June 2009 (Zakon č. 40/2009 Sb.), http://aplikace.mvcr.cz/sbirka-zakonu, access 15 May 2020

French Penal Code of 1992 (Acts No: 92–683; 92–684; 92–685 and 92–686 were published in Official Journal No. 169 of 23.07.1992. Act No. 92–1336 and published in Official Journal No. 296 of 23 December 1992)

German Penal Code of 15 May 1871 as published on 13 November 1998 (BGBl. I S. 3322). Gesetze im Internet

Penal Code of the Republic of Estonia (RT I) 2001, 61, 364, www.riigiteataja.ee, date of entry into force

Judgements

Decision of the European Commission of Human Rights of 12 October 1978, case *X v. United Kingdom*, Application No. 7215/75

Decision of the European Court of Human Rights of 29 June 2006, case Weber and Saravia (54934/00)

ECHR Judgement of 26 April 1979 on Malone v the United Kingdom, complaint No. 6538/74

ECHR Judgement of 23 September 1998, on *Steel et al. v United Kingdom*, complaint No. 24838/94

ECHR Judgement of 29 June 2006 on *Weber and Saravia v Germany*, complaint No. 54934/00

ECHR Judgement of 3 April 2007 on *Copland v the United Kingdom*, complaint No. 62617/00

ECHR Judgement of 1 July 2008 on *Liberty and Others v United Kingdom*, complaint No. 58243/00

Joined Cases C-293/12 and C-594/12

Judgement of the CJEU of 5 June 1963, *NV Algemene Transport en Expeditie Onderneming van Gend & Loos v Netherlands Inland Revenue Administration* (C- 26/62)

Judgement of the CJEU of 15 July 1964, – *Flaminio Costa v E.N.E.L.* (C – 6/64)

Judgement of the CJEU of 8 April 2014, *Digital Rights Ireland Ltd v Minister for Communications, Marine and Natural Resources and Others and Kärntner Landesregierung and Others*

Standards

ISO 3 – a standard unifying a series of values
ISO 2108 – International Standard Book Number (ISBN)
ISO 9407 – standard defining shoe sizes
PN-EN ISO/IEC 27000:2020–07 (Information Technology – Security Techniques – Information Security Management Systems)
PN-EN ISO/IEC 27001:2023–08 (Information Security, Cybersecurity, and Privacy Protection)

Internet sources

2018CeberhreatDefenceReport,https://cyberedgegroup.com/wp-content/uploads/2021/03/CyberEdge-2018-CDR.pdf; access 1 June 2024
ANts 2P2 project website, http://antsp2p.sourceforge.net, access 1 June 2024
Council of Europe website, www.coe.int, access 19 June 2024
European Commission against Racism and Intolerance (ECRI) website, www.ecri.coe.int, access 19 June 2024
Freenet project website, http://freenetproject.org, access 1 June 2024
GNUnet project website, https://gnunet.org, access 1 June 2024
https://en.wikipedia.org/wiki/Bluejacking, access 19 June 2024
https://en.wikipedia.org/wiki/EnCase, access 19 June 2024
https://en.wikipedia.org/wiki/Intrusion_detection_system, access 19 June 2024
https://en.wikipedia.org/wiki/Intrusion_prevention_system, access 19 June 2024
https://en.wikipedia.org/wiki/PTK_Forensics, access 19 June 2024
https://en.wikipedia.org/wiki/Rainbow_table, access 19 June 2024
https://en.wikipedia.org/wiki/Snort_%28software%29, access 19 June 2024
https://en.wikipedia.org/wiki/TippingPoint, access 19 June 2024
International Telecommunication Union (ITU) website, www.itu.int/itu-d/reports/statistics/2023/10/10/ff23-internet-use/, access 19 June 2024
ip2 Project website, www.i2p2.de, access June 2024
MUTE Project website, http://mute-net.sourceforge.net, access 1 June 2024
The Britannica Dictionary, www.britannica.com/dictionary/xenophobia, access 19 June 2024
The Encyclopædia Britannica, www.britannica.com/summary/racism, access 19 June 2024
Tor project website, www.torproject.org, access 1 June 2024
www.itu.int/itu-d/reports/statistics/2023/10/10/ff23-internet-use/, access 19 June 2024

Index

Note: References following "n" refer to notes.

FSC
www.fsc.org
MIX
Papier | Fördert
gute Waldnutzung
FSC® C083411

Kolibri 360 GmbH
Ferdinand-Jühlke-Straße 7
99095 Erfurt, Deutschland
produktsicherheit@kolibri360.de